SPANNING THE DECADES

1902-2002

The American Chamber of Commerce
of the Philippines

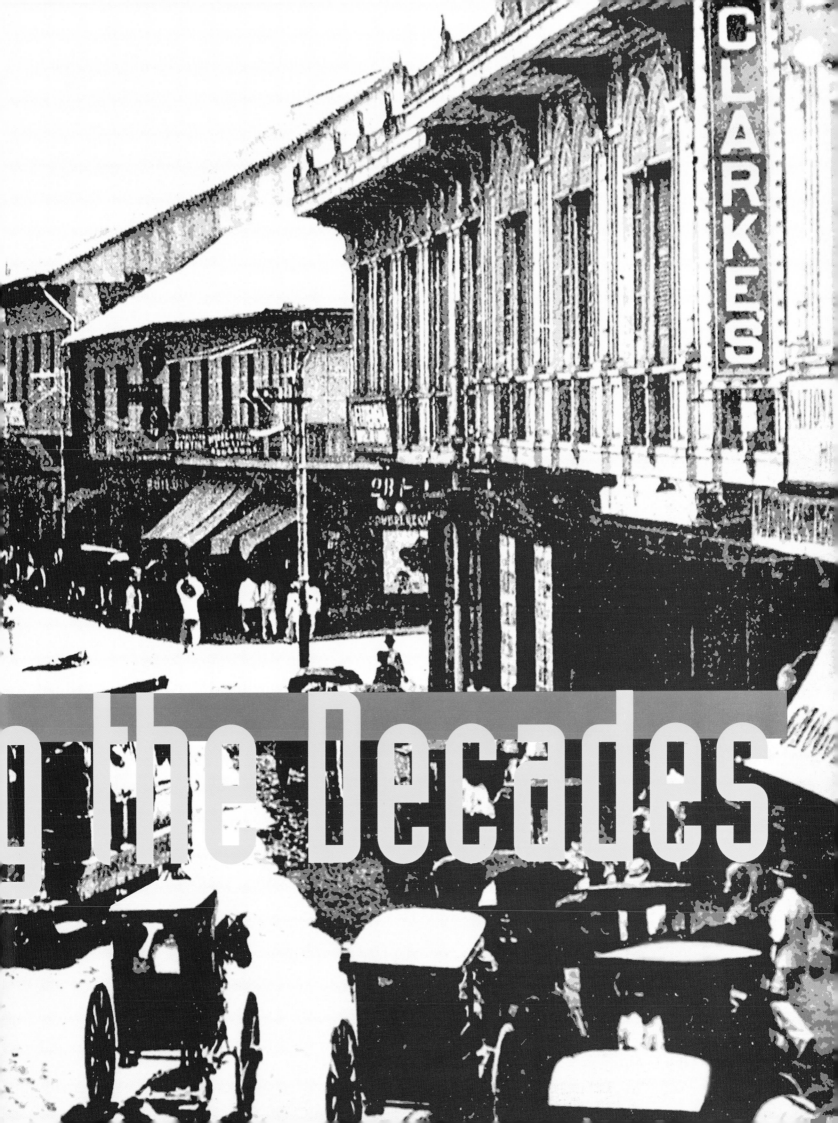

Philippine Copyright © 2003

Published by:
The American Chamber of Commerce of the Philippines, Inc.
2nd Floor, Corinthian Plaza, Paseo de Roxas, Makati City, Philippines
Tel: 63-2-818-7911
Fax: 63-2-811-3081
e-mail: amchamrp@mozcom.com
www.amchamphilippines.com

ISBN: 971-92709-0-X

AmCham Centennial Book Project
Editor-in-Chief: Robert M. Sears
Coordinators: Bobby Greenwood, Leslie Ann Murray
Editorial Coordinator: Guy Sacerdoti
Research Consultant: Leslie Ann Murray
Research Contributors: Tom Carter, Angel Solis

The views and opinions expressed in these essays are those of the individual
authors and not necessarily those of the American Chamber of Commerce of
the Philippines.

Design: Ige Ramos Design Studio
Printing and color separation by Island Graphics Corporation

Table of Contents

Daily around this
table from circa 1902 to 1920 sat
four members of the Manila Coffee Club
and one member of the Manila Merchants
Association. These five men became some of the
Founding Fathers of the American Chamber of Com-
merce of the Philippines when it incorporated in 1920.
The table was originally located at Clarke's -on-the-
Escolta from whose assets it was bought by the Manila Coffee
Club and moved to Tom's Dixie Kitchen on Plaza de Goiti, Sta.
Cruz District, Manila, where it remained until mid-1941 when
the Dixie Kitchen was closed prior to the Japanese Occupation.
Thought to have been lost during WWII, this Round Table was
discovered in 1984 in the Sta. Ana District of Manila.

Its purchase and restoration was funded by the Board of Directors and other interested members of AMCHAM who now
present it with pride, joy and satisfaction to AMCHAM
in its first owned home at Corinthian Plaza, Makati,
Metro Manila, this month of September 1984.

A full-circle homecoming.

The American Chamber's Round Table

Our cover features the brass plate affixed to the Round Table in the American Chamber's AmCham Hall.

The table top is of that heavy, naturally grained hardwood which used to carpet the archipelago. It is scarred and cracked, with just the right, circular coffee mug stains — some possibly from its early owners, others more likely caused by contributors to this book. Though it may appear unremarkable at first glance, this is no ordinary table.

The plate's inscription portrays a glimpse of Chamber history.

"Daily around this table from circa 1902 to 1921 sat four members of the Manila Coffee Club and one member of the Manila Merchants Association. These five men became some of the Founding Fathers of the American Chamber of Commerce of the Philippines when it was incorporated in 1920. The table was originally located at Clarke's-on-the-Escolta from whose assets it was bought by the Manila Coffee Club and moved to Tom's Dixie Kitchen on Plaza de Goiti, Sta. Cruz District Manila, where it remained until mid-1941 when the Dixie Kitchen was closed prior to the Japanese Occupation. Thought to have been lost during WWII, this Round Table was discovered in 1984 in the Sta. Ana district of Manila.

"Its purchase and restoration was funded by the Board of Directors and other interested members of AMCHAM who now present it with pride, joy and satisfaction to AMCHAM in its first owned home at Corinthian Plaza, Makati, Metro Manila, this month of September 1984."

Clarke's was a well-known restaurant and gathering place prior to the war, on a street that was at one time known as the "Fifth Ave. of Manila"— the Escolta. Tom's Dixie Kitchen, its successor, was located just around the corner at the base of the north end of what is now MacArthur Bridge.

The table was intentionally left in its less-than-pristine condition, as it was agreed that to refinish it would erase visible history. When the Dixie Kitchen closed, the table found its way to the home of a former employee of Tom's, where it remained safe during the Japanese Occupation. In 1984, its discovery — and subsequent return to the AmCham premises — was thanks in no small measure to the determined detective work of Tom Carter, long time member and AmCham historian.

Where was it finally discovered? Read on.

DEDICATION

This book is dedicated to the many American

businessmen and women

who did business in the Philippines

over the past 100 years.

Many failed, some succeeded.

Some stayed briefly, others a lifetime.

Together they made an indelible mark

on a country far from home.

Was it worth it?

PART 1

American Influences

The United States and the Philippines: LoveHate LoveHateLove HateLoveHateLoveHate

by Guy Sacerdoti

Mark Twain (Samuel L. Clemens) on a 1902 Pacific voyage. The famous US creator of characters Tom Sawyer and Huckleberry Finn was a vociferous advocate of freedom for the Philippines. (Photo: Mark Twain Library)

Right: President Theodore Roosevelt in 1902, the author of the US policy of "Manifest Destiny," became the youngest US president at age 42 following the assassination of President William McKinley. (Photo: Library of Congress)

Facing page: Early nationalist authors, frequently writing in Spanish, sought liberation from the US as seen in Zoilo Hilario's "Patria y Redencion," 1914. (Reproduced from "Tuklas Sining," courtesy Alice Guillermo)

The subtitle says it all. Like all nations that shed colonization, the Philippines has that strange, almost familial relationship with its former steward. But the Philippine-American relationship is unique.

It began at the close of the 19th century, just as European liberalism had finished planting the seeds of 20th century nationalism throughout the colonized world. The 1870s-90s brought sons of the colonized, malleable elite from their tropical plantation economies to the halls of European universities. There they excelled not simply in their studies and commitment to learning, but also in the grasp of equality, of freedom, and a determination to free their homelands. As a group, they performed better than their European counterparts. They had discovered the hypocrisy of foreign control.

Then America came out of its post-Civil War isolationism.

The US was the last of the newly industrialized nations of the "West" to venture into colonization. And it did so within the context of a great domestic debate. It was Mark Twain versus Teddy Roosevelt — independence versus "Manifest Destiny." After the Spanish-American War in 1898, Spain was expelled from Cuba and the country was given its freedom — Manila was not.

Twain argued in his famous speech "To the Person Sitting in Darkness" America's "mistake" in not using the Cuban precedent with the Philippines. The US was mimicking a time-worn

European paradigm, he said. Then poet Rudyard Kipling wrote the influential "The White Man's Burden," how it was a responsibility (!) to bring western civilization to the uninitiated — "Your new-caught sullen peoples, half devil and half child." At the time, it had greater impact.

US public opinion shifted in favor of 'Rough Rider' Roosevelt. But this was after Philippine General Emilio Aguinaldo was spurned, the Philippine-American War was underway and the "LoveHate" cycle started. The US colonial dilemma was just beginning.

Control was to come with palliatives of self-rule, a time-line to independence. But it came with conditions. We educate. We show you…this is the way we do things. This is the way things are done!

To Filipinos, it was a rose in a fisted glove. LoveHate.

Let's jump to 1986.

It was two and one-half years after the assassination of the exiled opposition leader and nemesis to Philippine President Ferdinand Marcos. Former Senator Benigno Aquino Jr.'s murder on the tarmac of the country's premier airport in August 1983 brought millions to the streets and the gradual disintegration of a dictatorship.

There were four "pillars of power" then, the four institutions whose support any president needed to govern — the military (muscle), the Catholic Church (populism — Muslims and minorities always excluded), the business community (money) and the US government (some strange sense of historical legitimacy). Since the 1946 independence given by the US, every successful Philippine presidential candidate lobbied for and received a tacit imprimatur from Washington.

The first "People Power" revolt in February 1986 — which led to a slew of similar anti-authoritarian revolts across the globe — spawned several book projects, including "Bayan Ko!" published in June, 1986. (Cover courtesy of "Bayan Ko!" editorial board)

And that included Marcos. Throughout the Vietnam War (1965-75), leftist and Muslim rebellions (since 1969), martial law (1973-81), the US pillar remained solid. And let's not forget US vice president George Bush Sr.'s comment as Marcos "lifted" martial law in January 1981, praising the dictator for his "adherence to democratic principles."

Aquino's murder, and an already brewing economic crisis, began to change all that. The US lobbied for a modicum of democracy. Marcos issued the palliatives this time. Nonetheless, Catholic, business and US pillars began to disintegrate. It came to a head during the "snap" presidential election in February 1986 between Marcos and Corazon Aquino, the martyr's widow. Voter intimidation and vote manipulation led to a last ditch effort by the US to broker a deal with Marcos, who had his parliament confirm his "victory."

But it was too late. A military revolt (that last all-important pillar) brought on the world's first "People Power" uprising and Marcos' exile — to the US, by the way. Freewheeling Philippine democracy was restored, only to suffer another half decade of coup attempts and political cacophony.

But the US relationship had changed. Its pillar of power had clearly begun to lose relevance. It was no longer crucial within the political firmament. No better proof of this occurred in 1991, when the Philippine Senate voted to expel the US from its two military bases at Clark Air Field and Subic Naval Base. Then politicians groused when US aid to Manila slumped. One commentator likened the attitude to a college student returning home after graduation. "I hate you. You were terrible parents. I will no longer listen. I will no longer be subservient. I'm outta here for good... Oh, and dad, can I have the keys to the car?" LoveHate.

Eleven years later, 2002, post 9-11, the Yanks are in "operational training" with the Armed Forces of the Philippines against terrorism on the southern island of Basilan. Some 74% of Filipinos approve, according to surveys. Filipino Muslims view the situation with resigned trepidation, hoping there will be no "spillover." Frequent leftist demonstrations against US "interference" occur in front of a US Consulate inundated by visa seekers. Yankee Go Home? An estimated 2.5 million, or 3.2% of all Filipinos, live and work in the US. The Philippines is second only to Mexico in annual migration to America. LoveHate.

Where does it all come from?

Then RP President Corazon Aquino with then US President Ronald Reagan six months after she assumed office. After her speech before a joint-session of the US Congress, House Speaker Eugene "Tip" O'Neal told her, "Mrs. President, you sure hit a home run." She replied, "Thank you. I hope the bases were loaded." They weren't. (Photo: US Embassy)

1897: Partners against Spain — Love

US business was pushing Washington to throw the Spanish out of Cuba. An 1895 indigenous rebellion there was continuing, and US opinion was swayed by tales of Spanish atrocities. While the US was preparing for war in late 1897, General Aguinaldo was talking with US officials in both Hong Kong and Singapore. They were tentative negotiations, but the US clearly gave him the impression he was their partner — an ally against Spain. The US would give Cuba independence, he was told. And he assumed the same would hold true for the Philippines.

April 25, 1898, the US declared war on Spain and Commodore George Dewey urged Aguinaldo to return to Manila quickly. Things moved very fast indeed.

Filipino intelligence dispelled rumors that the entrance to Manila Bay was mined, and Dewey entered May 1, finishing off the ill-equipped and obsolete Spanish armada in a few hours.

Aguinaldo arrived mid-May, took control of nationalist forces and pummeled Spanish garrisons around Manila. With 12,000 fighters he effectively trapped Spain's troops within the capital — waiting for US reinforcements expected in June. He also coordinated other armed movements throughout the colony to forge a unified revolutionary army. Aguinaldo felt Philippine independence was at hand — thanks in part to US support.

Admiral George Dewey, above, led the three hour Battle of Manila Bay, decimating the outdated Spanish fleet. (Photo: American Historical Collection - AHC)

Apache Tribe # 1

(Photos: LA Murray)

At the North Cemetary in Metro-Manila stands this memorial for the "Apache Tribe #1" of The Improved Order of the Redmen. The early US pioneers who came to the Philippines viewed themselves as settlers in an expanded US "West" — Manifest Destiny. Many expected Filipinos to be corralled on to "reservations" much as native North American "Indians" were at the time, opening up a new frontier for US expansion (3 new states?). The Redmen were a fraternity of "volunteers" who came to first fight the Spanish and then put down Filipino rebels during the Philippine-American War. Many from Fort Apache in Arizona, they petitioned the National Council of Redmen to transfer the charter of Apache Tribe #1 to Manila. Why ironically the Redmen? The group emenates from the "Sons of Liberty," the band of early US patriots who donned Mohawk Indian garb to "fool" the British when launching the Boston Tea Party in 1775.

Above, Spanish prisoners in 1898.

Below, US troops about to be ferried to their ship. (Photos: AHC)

Dewey Commemorative Medal

This Commemorative Medal is inscribed on the face (around the bust of Commodore Dewey): "The gift of the people of the United States to the Officers and Men of the Asiatic Squadron under the command of Commodore George Dewey".

The reverse side reads: "In Memory of the Victory of Manila Bay — May 11, 1898" with the name of the ship, the "U.S.S. Olympia" engraved beneath the figure of a gunner, seated on a cannon. The name "John L. Hallett" and rank "Ordinary Seaman" is engraved on the rim. The medal was found by a farmer working his field in Zambales province and was given to Mrs. Ceres Busa, formerly of the US Embassy in Manila, by her uncle, a resident of Zambales.
(American Historical Collection)

1898: Suspicions — Seeds of Hate

Aguinaldo asked the US to formally support independence, but the US refused to issue any statement. In fact, the US Navy ordered Dewey to distance himself from Aguinaldo — no commitments.

Within six weeks of Dewey's entry into Manila Bay, Aguinaldo decided not to wait for formal betrayal. He declared independence for the Philippines on June 12, 1898. The US decided to negotiate with Spain for Manila's surrender, excluding Aguinaldo's troops. On August 13, a ruse battle was staged, a predetermined signal allowing Spain's surrender. There were few casualties. It was face saving for Spain, but an insult to Aguinaldo's freedom fighters. The general was told bluntly that his troops were not to participate and would be shot if they tried. LoveHate.

Why the change in heart? Aside from manifest destiny and all that, there could have been a more practical and scintillating "what if" reason. Could others have been coveting the Philippines?

• • •

The first US flag raised on Philippine soil, Fort San Antonio Abad in front of what is now the Bangko Sentral ng Pilipinas (Central Bank). (Photo: AHC)

If Not A US Colony, Then German??

[How that could have altered history...]

from Richard Brinsley Sheridan's 1900 book on the early days of America's Occupation

The USS Raleigh firing its ordinance during the brief Battle of Manila Bay. (Photo: AHC)

...It is admitted that neither on the 1st of May, when the Spanish fleet was destroyed, nor on the 13th of August, 1898, when Manila was taken, was it America's intention to annex the Philippine Islands.

After Admiral Dewey had taken possession of Cavite, he had to await further instructions from Washington, his mission to the Philippines having been fulfilled. Meantime, he declared the blockade of Manila. Foreign vessels by Admiral Dewey's courtesy were permitted to remain in the bay, and it was at this time that Sir Edward Chichester, captain of the "Immortality," by his amiability and tact, assisted in removing whatever ill feeling may have existed before the war between the American and the English people. Whether ill feeling really existed between these two Anglo-Saxon nations is doubtful; but whether it did or not, when America urged war in the cause of common humanity, every Englishman in all Great Britain's colonies sympathized heartily with her, and all were prepared to support her in every way in every part of the world, in the great campaign of civilization.

England had stationed in the bay of Manila seven war vessels, Germany had four, and other nations also were fairly represented. Of all the powers assembled, Germany alone endeavoured to frustrate, embarrass, and make more difficult Admiral Dewey's maneuvers in the Philippine waters.

This appears almost incredible when we

1899 - 1901: Philippine American War — Hate

A group of "insurrectionists" from Pampanga in 1900. It took 126,000 US troops across the archipelago to subdue the freedom fighters. (Photo: AHC)

By the Treaty of Paris, December 10, 1898, the lines had been drawn. The cessation of Guam, Puerto Rico and the Philippines to the US came with a US$ 20 million "gift" to Spain. The US insisted it was not a purchase. "No question of honor or conquest was involved," writes historian Leon Wolff. On December 21 then US President William McKinley proclaimed a policy of "benevolent assimilation." The articulate Filipino revolutionary Antonio Luna wrote, "people are not to be bought and sold like horses and houses. If the aim has been to abolish the traffic in Negroes because it meant the sale of persons, why is it still maintained the sale of countries with inhabitants?"

During the night of February 4, 1899, two US privates killed three Filipino soldiers after an argument just outside Manila. In the two years that followed, 126,000 US troops fought throughout the Philippines. Over 4,200 US soldiers died along with 16,000 Filipino combatants. Worse, the disruption caused the deaths of an estimated 200,000 Filipino civilians, mostly due to famine and disease. Remember,

Adm. Dewey's flagship Olympia. Naval etiquette was breached by the Germans and Dewey was forced to fire across the bow of a vessel to force them to comply with international law. (Photo: AHC)

remember that the two nations were on friendly terms; but Admiral Dewey told me himself that at night the Germans would send their boats from ship to ship. He bore with patience this gross breach of naval etiquette until he found it necessary to prevent the continuance of such discourtesy. On one occasion, he told me, he was compelled to fire across the bows of a German vessel, in order to put a stop to further disobedience of International rules.

Admiral Dewey did not forget that when he was in Hong Kong, Prince Henry said that Germany would not permit America to annex the Philippine Islands.

It was generally reported in Manila at this time that the Germans were endeavouring to assist the Spaniards. On one occasion, Admiral Dewey, having a certain German vessels (sic), invited the German commander to meet him. At the interview, Admiral Dewey complained of German boats making visits at night, without special permission, to other ships in the harbor, and reminded the German officer that it was by his (the Admiral's) courtesy only, that his vessels were permitted to anchor in this blockaded port; that the action complained of amounted technically to an act of war; and, added Admiral Dewey, "as we are in for it now, it matters little to us whether we fight Spain, or Germany, or the world; and if you desire war, you can have it right here. You need not cable to Berlin, nor need I to Washington; you can just have war here and now." It is needless to say that the German commander, whether he had acted on instructions from Berlin or not, did not desire war then or at any other time; and Admiral Dewey in taking this bold and proper step saved himself all further annoyance and interference at the hands of that German commander…

the total Filipino population at the time was only six million (at 3.3% of the total, the relative number killed is slightly more than the total number of Filipinos residing in the US in 2000).

On March 23, 1901, Aguinaldo was captured in remote Palanan, on the eastern tip of Isabela province. He issued a proclamation ordering the end of hostilities. Still, small pockets of resistance continued for two more years.

1900 - 1916: Institution Building — Love

The US always thought of its occupation as "tutelage." Filipinos thought of it as… well… occupation.

But it was never a question of independence for the colony. It was a question of when. And the precursor to freedom was the formation of US-mirrored institutions — in education, politics, business, and in many ways, culture. As a famous 1950s era US high school history book explained —"The US had to teach the natives how to live."

Times have certainly changed. But in the Philippines during the first two decades of the 20th century, people for the most part were receptive to US institution-building, basically because the Spanish had done very little beyond enforcing religion.

It was not chance that the head of the First Philippine Commission in 1899 was Dr. Jacob Schurman, president of Cornell University. The five member group recommended a carbon copy of what the US was doing in its own less developed States and territories (there were only 45 United States in 1900). The Thomasites began the trek towards free elementary education and English language instruction as they spread throughout the archipelago.

It was the second Commission under William Howard Taft that lay the groundwork. From March 1900 through August 1902, with legislative and some executive authority, it issued 499 laws. It created a judicial system, a civil service,

"The policy which I had the honor to formulate and declare in these islands — 'the Philippines for the Filipinos' — continues to be the policy of this administration, and anyone who does not subscribe to it ought not to continue in its employ." – William H. Taft August 11, 1905.

McDowell O'Donnel Sellner Allen Bowditch JPH Heilbronn Derham Ray Hartigan Brown Claxe O'Reilly David Earnshaw
1 2 3 4 5 6 7 8 9 10 11 12 13

Edwards Taft Smith Langhorne

Taft and other US officials with members of the first Philippine Assembly, 1907. Several winners of those first elections began political dynasties which remain today. (Photos: AHC)

elected provincial and municipal offices. But it was the 1902 Organic Act that set the political stage — with a popularly elected lower House and an appointed Philippine Commission as upper house (later the Senate). First elections were in 1907. Two elected commissioners were sent to the US Congress as observers. The US Bill of Rights now covered all Filipinos. The Catholic Church was removed as State religion. And Taft became the colony's first civilian Governor.

First attempts at land reform were tried, with the US spending US$ 7.2 million to buy out 166,000 hectares of friar lands. Most went to estate owners, setting a precedent that led to the eventual creation of political-economic oligarchies.

Rapid "Filipinization" occurred during Governor General F.B. Harrison's tenure (1913-21), who saw himself as a "constitutional monarch" presiding over a "government of Filipinos." In 1913 there were 2,623 US and 6,363 Filipino officials in governance. By 1921 there were 614 US administrators and 13,240 Filipinos. The 1916 Jones Act passed by the US Congress replaced the 1902 Organic Act, promising independence when a stable government was established. No timetable was given, however. But it brought the legislature under Philippine control, with the executive and judicial branches still largely manned by US citizens.

• • •

The Moro Dilemma

from The Philippines, 100 Years

But it was a harsh military crackdown led by General John J. Pershing (shown with his family in Zamboanga, right) that stopped the Moro uprising — at least for a brief moment. Pershing later became a WWI legend.

Superintendent of Education David P. Barrows, left, with the Sultan of Sulu in 1903. (Photos: AHC)

The Moros on Mindanao and on the Sulu archipelago, suspicious of both Christian Filipino insurrectionists and the US, remained for the most part neutral (during the Philippine-American War). In August, 1899, an agreement had been signed between General John C. Bates, representing the US government, and the Sultan of Sulu, Jamal-ul Kiram II, pledging a policy of non-interference on the part of the US.

In 1903, however, a Moro province was established by the US authorities, and a more forward (sic) policy was established. For example, slavery was outlawed. Schools that taught non-Muslim curriculum were established, and local governments that challenged the authority of traditional community leaders were organized. A new legal system replaced the Sharia, or Islamic Law. US rule, even more than that of the Spanish, was seen as a challenge to Islam. Armed resistance grew, and the Moro province remained under US military rule until 1914, by which time the major Muslim groups had been quieted, but only for a time.

F.B. Harrision, the "Constitutional Monarch" over a "Government of Filipinos." (Photo: AHC)

1903 - 1941: Feudalism and the Oligarchs — Hate

While the rapid absorption of Filipinos in both education and politics was viewed with pride, the economy bore mixed results. The relative lack of economic "tutelage" is still visible today. The Spanish left a feudal sharecropper culture in the predominant rural areas, keeping workers from owning land, yet constantly in debt.

The US Congress, despite its initial "land reform" purchase of friar lands, actually worked to maintain the status quo, originally fighting against tariff-free Filipino imports to the US, citing competition with domestic agricultural products such as sugar, vegetable oils and tobacco.

When the US Congress finally lifted the restrictions in 1913, the US rapidly dominated the export market for Philippine goods. By 1939, fully 85% of all exports were shipped to the US.

But that was not the only problem. The US took control over the archipelago in the heyday of its own industrial, railroad and financial "robber barons." Carnegie, Rockefeller, JP Morgan typified the success of early US big business. Ford's Model T

1907: Speaker Sergio Osmeña, left, leads the first Philippine Assembly, right. (Photo: AHC)

US "tutelage." A political cartoon from 1910. (Cartoon, Lipag Kalabaw, November 14, 1908)

had hit the roads. Procter and Gamble and Del Monte were processing consumer goods out of plantation economics. What works… works.

Large landholders were plucked from the rural areas as agents for supplying raw materials for processing, a thin veneer of manufacturing, and even a little industrialization. These scions of the former Spanish *mestizo* elite were mixed with successful traders of Chinese descent to form a backbone of raw material suppliers to US corporations. The firms helped finance and support the development of these family-based oligarchies. It was landed gentry first, then a processing base.

To finance the processing one needed a bank. Logistics (shipping) and utilities (power, water, telephones, etc) became another few companies in the oligarch's growing empire. But control over the regional masses was essential, so one family branch would veer into politics (for protection), while another would move into media (radio, newspapers and later TV) to maintain propaganda control over their "feudal" subjects — "let them know only what we want them to know."

That business footprint remains today. And efforts to reform, privatize and deregulate consistently come up against the powers of warlords, protectionists and oligarchs in legislative, judicial and executive branches. Profit margins are not targets. They are usually preset with consumers bearing the cost and risk of changing economic realities, which is why the cost of business in the Philippines remains so high compared to the rest of the region. It is also why the band of attainable economic growth today remains so narrow as it is relatively slow.

The chosen few did very well, thank you. But the *masa* remained constantly in debt, frequently relying on usury lending to survive. LoveHate.

• • •

"Beautiful afternoon! How about a spot of fishing?"

The clash of cultures was evident from the start. An American with friends outside Zamboanga, c. 1910. (Photo: AHC)

1935: Timetable to Independence — Love

General Douglas MacArthur, Commandant of the Philippines prior to the outbreak of WWII, in his "civies." The gentleman behind him with the same hat was his chief aide at the time, then Col. Dwight D. Eisenhower. (Photo: AHC)

It was actually a confluence of love and hate that brought on the Commonwealth with the US on a ten-year plan towards Philippine independence. But the hate seems to have come from the US this time. US farmers once again saw competition from low-tariff Philippine exports. Also, those US businessmen operating in Cuba viewed Manila as a threat to their sugar exports. They both lobbied Washington. Simultaneously, the US was retrenching into one its isolationist periods, primarily due to the Great Depression. Labor unions lobbied for strict limits on Philippine immigration, with unemployment hounding the nation.

Many legislators wanted the US to withdraw across the Pacific to Hawaii, then a US territory, in the face of an expansive Japan. The Tydings-McDuffie Act of March 1934, negotiated by Manuel Quezon in Washington, became the timetable to independence.

By July, 1934, a constitutional convention was convened in Manila and eight months later, the resulting document was overwhelmingly approved in a national plebiscite. In July 1946, it was to become the Constitution of an independent Republic of the Philippines. In the meantime, a Commonwealth was to be

Paco Station designed and built by William Parsons (1914) resembles New York's Penn Station with its four-garlanded eagles. All that now remains is the facade and the abandoned building site of yet another shopping mall. (Photo: Lico collection)

US President Franklin D. Roosevelt signing the 1935 Philippine Constitution. (Photo: AHC)

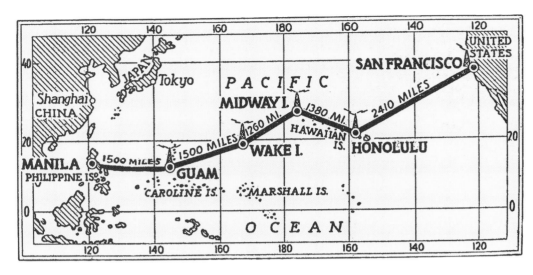

Above: Ruth Law, who delivered the first transpacific airmail to the Philippines in 1919. "Barnstorm" aviation shows drew huge crowds at the Luneta around that time. By the 1930s, long-haul passenger services reached Manila. The route of the Pan American Airline Clippers is shown at right.

established. Manila would govern itself, but the US would hold sway over foreign policy, immigration to the US and monetary policy (an interesting note – Philippine immigration to the US was limited to 50 people a year). Commonwealth elections were held in September, and Quezon was elected president with erstwhile rival Sergio Osmena as vice president.

Moros of the South

US military contingents (above) tried to control culturally independent datus (right). Muslim leaders asked the US for protection against the growing Catholic migration south into Mindanao in the 1920s-1930s. The historical seeds of conflict had long been planted. (Photos: AHC)

Although the Jones Act did not transfer responsibility for the Moro regions (reorganized in 1914 under the Department of Mindanao and Sulu) from the US governor to the Filipino-controlled legislature, Muslims perceived the rapid Filipinization of the civil service and US commitment to eventual independence as serious threats.

In the view of the Moros, an independent Philippines would be dominated by Christians, their traditional enemies. US policy from 1903 had been to break down the historical autonomy of the Muslim territories. Immigration of Christian settlers from Luzon and the Visayan Islands to the relatively unsettled regions of Mindanao was encouraged, and the new arrivals began supplanting the Moros in their own homeland. Large areas of the island were opened to economic exploitation. There was no legal recognition of Muslim customs and institutions.

In March 1935, Muslim datu petitioned US President Franklin D. Roosevelt, asking that "the US people should not release us until we are educated and become powerful because we are like a calf who, once abandoned by its mother, would be devoured by a merciless lion." Any suggestion of special status for, or continued US rule over the Moro regions, however, was vehemently opposed by Christian Filipino leaders. When the Commonwealth of the Philippines was established, they gained virtually complete control over government institutions.

1941 - 1944: Abandonment — Hate

Despite the courageous defense of Corregidor by US and Philippine soldiers in the four months following the Japanese attack on Pearl Harbor — with Imperial planes bombing Baguio a mere three hours after the US Pacific Fleet was decimated — many Filipinos felt the US simply abandoned the country in the face of Japanese aggression.

In less than a week, Manila was declared an open city, with senior officials escaping with General Douglas MacArthur to the island base. They were later evacuated to Washington to run a government-in-exile, while MacArthur slipped out to Australia to begin picking up the pieces and plan his famous "return."

Deprivation and suffering were widespread. Yet Filipino guerillas worked with US spies (surreptitiously landed by submarine) to mark Japanese positions and movements. They were so efficient in their jungle and hillside hideouts with coded radio contact that they provided the US with meticulous intelligence (every take off or landing in the months leading to the Battle of Leyte Gulf was monitored — throughout Luzon and most of the Visayas).

But for the general public, both urban and rural, the feeling of abandonment, and in some cases betrayal, was paramount.

• • •

Were those carefully crafted "institutions" about to crumble? Above, the damaged Philippine Legislature Building, 1945. (Photo: AHC)

Sayer - MacArthur: A most Bizarre Meeting

Upon the declaration of Manila as an Open City, for safety High Commissioner Sayer and family evacuated to Corregidor, along with President Quezon and his family, on orders of General MacArthur.

Ralph Graves, Sayers' stepson, relates an amusing anecdote about his stepfather and General MacArthur that took place on Corregidor. "Before the war, when my father was the chief civil authority, he had outranked MacArthur, but now in wartime, MacArthur outranked him.

"General MacArthur had posted an order in the Malinta Tunnel that if anyone was caught out in the open during a Japanese air raid, he was to lie flat on the ground until the 'all clear'. My father and MacArthur were discussing some problem out in the open when the 'red alert' sounded. My father, dutifully obeying the orders of the commanding general, lay down flat on the

ground. MacArthur, of course remained standing. They continued their discussion without either of them acknowledging that this was very bizarre conversation. That was my father. That was MacArthur."

Philippine Commonwealth President Manuel Quezon (left) with Sayer in a more peaceful setting. (Photo: AHC)

1944-1946: "I Shall Return" and Independence — Love

President-in-exile Quezon died August 1, 1944, with Osmeña assuming his post. MacArthur, by then the 64 year old commander of the US Pacific Army, argued vociferously that the Philippines needed to be retaken before the onslaught against Japan.

The US Navy wanted to bypass the islands in favor of Taiwan, which it felt was a better base. MacArthur convinced President Franklin D. Roosevelt during a briefing in Hawaii to go for the Philippines first, for both tactical and propaganda purposes. While the October 1944 landing just south of Tacloban, Leyte, is commemorated annually at an impressive memorial at the site, the irony is that it was the naval Battle of the Leyte Gulf prior to the invasion that decimated Japan's sea power. It placed Japan in a serious tactical retreat, from which it never recovered.

But for the Philippine public, it was indeed liberation, a promise kept, and an injection of hope that the road to independence was nearing its end. July 4, 1946 was the date set. But first, an election was needed, and the issue of collaboration with the Japanese settled. That proved difficult, primarily because Manuel Roxas, a minister during the Japanese occupation, had also been feeding the Allies intelligence and was clearly a patriot. Roxas was also organizing a Liberal wing from the Nacionalista Party to back him for a run at the presidency.

MacArthur publicly backed Roxas to much local criticism, but Roxas won the polls against the aging Osmeña, just two months before the formal raising of the Philippine flag at the Luneta.

• • •

1946 and 1955: The Bell Act & Laurel-Langley Agreement — Hate

Independence in some ways proved a double-edged sword. Political independence was assured. During the immediate post-war period, aid for reconstruction was critical. And the bargaining chip became economic dependence, primarily induced by the oligarchs to ensure control and profits, but grasped by nationalists as a hollow agreement that led to a leftist revolt in the mid-1950s.

At the time US$ 620 million was a lot of money. And that was for the rehabilitation and war damages. Contingent upon this Rehabilitation Act of 1946 was a Philippine acceptance of "parity" — that US citizens and US firms had the same economic rights as Filipinos, with free trade between the two countries through 1954. The peso remained pegged to the dollar.

The Laurel-Langley Agreement in 1955 removed that condition, and it made parity provisions reciprocal. But it also added graduated duties on exports to the US. It fell into the category of agreements of the times that aggravated nationalist tendencies among the rural population in favor of an elite that was viewed as puppets of former colonizers. It lent sympathy for communism and its agitators, and became the seed for the guerilla wars of the 1950s to the 1970s. LoveHate.

• • •

The phrase "economic colonialism" emerged during the early 1950s, though it's doubtful this 1952 ice cream stand at Clark Air Field left much of a bad taste. (Photo: Bob Flanders)

Jeep to Jeepney

servicemen who decided to stay. Most infrastructure had been destoyed during the war, and transportation for both supplies and people was at a premium. US Jeeps, many still unassembled and crated in grease, became the backbone of what grew into an entire industry. Today they are stainless steel shells powered by reconditioned (mostly Japanese) diesel engines. Their heyday has passed, but the WWII Jeep has made an indelible mark on Philippine culture.

The ubiquitous Philippine Jeepney had its origins at the close of WWII. The Americans had tons of war surplus material landed following the invasion. In December, 1946, it was officially handed over to the newly independent Philippine Government. But many entreprenuers had already made private deals, securing the assets from a variety of sources, including several US

Above left, celebrating victory aboard a US Army jeep (Photo: AHC). Above, modern day jeepney (Photo: courtesy American Women's Club Philippines). Left, Antonio Austria's "PUJ", 1970 (Reproduced from "Tuklas Sining", courtesy Alice Guillermo).

Postwar-1965: Aid and Development — Love

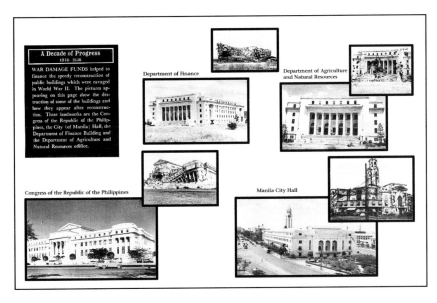

A Decade of Progress
1946 1956

WAR DAMAGE FUNDS helped to finance the speedy reconstruction of public buildings which were ravaged in World War II. The pictures appearing on this page show the destruction of some of the buildings and how they appear after reconstruction. These landmarks are the Congress of the Republic of the Philippines, the City (of Manila) Hall, the Department of Finance Building and the Department of Agriculture and Natural Resources edifice.

Department of Finance

Department of Agriculture and Natural Resources

Congress of the Republic of the Philippines

Manila City Hall

Aside from the massive reconstruction needed in Manila (above), the Philippines embraced the post-war culture of the US. Theater, music and art reflected the happier times. (Photo: Lico collection)

The other edge of that sword was an influx of US business interests in the country and partnerships in the development of infrastructure, commerce and the building of some manufacturing competence. Although many US observers following the war saw the Philippines as the next economic powerhouse of Asia, the democratization of Japan and supplying the Korean conflict brought far more development and energy to Tokyo. Still, in terms of roads, power, water, communications, shipping and private sector investment, the US helped Manila prosper during the period. US companies joined their Filipino counterparts in boosting consumer spending through both job creation and product availability.

By 1954, educational attainment in the Philippines in terms of participation and achievement scores was ranked second only to Japan within the East and Southeast Asia region. The banking system expanded with several start-up banks gaining new customers and confidence. Several Philippines presidents during the period, most notably Ramon Magsaysay (1954-57), provided a plethora of local projects aimed at bringing more of the rural population into the economic system. He did much of this with US support, both financially and via advisors, who helped develop a plan to neutralize the worrying communist Hukbalahap rebellion spreading in central Luzon.

Gross National Product grew steadily during the period as did per capita income — although it is critical to note that rapid population growth eroded a good deal of the ultimate benefits of this growth over time.

• • •

Right, Bayani Casimiro, the Filipino Fred Astaire, shows off his talents in a "bodabil" act. (Reproduced from "Tuklas Sining", courtesy Alice Guillermo)

Postwar-1965: Nationalism & Protectionism — Hate

The problem, as viewed by new businessmen, new politicians and academicians, was that all this economic activity was making large profits for the elite oligarchs (viewed as having strong ties with traditional or US interests), with the costs of inefficiency being passed down to the consumer. From cement to steel, vehicles to appliances, the fear of competition brought on a rash of protectionist measures. The perennial issues of parity (equal treatment for US business) and US military presence compromised sovereignty, the argument went. LoveHate.

Worldwide, former colonies were flexing new-found political muscle in foreign relations. The Gamal Abdul Nassars and Sukarnos laid the foundation of what would become the Non-Aligned Movement in the face of the escalating US-Soviet Cold War, while others shifted more directly into a Soviet embrace. The Philippines was considered clearly in the American camp (with its military bases), thus forcing policies towards a nationalism that would mollify critics who felt sovereignty was compromised. At the same time, the US was beginning to shift its Cold War attention to mainland Southeast Asia, and certainly did not want to lose its influence on Manila.

After Magsaysay died in a 1957 plane crash, Carlos Garcia assumed the presidency. He adopted policies of "Filipino First" and sought a "respectable independence." The US negotiated the return of several military base lands, the main one being the city of Olongapo adjacent to Subic Naval Base. The US in effect built a moat between the base and contiguous areas of the city for security.

Several senators and politicians, most notably Senator Claro Recto, sought and won expulsion of Americans caught bribing politicians to secure protection against several borderline or outright illegal businesses. LoveHate.

Nationalist art showed itself in many forms from the 1930s. The Philippines followed the regional trend of building monuments depicting heroic acts, while extolling the virtues of freedom and independence.

Above left, Constancio de Guzman's "Bayan Ko." Below, the Bonafacio Monument. (Reproduced from "Tuklas Sining", courtesy Alice Guillermo)

Lyndon Baines Johnson talking to Ferdinand Marcos as his wife Imelda looks on. (Photo: LBJ Library)

1965 - 1972: Early Marcos — a wily Love

Ferdinand Marcos was touted in his early years within the US as Asia's John F. Kennedy. Young, bright and handsome, he topped his law class and held the national sharp shooting title. He promoted himself as a decorated WWII guerilla commander (much later proved false), married a beauty queen and was a skilled campaigner. Comic books depicting his military exploits were sent out to the provinces to idolize his image before the 1965 election.

The Yanks loved him.

In the midst of US escalation in Vietnam, the pressure from advancing communism within the then "Third World," and the need for enhanced use of existing military bases, the US government embraced Marcos, as it did several other future dictators around the globe.

He was brilliantly manipulative from the start, both domestically and in foreign affairs. From his staunch support of the US Indochina effort, he lobbied for substantial aid increases in return for a 2,000 man Philippine Civil Action Group sent to Vietnam. He used budget resources on a vast infrastructure program throughout the provinces. Roads, bridges, civic centers, market plazas, were all part of the plan.

But it was all "pork barrel". Local politicians received the money and could "bid" to contractors as they pleased. It was not uncommon for a muddy, nearly impassable mountain pass to suddenly become a concrete two lane "highway" — for about four kilometers — before dropping off again into mountain muck. Patronage politics won political support. And as the more successful entrepreneurs with inside access expanded their business on political largesse, so too did the symbiotic relationship of cronyism.

Clark Air Field and Subic Naval Base were key logistics and training sites for the US military during the Vietnam War. Below, a group of couriers in 1967. (Photo: John Hagler)

His strategy worked well. He became the first Philippine president to win a second term. But the elections, which included Senate, Congressional and provincial positions as well, resulted in unprecedented political violence and accusations of fraud, intimidation, and vote-buying.

Marcos used his second term to tighten his grip on power, and to increasingly use the military to scare the population into submission. Marcos was using Constitutional Democracy to consolidate power — nothing wrong about that. But he was being increasingly nagged by influences outside his, or US, control. And that was the story behind many leaders seeking US support for a stand against communist expansion. Whether in South Korea, Singapore, Taiwan or Indonesia, autocracy was tolerated by the US — dictatorship was the norm for all four. What made the Philippines different was that Marcos took a freewheeling democracy and turned it towards a military enforced dictatorship — and with US blessings.

A fledgling Maoist communist party started in 1968, uniting leftist academics with remnants of the Stalinist Hukbalahap fighters, who had resorted to banditry in rural central Luzon. Marcos also ignited the fury of the Moros in Mindanao after a massacre of Muslim soldiers being trained on Corregidor — to infiltrate and destabilize the Malaysian State of Sabah (based on a 150-year-old claim Marcos publicly reasserted in 1969).

As demonstrations from students and Muslims rose, Marcos increasingly used violence to maintain control. His actions actually brought the dissidents greater support — the communists from activist university students, the Moros from their deep-seated feelings of entrapment, encroachment and Catholic ignorance of Muslim affairs. Moro National Liberation Front (MNLF) founder Nur Misuari was a leftist leader at the University of the Philippines at the time.

Violence bred more violence, which Marcos exploited to rationalize tightening the noose on democracy. A bipartisan desire to rewrite the 1935 Constitution was used to define a parliamentary structure whereby the two-term limit on the presidency was nullified. The Opposition managed to pass a motion banning Marcos or his family from running again, but that was reversed within a year.

The problem for Marcos was that if elections were held as scheduled in 1973, then Senator Benigno Aquino would probably have won.

Jose Joya's "Granadean Arabesque", 1968.
(Photo: The Ateneo Art Gallery)

The pensionado system of US study aided Filipino artists as well. Two outstanding pensionados in the field of the visual arts, Jose Joya and Constancio Bernardo returned from the US in the late 1960s. Joya's homecoming exhibit bore the stamp of the New York School, the postwar generation of Jackson Pollock and Franz Kline, bringing kinetic painting and abstract expressionism to the fore. While Pollock created thickets of overlapping lines in paintings in which all parts were of equal value, Joya worked in dense masses of brushwork played against spaces or passages of color and tone.

(Cartoon: Philippine Free Press, 1969)

1972 - 1981: Martial Law — LoveHate

There was a slew of other reasons for Marcos to declare martial law on September 21, 1972. But he used a staged ambush of Defense Minister Juan Ponce Enrile to unleash the troops that would detain some 30,000 politicians, businessmen, journalists, students and other people with influence opposing his rule.

By blaming the fledging communist movement, he stoked the flames of the insurgency. The business elite, the US and the Church did little more than a quick shudder before their pillars of power were back in place.

Despite the declaration of martial law, US relations with Manila remained cordial, and many in the business community welcomed the discipline. Above, then US Secretary of State Henry Kissinger stands between UN Ambassador Carlos Romulo and Philippine Secretary of Defense (and martial law administrator) Juan Ponce Enrile. (Photo: AHC)

The chaos of the time was part of the reason. The US was in the middle of a presidential election in the face of protesting youth, academics, several politicians and much of the press. US President Richard Nixon knew very well what it was like to be pummeled from all sides. And he understood what would stop it (as was unraveled during the Watergate revelations two years later — Nixon would have relished having Marcos' powers then).

A financial crisis in Manila two years earlier created an economic downturn. Investor interest from abroad waned due to the instability caused by the violence (in favor of other more stable environments in Thailand, Malaysia, Singapore, Indonesia). So oligarchs and businesses generally supported the initial stability martial law created.

Marcos joins a briefing at Subic Bay Naval Base with Adm. Frederick Barshar. (Photo: US Navy)

As with all international celebrities, Imelda just had to meet Ali. But as the obligatory photo-op splayed across US sports pages the next day, Ali's wife, at home in the US, noticed a different kind of competition in the photo. She flew immediately to Manila to "clear up" the matter. (Photo: Ted Lerner collection)

Businessmen associated with the Opposition did not fare as well, however. Companies were taken over, family scions either arrested or went into exile (most to the US). The Laurel-Langley Agreement expired in 1974, and Marcos attacked US companies in strategic industries with a passion. Utilizing decreed tariffs, excise levies, fees, litigation and sometimes simple harassment, Marcos favored his handpicked cronies and family. Many US firms opted out, but in the end still dealt with the new owners as suppliers.

The Marcos "New Society" was a "revolution from the top", as Marcos described it. In actuality, it was simply a mix of political suppression and crony capitalism. LoveHate.

For the first few years, things went well. Stability returned, the economy grew faster than ever. One reason was Marcos' clever use of respected technocrats to define "public" policy. Behind the scenes it was different. The inefficiencies of corruption and mismanagement began to take their toll. Politically, US President Jimmy Carter pressed all dictators in the region on human rights. In the Philippines, it was parliamentary elections and a timetable to the lifting of military rule, along with the release of Aquino, now sentenced to death by a military tribunal, and already a symbol of democracy and reform.

Marcos allowed Aquino to travel to the US for a bypass operation in 1980 — where he remained in exile at Harvard — while Marcos lifted martial law January 17, 1981. US President Ronald Reagan applauded the move (via VP Bush Sr.). But the cauldron kept simmering.

Boxing: The Thrilla in Manila

Marcos was intent on "softening" the international image of Martial Law. He vied successfully to host widely publicized international events such as an IMF annual meeting and an UNCTAD conference. But his most prized event was the Ali/Frazier "Thrilla in Manila" in 1975, which became a classic in boxing history. The Ali Mall in Cubao was named to commemorate the fight which enthalled a nation with a proud history of world boxing champions. The Philippines remains a boxing training ground for boxing title-holders, particularly in the lighter weight categories.

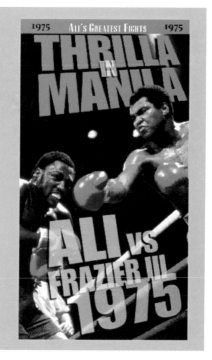

1981 - 1983: Crisis Builds — LoveHate

Marcos formally returned the government to civilian control. He appointed a respected, if unthreatening prime minister, named a province mate as Armed Forces chief of staff over a West Point graduate (the West Pointer had great rank and file respect — and US support), and demoted his martial law administrator back to "only" defense minister. Rather than ameliorating his problems, however, they were only beginning. Nine days before returning to civilian rule, a favored financial wheeler-dealer ran off to Canada carrying much of the US$706 million he left behind in debt.

The 1981 Dewey Dee affair shook the financial timbers of the economy, because the majority of those left in the lurch were Marcos cronies. None had been left out of the misconstrued scheme. Crony empires had been built similar to the elite oligarchs, but with few exceptions, without managerial expertise or entrepreneurial talent. Each owned equity in financial institutions, banks, investment houses or other finance companies. "Behest" loans were the name of the Malacañang game, where funds were diverted to pet projects or personal investments. Duped or not, balance sheets suffered. IMF emergency bailouts came with harsh conditions. On top of that, prices of traditional export commodities such as sugar and coconut oil plummeted below production costs. Cronies controlling those industries came under increasing criticism from activists supporting farmers whose incomes suffered most. In industry, the shells of crony enterprises collapsed leaving Marcos' friends in unsustainable debt. Business began lobbying for change as well, supporting "restructuring" and more responsible management.

The economy contracted. Political insurgency intensified. The communist National Democratic Front (NDF) and its military wing, the New People's Army (NPA), gathered strength from displaced rural farmers and their families, egged on by a steady stream of politicized students visiting their rural and mountain enclaves for

Ronald Reagan and Marcos were friends since he inaugurated the Cultural Center of the Philippines while Governor of California in 1969 (right). As President, he remained supportive of the dictator, but had to tow a careful line as more of Marcos' excesses hurt both the economy and his political base.

The controversy surrounding the US$ 2.1 billion Westinghouse-contracted Bataan Nulcear Power Plant was debilitating for Marcos. First was the cost, with charges of corruption and favoritism towards crony Herminio Disini. Then there was the site of the plant — nearby an earthquake fault. It became a target for the expanding anti-Marcos Left — students, environmentalists and the Communist Party of the Philippines, which was active in building support in the impoverished region. Construction was interrupted, then halted as the plant neared completion. The debt, however, still had to be paid. And it led the Government to seriously consider a partial moratorium on sovereign debt even before the 1983 assassination of opposition leader Benigno Aquino Jr.

political indoctrination — and an introduction to life with the *masa*. Strong-armed military tactics in the regions further exacerbated the rebellion.

Marcos continued to use the communist bogey to maintain US support, and this was well after US focus had shifted away from Indochina. Thus, criticism was on the rise in Washington. But it was becoming clear as two critical events approached that a full-fledged crisis loomed.

The first was the debt of a US$ 2.1 billion nuclear power plant on the shores of the Bataan Peninsula. Since the contract was awarded in 1976, Westinghouse, the US contractor, and a business crony who acted as agent for the deal, became targets for incessant harangues on nuclear safety and corruption. To this day the plant has not operated. But it became clear by mid-1983 that a selective moratorium on sovereign debt payments was a distinct possibility.

The second involved Marcos' kidneys. He needed a transplant but forced himself to maintain the image of total control. Reality was quite different. His political nemesis, Benigno Aquino Jr., was set on returning from his US exile August 21. Everything was tried to stop him, or at least delay him from coming home. The kidney operation was done in the utmost secrecy, carried out four days before Aqunio's surreptitious return — few knew what flight he would take. Marcos body initially rejected the new tissue, and his aides panicked. The Aquino assassination plot was hatched.

Things had gone way out of hand, as a senior US official confided the day before the murder.

• • •

1983 - 1986: The Pillars Disintegrate — LoveHate

A healthy Marcos would have sent a palace limo out to the tarmac to welcome back his political adversary, inviting him to lunch at Malacañang, thus destroying Aquino's credibility as viable opposition (rumors of a "deal" with the president were already circulating). That was Marcos' style. But the assassination was clearly a desperate bungle to cover for a sick man. It turned a meager 2,000 supporters out to greet Aquino at the airport into 2 million people massed along the 20 kilometer funeral procession ten days later.

For the next 30 months, Marcos hung on, as the US tried to coax and cajole, while still supporting his efforts against the growing insurgency. It was a gradual process that saw the disintegration of the four pillars of power giving Marcos, or any Filipino president, his legitimacy.

First to go was the economy. Already teetering on the verge of a debt crisis, Aquino's murder coupled with an ill Marcos — who called the assassination a "communist rub-out job" — did little to inspire confidence among the international finance community. By mid-October, a moratorium on debt servicing was called when foreign banks — many of them from the US — stopped rolling over short term obligations. Some 483 banks were effected, and virtually all international financing, including import letters of credit, stopped.

Next to crumble was the populist Catholic Church. Close to the devout widow Corazon Aquino, Manila Archbishop Jaime Cardinal Sin towed a delicate line with Marcos and the growing opposition. Rallies against the regime flourished, with the Church urging peace. But liberation theology, in vogue at the time, had penetrated the ranks of leftists and the NDF with several prominent "rebel priests" going underground to fight with the communists. That gave Marcos the fuel he wanted to hit back. Violent dispersals marred demonstrations even as moderates joined the rallies. Pastoral letters read during Sunday mass became more frequent and more critical. Sin began trying to help unify disparate opposition groups and leaders.

Few can forget the images of confetti showers throughout the Makati financial district on Fridays and the speeches uttered at the Ugarte field, adjacent to what is today the Ayala Tower. Gradually more and more business leaders jumped on to the opposition bandwagon, including the new, yet influential Makati Business Club, followed over time by local business chambers.

All groups — including the US — called for an impartial investigation into Aquino's murder. After a false start (Marcos appointed a commission led by a Chief Justice, also a family friend), he allowed an independent fact-finding commission to investigate. The majority report found a coterie of military men led by then Armed Forces Chief of Staff Fabian Ver indictable. A high profile trial was held, acquitting Ver in December 1985, creating yet another uproar.

Throughout his gradual loss of institutional support, Marcos played his US card to the hilt. The US alternately lobbied for change and compromised with his manipulative political deals and grandstanding. The US tried to be "proper" in its dealings with the beleaguered president, at the same time pushing for greater reforms, both political and economic. The result was that it really pleased no-one.

LoveHate.

Those who favored quick change and new leadership were angry with the US for not forcing the issue, while leftists and other anti-US factions lambasted Washington for propping up the ailing dictator, proving "once again" US imperialism.

The Aquino assassination in 1983 brought an increasing number of protests and protesters to the streets, melding the traditional political opposition with more radical leftist groups. The US found itself both courted and disliked by all sides as it took on a tentative policy of not actively supporting anyone, but pressing for democracy — in the halls of Government and in the streets — to play itself out.

Marcos used his US "card" almost as a threat to detractors. Image grew more important than substance — a lot of icing, no cake. Parliamentary elections in 1984 gave the opposition a minority say, but it remained fractured and merely a political vent. Then In November 1985 Marcos announced — live on ABC's "Nightline" — that he would call a "snap" presidential election to prove once and for all he maintained popular support. He believed the opposition would never unify over one candidate, and that his control over election machinery would suffice.

But after tense negotiations, the opposition united behind Corazon Aquino, who stood as an anti-Marcos icon, regardless of her political inexperience. The prime poll watching organization — the National Movement for Free Elections (Namfrel) — expanded its coverage nationwide, and foreign observers, many from the US, were invited. It was a hectic month of campaigning for both sides before the February 6 vote. It was obvious that Aquino was drawing huge spontaneous crowds against Marcos' stage-managed campaign. Marcos was so ill he had to be carried through the crowds to the rally grandstands.

Had votes been properly counted, the result would have been close. But Namfrel's tally varied from the official tabulation. Commission of Election computer workers walked out en masse after they discovered manipulated data. The parliament read its fixed count and declared Marcos president.

The US sent senior diplomat Philip Habib to broker a deal as massive demonstrations and boycotts of crony businesses mounted. The US Embassy was almost a daily target, its security fence splattered with red paint and graffiti.

But events moved well beyond US influence, and caught Washington off guard.

Lt. Gen. Fidel V. Ramos was Vice Chief of Staff when Ver won the top job in 1981. Ramos replaced Ver while the latter was on trial, but became incensed when Marcos reinstalled Ver — rather than retiring him — upon his controversial acquittal two months before the snap election. Defense Secretary Juan Ponce Enrile also saw his power gradually reduced since he was removed as martial law administrator in 1981. And he became political guru to a group of disenchanted officers known as RAM (Reform the Armed Forces Movement).

Marcos, learning of a plot to remove him from the palace, pre-empted a putsch by arresting several plotters, including the bodyguards of the trade and industry minister. Afraid of a sweep against them, RAM officers, led by Col. Gregorio Honasan, met at Enrile's home on Saturday morning, February 21.

By late afternoon, Ramos and Enrile, protected by RAM, entered the main military camp at Camp Aguinaldo. The revolt was on.

Ramos that night moved to his office across the EDSA highway at Camp Crame, working the phones with provincial commanders for support. But by the following afternoon, a Sunday, Sin's call to show "the people's power" brought millions of people to the streets — the largest group on EDSA between the two camps. Orders to lob shells into the camps were refused, and Marcos quickly lost his last pillar, the military.

The US pressured Marcos to escape into exile (he brought along family, friends, boxes of money and jewels). But first Marcos wanted his "inauguration" on the veranda of the tightly guarded palace, minutes after Aquino was "inaugurated" in a ceremony across town.

• • •

Manila Archbishop Jaime Cardinal Sin tried to mediate peace while supporting and helping coalesce the disparate opposition groups. But it was his call over the radio the night the military revolt began – for the public to go to the streets to show "the people's power" – that rapidly became a mantra worldwide for popular uprisings against dictatorial or authoritative regimes.

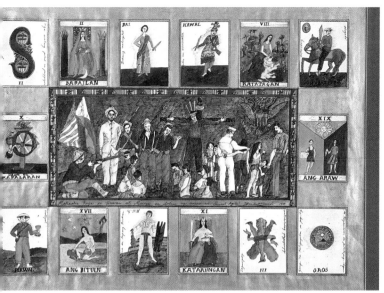

1986 - 1992: Political Cacophony — LoveHate

There was a palpable, almost giddy euphoria upon the restoration of democracy that lasted several months. Aquino's problem was twofold. First, her "coalition" now included not merely disparate opposition groups and politicians, but the business community, religious groups and — her murdered husband's jailers — the military. She had to get all of them represented and heard, to keep them on her side.

The second was her stature as an icon of democracy. The trusted few inner circle included her family, a group of human rights lawyers, a few religious-minded businessmen and Cardinal Sin. She was not keen on complex issues and used a great deal of instinct in making decisions.

In short, she needed to become a reasoned, human administrator and political leader rather than a symbol of ideals. It was a nearly impossible shift.

The US was oozing praise — a populist-led victory for democracy for a change. The US Congress was ecstatic. During her late summer trip to the US, she was greeted by House Speaker Eugene "Tip" O'Neal after her warmly received congressional speech. "Mrs. President, you sure hit a home run," he said. Aquino smiled back, "I just hope the bases were loaded."

Debt rescheduling, new financing, investments, an IMF program all helped get the economy moving (it had a lot to catch up — just to its prior self, let alone to the rest of the booming region). A new Constitution was in the works. Political prisoners were released. Steps were taken to bring Moro separatists home to start the process towards peace in the Muslim south.

For the RAM officers, however, they had a huge problem with all this.

Foremost, they felt they were the ones who finally bit the bullet and got rid of Marcos. They had taken the immediate, and ultimate, risk. And they did so not for any reasons of pure democracy, rather to reform what had become a personalized military — that bypassed them in the process of promotion by the way. They had fought leftists, communists and the Moros for 15 years, and here she goes and releases everyone they fought so hard to capture. True, Ramos was AFP Chief of Staff and Enrile Defense Secretary. But the power had gravitated towards the so-called Mabini human rights lawyers, their adversaries for years. It was the exact opposite of martial law. The military had to remain the strongest of the pillars of power, they said. Yet it seemed that an amorphous fudge of religious and liberal zealots had taken control — with no direction except dismantling anything Marcos created.

It was Aquino's autumn trip to Tokyo that set the tone for the next four years of political instability. "God Save The Queen" was the name

"Makaalis kaya si Huwan at Mariya sa Ilalim ng Anino ni Samuel Agila?" ("Can Huwan and Mariya Flee from the Shadow of Samuel the Eagle?")...is a part of Brenda Fajardo's Tarot Card series. This series by Farjado, painter and printmaker, has strong historical and nationalistic themes, along with folk and surrrealist aspects. The tarot images have been indigenized to convey a narrative of anti-colonial struggle, according to Alice Guillermo. (Photo: The Ateneo Art Gallery Collection)

Long-time Social-Democrat Raul Manglapus, a nationalist from the 1950s, assumed the Foreign Affairs portfolio during the Aquino administration just in time to begin negotiating on the extension of the US Bases. His views clashed directly with no-nonsense negotiator Richard Armitage of the US. Some say Manglapus should have kept playing the drums with Duke Ellington, as he does in this vintage photo from January, 1972. (Photo: Richie Quririno)

of the plot. In essence, Aquino would be made a figurehead, with the Edsa revolt leaders taking control. Ramos refused to lend support, however. Political power is won by election, he argued. So retire from the military and run for office. That was very much Washington's line as well. The putsch was stillborn. Enrile was replaced by Ramos as Defense Secretary.

But it antagonized RAM leaders to the point of resigning themselves to an outright *coup d'etat,* the first overt attempt in late August, 1987, as the economy was showing solid signs of growth. That was, of course, abruptly stunted.

US Secretary of State George Shultz signing an interim agreement on the US bases in 1987 with Philippine Foreign Secretary Raul Manglapus. At right is Richard Armitage, who led the final negotiations into 1991. The Philippine Free Press cartoon below illustrates how the Philippine Senate reacted. (Photo: US Embassy - Public Affairs Section)

US relations ran hot and cold as well. It saw the political floundering weakening a reborn democracy at a time when institution building was paramount. Yes, there was a new Constitution, a freely elected Senate and Congress, and cooperation with multilateral institutions on economic issues. But within those walls was political mush, not exactly President Ronald Reagan's favorite. And negotiations over the future of the bases at Clark and Subic were needed prior to treaty expiration in 1992.

RAM struck again in December, 1989, and almost won. After a frenetic morning of consultations within Malacañang, and with Washington, the US scrambled its fighter planes to fly over Manila airspace in support of Aquino (and Ramos, who adamantly stuck to Constitutional process). The tide turned against the rebels, although a weeklong standoff in the Makati financial district added prime time drama. Foreign investors — particularly Japanese — had been told two weeks earlier Manila was stable enough for rapid growth and investment. After the coup attempt, all was lost — another three years before anyone would take notice again. More economic opportunity gone.

The US over-flights had been critical, even though they were mostly for show. Several points were being made. One ultimately succeeded, the other failed.

The failure was in proving the importance of US bases as a protector of democracy, at least in the Philippine context. As early as 1988 US foreign affairs forums with high level Filipino participation were concluding that a phased return of Clark was likely, with the Yanks retaining the secure deepwater Subic Bay for naval logistics and repair. A new Treaty was needed, not any agreement. And it thus required approval of both US and Philippine senates.

The US chose the tough, no nonsense Richard Armitage as its

negotiator. Aquino chose newly appointed Foreign Secretary Raul Manglapus, an aging social democrat on the coalition fringe with ideals from his heyday in the 1950s and pre-Marcos '60s. Given the forward-looking nature and diplomatic sensitivity required for these talks, neither side could have chosen a more conflicting personality. Neither could empathize with the other. They spoke at different levels. The draft treaty was delayed past the self-imposed deadline of January, 1991. LoveHate.

Then came the eruption of Mt. Pinatubo in June. The most massive volcanic eruption of the 20th century left millions of tons of ash and lahar around Clark, its accompanying tremors weakening runways. A storm passing through at the time blew up to six feet of ash on to Olongapo City and Subic. The cleanup hounds the region to this day.

But it was the nationalists in the Senate who won the day, and the proposed Treaty was voted down. The US had until November, 1992 to leave both bases. Some called it the first true independence from the US. Others called it folly. The critical role both Clark and Subic played as a staging area during the Gulf War in early 1991 was lost to the US. But so was hundreds of millions of dollars a year in aid and direct contributions to the Philippines GDP.

The success was Ramos. He proved to the skeptics in the military that a general can earn political power via the electorate, not coups. Aquino supported him during the 1992 elections. He won a plurality in a multiparty campaign for the presidency. Since then, several retired military officers have been elected to Congress, with two — including Honasan — winning Senate seats. Enrile also won a Senate seat, but lost reelection in 2001.

• • •

The US Navy Battleship New Jersey (above), an occasional visitor to Subic Bay, below. Subic was critical in logistics support during the Gulf War, but it was US Air Force flyovers across Manila's military camps that changed the tide during the 1989 RAM coup attempt. (Photos: US Embassy - Public Affairs Section)

1992 – 1998: Political Stability/Economic Reform — Love

Despite losing the military bases, the US saw the Ramos presidency as a sign of political maturity. He was a methodical, meticulous president almost to the point of micro-management. There was a dearth of new infrastructure during the Aquino years, and it showed itself most profoundly in the 6-8 hour blackouts faced almost daily in and around Metro-Manila. He created a Department of Energy, fast-tracking new build/operate/transfer plants to get the lights back on. But more important, he sat down with advisors and built a vision of what he wanted the country to be in 1998. Then step by step he set out to fulfill it. He didn't get all the way there, but at least had significant achievement to show for the attempt.

San Roque hydro-electric project. "Turn on the lights" was the early credo of the Ramos administration, which restarted infrastructure investment during a period of economic growth. (Photo: San Roque Power Corp.)

He used US president Lyndon Johnson's characterization of politics as a tent: "I'd rather have 'em on the inside pissin' out than on the outside pissin' in." Ramos began or restarted negotiations with the communists and Moro MNLF (the Jakarta accords of 1996 bringing most of the MNLF back into the fold). He accommodated political aspirations of RAM and other retired military men by either giving them a voice or being lenient on their past roles in coup attempts — allowing them to run for office. They did, and some won. Ramos worked hard — and with US support — to help give the military greater professionalism.

Deregulation and privatization was his economic mantra. Shipping, finance, retail liberalization and power were all placed on the road to better efficiency. The business sector responded and steady growth ensued. US business took notice and contracts with Filipino suppliers boomed. Sub-contracting flourished, but direct investment also increased. Ramos emphasis wasn't the US, however. It was to get the country back in competition with the rest of ASEAN. That was a refreshing sign, not merely because it was needed, but because the US was itself dealing with Asia as a partner and not as policeman around the Pacific Rim.

Still, steady US economic growth during Ramos' tenure brought a surge in new overseas employment opportunities in the US itself, and Filipinos grew to become the second largest annual immigrant group in the US behind Mexicans.

The Asian financial crisis beginning in 1997 took its toll, but less forcefully than other ASEAN nations. Manila was still on a "recovery" path so had less to lose. The lost decade of the 1980s left the Philippines way behind its core ASEAN neighbors in terms of economic infrastructure. So it was also less vulnerable to a fall.

Philippine and US Presidents Fidel Ramos and Bill Clinton at the Seattle APEC meeting, above. Thumbs up was the mood in both countries, particularly in the economic sphere. The Philippines began catching up with the rest of its ASEAN neighbors, while the US enjoyed the flowering of the information age.

Then US Ambassador to the Philippines John Negroponte, right, at a meeting of Republicans abroad. He, like many US ambassadors posted to Manila, rose to major portfolios within the US Government. Negroponte later became US Ambassador to the United Nations during the administration of George W. Bush. (Photos: above, US Embassy; below, AmCham)

There was even some political hankering for ways to allow Ramos to continue as President for another term. But always the constitutionalist, he vowed to abide by the one-term limitation. His opposition vice president, Joseph "Erap" Estrada, a Robin Hood-like matinee film idol from the 1960s and pro-Marcos Mayor of Mandaluyong during martial law, was considered a shoo-in to replace him. Extremely popular with the *masa* — both urban and rural — they saw him as champion of the poor. This was now grass-roots democracy. And Estrada won a landslide against several opponents who split Ramos' coalition vote.

• • •

1998 - 2001: "A Man of the Person" — LoveHate

US-Philippine relations remained proper. And it was clear from the beginning of the Estrada presidency that most were willing to see if the mayor, with his late night carousing, gambling instincts and his buddy system would grow into the job.

He didn't.

The US "card" had weakened as its "pillar" of power had disintegrated. Filipinos still thronged to the consulate for visas, but politically there was little need to curry Washington's support on domestic issues.

From the US side, the main issues were intellectual property rights, the application of a new extradition treaty to hand over an Estrada crony for fraud and illegal campaign contribution indictments, and a new visiting US forces agreement for joint military exercises.

It was all peripheral to the fact that the former movie star was systematically eroding most of the confidence and credibility the country had worked so hard to achieve. He initiated a "war" in central Mindanao against the Muslim Moro Islamic Liberation Front (MILF), celebrating his "victory" by flying in roast pig to troops who had taken its main camp. Great diplomacy! An international hostage crisis by the mafiosi-like Abu Sayyaf, kidnapping mostly European tourists from a Malaysian diving resort, didn't help his image as they were gradually released after negotiated ransom payments.

But it was an illegal gambling scandal in which he was alleged to be siphoning off money from the poor that led to his impeachment in late 2000. A Senate vote not to see crucial evidence led to a middle class uprising at a monument commemorating the 1986 Edsa revolt. The military withdrew its support and vice president Gloria Macapagal-Arroyo, became President.

• • •

Joseph "Erap" Estrada at an AmCham luncheon. Early on, he was refreshing with his populist touch. But he ran the country as if he were mayor, not President. And his penchant for back door deals antagonized both the legislature and the business elite. (Photo: AmCham)

2001 – : Ally Against Terror — LoveHate

Brought up in a presidential household, President Macapagal-Arroyo has to mix traditional politics with economic common sense. That is no easy task in a country coming to grips with a gaping chasm between rich and poor. Immediately following the September 11, 2001 terrorist attacks on New York and Washington, she declared her support for the War on Terror. And this came despite her sincere attempts to move forward in working out agreements with the predominantly Muslim Moros in central and southern Mindanao.

The Philippine/US relationship has grown stronger in the months prior to this essay. And it has rekindled a now miniscule leftist antagonism in the process. But the US — and the Philippine Government — must tread a delicate line. Terror must be vanquished. But it must be done within the context of a centuries-old, valid Moro right to religious, cultural and political legitimacy, as well as Filipino pride and nationalism.

• • •

Three Philippine presidents — Corazon Aquino (1986-92), Fidel Ramos (1992-1998) and Gloria Macapagal Arroyo (2001-) lighting the "Freedom Flame" commemorating the "People Power" revolts which toppled the presidencies of Ferdinand Marcos (1986) and Joseph "Erap" Estrada (2001). (Photo: Agence France Presse)

Where Do We Go From Here? — LoveLove?

Doubtful. Can't think of a country that had two colonizers during the so-called "colonial" period. Also can't think of a country that didn't win its war for independence. Malaysia never fought, and it's a rotating Muslim monarchy over a federated, parliamentary system. The Kingdom of Thailand was never a colony. Singapore is a city state, ejected from Malaysia in 1965 so Kuala Lumpur could keep its population…well…Malay. Indonesia fought the Dutch in 1945 with US help and won.

The Philippines was given independence piecemeal, after losing its war in 1901. US culture penetrated the archipelago far more in 48 years than Spain did in 336 years.

There remains a popular antithesis against the US for its "haughty" attitude, its "wealth," its world "power," and its "sideshow of the sideshow" view of the region. "The Philippines is crucial logistically, but for little else," so people feel.

Yet, there are few *barangays* in the country without at least one family with a relative thriving in "the States." And they say this with pride.

US-Philippine relations will remain an unrequited LoveHate for years to come. And perhaps that's how it should be. After all, most familial relationships are.

"Where do we go from here??" US and Philippine "Balikatan" joint-exercise Commanders ponder the question in 2002. (Photo: by 1st Lt. Neil A. Peterson, USMC, Balikatan 2002)

Philippine Political Parties — a lack of US influence

by Beth Day Romulo

Some Filipinos like to say that their justice and political systems are based on the US system. But one of the first things that strikes an American expatriate living in the Philippines is the absence of political parties as we know them. There are names of parties but as one western observer commented, Filipino politicians change parties as casually as they change their shirts. The parties have no meaning — beyond the "Ins" and the "Outs."

There are no clear political party platforms such as we see in the two major political parties in the United States — the Democrats and Republicans — which have very real differences in how they believe the nation should be governed, starting with "big" government versus "small" government. In the main, the Republicans stick to the idea that less is better, also favoring lower taxes for example, while the Democrats cling to the notion that government should provide a range of social services for the people and that taxes should be high enough to cover costs.

Leonard Wood addressing the Philippine Legislature 1921. (Photo: AHC)

But in the Philippines, we see no such philosophy of governance. While initially parties took some stands in political philosophy (read the speeches of Quezon and Osmena and Recto), the Marcos years of martial law in which parties not aligned with the presidency were considered subversive and there was no public debate, killed off what nascent political philosophy there had been.

Thus the country developed the parties of "personality and patronage," which are actually antipathetic to the foundation of a sturdy democracy. Campaigns are a personality contest, nowhere more evident than in the fact that movie stars and TV personalities and sports heroes often prove to be the most popular candidates. Speeches on policy are virtually non-existent. Candidates are expected to dance and sing, play the guitar and in many cases act the fool. Even the very serious present President Gloria Macapagal-Arroyo has been known to dance on stage, as did Letty Shahani, who "cha-cha'ed" her way to senatorial popularity. These women, both immensely serious and informed, should not have to do that to get votes. But in the Philippines it is par for the course. One "performs" in the theatrical sense during a

(Cartoon: Philippine Free Press, May 2, 1931)

campaign, or is politically dead. People walk away.

Nor are the so-called "privilege" speeches in the Senate anything worth studying. They are also platform pleasers with little substance. The most impassioned are usually the nationalists who unfortunately are also likely to be protectionist, which does not suit the needs of today's global society.

Politics, to a great extent, is perceived by aspiring politicians as a sinecure — an income for life. Family dynasties control provinces. Payoffs at every level are expected. Corruption is not only countenanced but often institutionalized. One small town mayor estimated that of funds earmarked for a project (roads, bridges, and schools) no more than a tenth of the original amount actually goes to the project.

The so-called party system is relatively meaningless by US standards. The earliest political parties in the Philippines in 1906, organized for the first Philippine Assembly, were simply pro-American and nationalist. By the Commonwealth period, there was the leading Nacionalista Party (the party of President Quezon and Vice President Osmeña) and soon thereafter the Liberal Party. President Roxas left the Nacionalista Party to form the Liberal Party, and upon his death (in office) Vice President Quirino succeeded him as the Liberal Party leader. President Garcia, who as vice president to President Magsaysay (who also died in office) was a Nacionalista, but the disenchanted young followers of Magsaysay formed the Progressive Party to disassociate themselves from Garcia's administration.

Both Nacionalista and Liberal parties were controlled by wealthy cliques and landowners. There was little difference in policy between them. The system of political patronage emerged early on, so that the allegiance of voters was to the leader of the party rather than to the party itself. Presidents Roxas, Magsaysay and Marcos all switched parties for political gain, to no one's surprise. In 1965 Marcos won as a Nacionalista, the same year that Raul Manglapus formed a Party for Philippine Progress which went nowhere.

From 1965, when he took office, till he fled the country in 1986 during the EDSA revolution Marcos' Nacionalista Party ruled — though he called it the KBL (Kilusang Bagong Lipunan) — but any opposition to it was simply considered subversive.

Since the first EDSA revolution, parties have been negligible in face of a contest of leaders — Aquino, Ramos, Estrada, and Macapagal-Arroyo. Philippine democracy according to British historian Raymond Nelson more nearly resembles Latin America than the US in the fact that regardless of how the economy and services of the country are run, the sub-stratum is Spanish in origin — a system of political patronage, based on wealth.

Although congressmen supposedly represent the interests of their districts, the Philippine Congress has seldom been representative of the majority of the people.

Most political leaders have come from the same, landed class, originally established under Spanish rule. Four centuries of Spanish rule left a nation of Spanish masters and Filipino serfs which, when the Spaniards left, was replaced by an internal, almost feudal, colonialism.

Ferdinand Marcos after winning the Nacionalista Party's nomination for president 1965. (Photo courtesy Beth Day Romulo)

Filipinos, through crown grants or the acquisition of church lands, took over from the Spaniards and became the master class, and their members, or politicians backed by them, won the congressional seats. For those without inherited wealth, the avenue to power has been to study law, and then run for political office. Once elected, professional politicians were expected to dispense jobs and favors to their constituents and relatives (which accounts in part for the bloated and inefficient bureaucracy). Businesses were forced to hire workers they did not need nor want. Since all the politicians came from the same class, they and their parties were relatively interchangeable, as alike — the saying went, as "Coca-Cola and Pepsi Cola."

Without personal wealth or the support of a wealthy patron it is still impossible to win political office in the Philippines.

And political corruption is endemic and can be traced back as far as a 1920 survey which found that all civil service positions at that time as well as political office were "bought."

Unfortunately, while US rule did introduce public education and sanitation, it did not lay down the roots of a healthy, working democratic political system. American administrations initially dealt with the Filipino elite, reinforcing the landed aristocracy rule, inherited from Spanish times.

Later, during the Cold War years, the US simply supported whoever appeared to them to be anti-communist. Ramon Magsaysay was strongly supported by Washington, as was later Ferdinand Marcos, primarily because of their anti-communist position, which the US felt was essential to the stability of Asia at the time.

Another weakness in the Philippine political system lies in the manner of electing members to the Senate. They are elected at large and thus have no constituency to answer to. They proceed on the basis of personal agenda that has little effect on society as a whole. Frequently, the Senate is used as a springboard to the presidency. They can do this with impunity since they have no constituency to monitor their actions. "Write your Senator" has little or no meaning here.

So long as poverty and corrupt political practices prevail, the country has a limited chance to develop a democratic political system. On the other hand, there is today a growing awareness of the effects of corruption, and a growing public cry for good governance. A lot of this comes from young people — those professionals with their cellphones attached to their ears, who are constantly sending text messages to one another. Fortunately for this intercommunication among citizens, politicians are more vulnerable than they have ever been. During the first EDSA revolt in 1986, it took twenty hours to assemble a crowd. The second EDSA revolt (2001) created a crowd within twenty minutes.

The foreign media greatly misjudged what EDSA II was all about and who was present. They were not the elite. They were not the military. The hard core was composed of relatively anonymous young professionals, awakened to the problems of the country through the live coverage of the impeachment trial of then President Joseph Estrada. For once the public could see the politicians and the lawyers in action. And they turned off their television sets in disgust when the 11 wily senators succeeded in getting a vote to withhold evidence, just as the Chief Justice was about to rule that the evidence should be opened. This was as good a lesson in political chicanery as a voting public is likely to get. Within that twenty minutes of the closure of the impeachment trial without resolution, crowds were forming on EDSA.

While impeachment had been threatened before, the first impeachment trial that actually got underway was the one against Estrada. If it had been allowed to run its course, there would have been no need for a subsequent trial. But as there was no closure and no verdict, the trial of the President before the Sandiganbayan (a judicial court dealing with cases filed against government officials) must proceed, on the corruption and plunder charges introduced at the impeachment trial.

This is a first in Philippine history. And it augurs well for the political maturity of the country. It also reflects a growing awareness and acceptance of the necessity of the rule of law in Asia.

The Asian breakthrough occurred in South Korea when two former presidents were charged, tried and imprisoned for the sort of corruption that has been going on in most Asian countries for decades. When the then President of South Korea, Kim Dae Jung (who had been harassed and imprisoned by his predecessors) took office, he pardoned them and they went free — to live out their days in infamy.

In other parts of the world, we find Chile's Augusto Pinochet on trial for violation of human rights, and Slobodan Milosevic finally being tried for war crimes in Yugoslavia. Individual members of the legislatures of India and Japan and Thailand have recently been forced from office on charges of corruption. And let's not forget Indonesia.

An alert citizenry is demanding good governance. And only when governance is good, can any country develop to its full potential. It is hoped that the level of public awareness and public protest in the Philippines will be maintained until the political system is reformed to reflect the public will, and truly becomes a democracy. At this stage, it is still a work in progress.

Education and the American Legacy

By Andrew Gonzalez, FSC

Students of Philippine post-colonial (July 4, 1946) history are almost unanimous in their opinion that the most lasting positive legacy of the US period (1898-1946) was the nation's educational system.

Excellent studies about education during the period trace its growth, development and its immediate impact on the educational plans of the Philippine Commonwealth (1935-1946) — Alzona 1932, Aldana 1930, Hayden 1947, Larson 1963.

Less examined in detail is the development of the system built by the US government since the July 4, 1946 independence, for in studying the history of institutions, it is important not only to examine the legacy itself, but likewise to see what the heirs of that legacy did with their inheritance.

The analysis of the continuing influence, if any, of the American system set up by the colonial government takes on special relevance this year 2002 as we mark the centennial of the American Chamber of Commerce. The Chamber continued its work after Independence and has taken a continuing interest in education ever since.

It likewise takes on special significance at this time as the American community in the Philippines observed the centennial of the Thomasites in the year 2001. For it was the Thomasites who set up the system of education in the country after they began arriving on August 21, 1901 and exercised their influence (albeit in reduced numbers) afterwards.

The end of the Francis Burton Harrison governor-generalship saw a civil service almost totally Filipino, including the middle level bureaucracy and the teaching force of what was then called the Department of Public Instruction.

• • •

The Legacy Itself

The school system, established via the Organic Act of 1901, initially began with the Bureau of Public Instruction under a Director; subsequently, it became the Department of Public Instruction under a Secretary. Traditionally, through the end of the Commonwealth period,

Thomasite teachers relaxing inside an early 20th century Philippine home. They overhauled the Spanish colonial system of selective enrollment by instituting public education throughout the archipelago. Using English and initially US textbooks, their cultural influence was profound. (Photo: AHC)

William Howard Taft with Thomasites and children in Baguio. (Photo: AHC)

the office of the Department of Education was deemed so important that its Secretary was concurrently the Vice-Governor General and, under the Commonwealth, the Vice-President.

Elementary schools were established in every municipality; secondary schools in every province. To staff these institutions, the Philippine Normal School was set up in 1901, initially to offer a two-year post-secondary teacher training program. Subsequently, the liberal arts sequence of the Philippine Normal School was expanded to a full four-year program of liberal arts and became the nucleus of the College of Arts and Sciences of the University of the Philippines in 1908.

By then, Philippine Normal School offered a two-year program for Elementary Teaching Certificates and subsequently, a full four-year program for Bachelor of Science in Elementary Education. The four-year program, leading to a Bachelor of Science in Secondary Education, was offered by the College of Education of the University of the Philippines. The University of the Philippines itself started out as the liberal arts unit of the Philippine Normal School, the College of Medicine in Manila, and the College of Agriculture at Los Baños, all established in 1908.

The Department of Public Instruction was staffed by well-trained educators. They came from the best universities in the US; the initial Directors of Education later became college university presidents or important education officers in the US.

In addition to setting up basic academic programs, special schools were organized: at the secondary level; provincial agriculture high schools in rural areas, schools of arts and trades, and commercial courses. To train teachers for these special schools, the University of the Philippines at Los Baños prepared agriculture teachers; the Philippine College of Commerce trained teachers and practitioners in the "distributive arts"; and the Philippine School of Arts and Trades, teachers for vocational-technical education.

Thus basic education for all levels and for different kinds existed, with the University of the Philippines beginning to offer graduate programs to the MA level beginning in 1922.

Research was conducted at the Bureau of Science; Bureau of Plant Industry, Animal Industry, Public Health, Forestry; and the Weather Bureau. The Bureau of Science had special research institutes: Food and Nutrition Research Institute (FNRI), Forest Products Research and Development Institute. In 1933, by special law, the National Research Council of the Philippines was established and the *Philippine Journal of Science* began to enjoy an international reputation throughout the decade.

During the period, sectarian (including Catholic and Protestant schools) constituted the nucleus of the private school system operating all grades, especially at the secondary and tertiary levels.

Early on, the US colonial government insisted on universal use of the English language throughout the system, except at private schools which continued to use Spanish. By the 1920s even Spanish-era institutions switched to English, with Spanish relegated to a foreign language.

The use of English was a practical expedient as none of the local vernaculars could claim a majority of speakers. There was also the obvious problem of lack of materials and teachers. President William McKinley actually instructed the Second Philippine Commission to use local languages and English (as the "language of democracy"), but a multilingual primary system was simply not feasible. Secretary of War Elihu N. Root, who was in charge of governing the colony at the Insular Desk, finally chose English as de facto the only language in the classroom.

With English taught as a subject and as the medium of instruction, a fully developed system was built on three levels. Seven years of elementary schooling, 4 years of secondary schooling, and 4 to 7 years of tertiary schooling became the norm. The usual courses ranged from 2 years for certificates (elementary education, practical courses in agriculture, arts and trades, and distributive arts i.e. commerce) — to 4 years for bachelor's degrees. Master's degrees were open-ended, with no doctorate except in medicine. Other available programs were in education, law, divinity, commerce (including accountancy), engineering, the natural sciences, pharmacy and optometry).

• • •

Training Filipino Teachers, Thomasite-Style*

by Mary Racelis

When older Filipinos remember the Thomasites, what they recall most vividly is the influence these early American teachers had on their own generation, and carried well into their adult Filipino lives. By contrast, many contemporary Filipino educators believe that the Thomasites' greatest legacy lies in the professional standards they instilled for generations of Filipino teachers.

As early as 1900, there were 2,167 Filipino educators augmented by 889 US teachers — many of them academically qualified ex-soldiers temporarily drafted to launch the new school system. By 1902, the 1,074 American teachers who disembarked from the transport ship *Thomas* the previous year found themselves organizing schools in 44 provincial capitals and in Manila. Three years later there were 3,414 Filipino teachers supervised by 826 Thomasites, actively honing their skills in English and learning to promote "the American way of life" in classrooms the length and breadth of the archipelago.

From the very beginning, the colonial administration knew it could never muster enough US teachers to cover more than a fraction of all the classrooms it intended to open. Its strategy, therefore, was to assign Thomasites to provincial urban centers, where they opened and ran public schools patterned after the first four grades of American primary education. Filipino teachers handled the barrio or village-level primary schools, continuing to teach in the local language or Spanish until they could make the shift to English instruction.

Early problems arose as recalcitrant

SS Thomas (Photo: AHC)

Note "Thomasites" has become the generic term for all American teachers recruited by the colonial government into the public school system, whether or not they actually arrived on the transport SS Thomas.

Opposite page: Pre WWII Buildings of the UP College of Fine Arts on Padre Faura.

This page, above and right: Philippine Normal School, circa 1915. (Photos: Lico collection)

Thomasites waiting to unload boxes of textbooks for their schools. (Photo: AHC)

teachers from the Spanish era persisted in using rote-memory methods, sometimes reinforced by harsh discipline. The Thomasites soon began seeking out young people in the town with adequate schooling, who were interested in becoming professional educators and willing to undergo training in the new pedagogy. In larger cities, like Manila and Cebu, locating likely candidates proved easier than in the more remote, sparsely populated areas, where educated young Filipinos were still few. Moreover, those among them who showed potential frequently opted to go into business or take better paying jobs rather than go into teaching that offered a meager P6 – P10 monthly salary.

Nonetheless, the Thomasites soon attracted a growing number of Filipino applicants. Some started off as assistants to the US teachers and, upon passing the required tests, assumed formal teaching positions. To reach that point

meant a daily after-school study program over a period of several months featuring two- to three-hour afternoon or evening classes with a Thomasite. For barrio teachers, regular visits from their supervising Thomasite in town would have the latter observing classroom manner and methodology and the conduct of outdoor calisthenics and sports programs. A concluding feedback session would find the American giving the Filipino teacher suggestions for improving his or her performance. The session would end with the local teacher happy and relieved at the support and encouragement coming from the *maestro americano.*

Becoming a professional educator required not only teaching subject matter but also an understanding of democratic values. The Thomasites enjoined Filipino teachers to inculcate in their students the spirit of intellectual inquiry and critical thinking. Crucial, too, were traits like honesty, perseverance, industriousness, cleanliness, justice, fairness, cheerfulness, courtesy, equal treatment of others, sportsmanship, the dignity of manual labor, citizenship and love of

What's happened since (1946-2002)?

World War II largely disrupted the entire system. But in the post-War period, the single biggest factor influencing education was the rampant population increase.

During the last census (1939) of the American Period, total population was 16 million. In the 2000 census, initial results show the Philippine population at 76.4 million. That's nearly a fivefold increase in just 60 years, discounting widespread death associated with WWII.

From 47 tertiary level institutions in 1946, there were 1,353 in 2001. These are composed of state and private colleges and universities, technological institutes, post secondary and non-degree programs.

The 1987 Constitution declared secondary education free for all; the proportion of the high school population was 40% public, 60% private in 1987. However, over the last 14 years, the shift has been dramatic in favor of the public high schools, now serving 76% of the total high school population of 5,022,830. The private sector is down to 24% and dropping further.

The education budget during the presidency of Diosdado Macapagal reached a high of 26% of the budget total. But it went down progressively in favor of military expenditures under the dictatorship of Ferdinand E. Marcos. Of the total budget for FY 1985-1986, the education slice was a mere 10.37%.

country. Morality was essential and visible in Filipino teachers' avoiding vices, and paying their debts on time.

Communicating these noble ideals would be difficult under any circumstances, but more so when in the early years, neither teacher nor pupil understood the language preferred for transmitting these values! The Thomasites persisted by example. Gradually these norms became staples of value systems taught to generations of public school students, sometimes in contradiction to countervailing values simultaneously promoted at home and by the community. Belief in the honesty, fairness and integrity of public school teachers persists to this day, evident in their continued designation as election administrators and the respect they command in their communities.

The zeal with which Filipino teachers pursued the aim of becoming true professionals appeared as early as 1905 during the teacher-training summer institute conducted at the Manila Normal School. While 200 participants had been expected, 800 turned up from all parts of the country,

eager to know the latest in "modern education." New approaches to teaching, and reading widely about the world became increasingly important as one moved up to the upper grade levels. Several incentives fired their enthusiasm, like having a regular salaried job, the prospect of promotion, and the prestige of speaking English and even being called upon to translate at meetings between the *presidente* (town mayor) and visiting Americans.

On the eve of World War II in 1940, 43,682 Filipino teachers were running their classrooms, a few of them still assisted by the remaining 97 US teachers. In another six years, Filipino educators would face the task of charting on their own the education system for an independent Philippines, building on the Thomasite heritage of a democratic education, while exorcising its underlying colonial content and orientation in favor of a nationalist-oriented system. For the Thomasites the job was done; for the Filipino teachers the task was just beginning.

The books are on their way.
(Photo: AHC)

Early 1900s classroom.
(Photo: AHC)

The Gabaldon schoolhouse.

William Parson's most recognizable architectural legacy was the Gabaldon schoolhouse, one-meter above ground, with walls and foundation of reinforced concrete and roofs of galvanized sheets. Named after Isauro Gabaldon, member of the Philippine Assembly and Resident Commissioner to the U.S. (1920-1925) and known for the Gabaldon Bill which provided one million pesos for the building of concrete public schoolhouses throughout Philippines. (Photo: Lico collection)

The 1987 Constitution dictates the biggest item of the budget is to go to education, a policy that has been followed ever since. For the proposed 2001-2002 budget, the share of education is P102 billion out of P780 billion or 13% just for basic education operations.

Despite the seemingly large allocation, necessary inputs for education have dropped such that the backlog has become almost insurmountable unless the current and future administrations have the political will to prioritize education.

By school year 2001-2002, there remained a shortage of 35,000 teachers and 8,443 classrooms. Only 25% of the 36,000 public elementary schools had full time principals; the rest run by head teachers or teachers-in-charge. Only slightly over 51% of the 4000 public high schools had principals. In 1998, at the start of the Estrada Administration, the proportion of books per students was 1:8 for high school and 1:6 for grade school.

By reducing the number of major subjects to 5 (English, Filipino, *Araling Panlipunan* [Social Studies], Science and Mathematics), streamlining bidding to maximize books printed and through soft loans, the Department of Education, Culture and Sports (DECS) wants to achieve a 1:1 ratio at the end of 2002.

Shortages of teachers, classrooms, and administrators continue, as well as desks — another priority for 2002.

What's left of the US legacy is the continuing use of English as a medium of instruction. This allows the continued large deployment of Overseas Foreign Workers possible.

In 2000, the number of Filipinos estimated with competence in English was expected to be 78.7% (Gonzalez 1977). A small survey done for the Linguistic Society of the Philippines in 1994 showed that 73% claimed that they could read English, 59% claimed that they could write English, and 56% claimed that they could speak English fluently.

When people claim that English is 'deteriorating,' they neglect the evolution of Filipino English, modified structurally because it is learned more often as second language, a situation similar to English in all non-English speaking countries. Linguistic sounds or literal translations from Filipino to English, produce phrases like "open the light" (from the Tagalog *'Buksan mo ang ilaw'*) instead of "turn on the lights."

Grammatically, however, Philippine English tends to be conservative; there is an attempt among users to try to maintain the rules although there are evolving subsystems of verb/tense, use of articles, special combinations of two-word verbs (*get up, get on,* etc.) which are peculiarly Filipino. As English is learned in schools, the written style of most Filipinos, including our fiction writers, tends to be conservative, less colorful, less creative (unlike Australian English). It follows what I have called elsewhere 'a monostylistic classroom style' or essay writing which is more akin to the writing done by the Victorians rather than modern day Americans.

There is now a derivative of English switching between Filipino and English. It is used even by educated Filipinos in ordinary conversation, in classrooms and at recreation. The emerging vernacular Taglish is a pidgin of Filipino and English the same way the Spanish period saw Chavacano develop — a mixed variety of Tagalog or Hiligaynon or Cebuano and Spanish, now used by children as a first language in some parts of the Philippines. No one is certain if this pidgin will become naturally institutionalized. Many believe that with the dominance of mass media in people's lives, there is enough control of the dominant educated variety to minimize the need for the language mixture.

In schools, one modification in the language use policy is the use of the bilingual education scheme (since 1974), whereby English is used for the English Language, Mathematics and Science, with Filipino for the rest of the subjects. In reality, however, based on classroom observations and surveys, a code-switching variety is used for explanations during content classes (see Santos 1984). Economics (supposedly taught in Filipino) is still for the most part taught in English. Among the performing arts and even Physical Education, English is still used, especially for terminology. Print media is dominated by English usage with others (including cinema, TV and radio) predominantly Filipino.

English continues to be used in education, business, and international trade and communications.

Early Philippine textbook, circa 1932. (Reproduction courtesy Ige Ramos)

The First Pensionados to the US

Fulbright scholars are the modern-day version of the first Filipino scholars to the US — or *"pensionados".* As early as 1900, the American colonial government recognized the importance of investing in education and training of Filipinos.

"It is in our opinion that there is no other object on which liberal expenditure could be made with such certainty of good returns," the 1900 Report of the Philippine Commission to the President noted. The Report concluded that it would be "impossible to provide in the Philippines a substitute for the object lessons in American civilization which they will receive in spending three or four years in different parts of the United States." The passage of Act No. 854 by the Philippine Commission on August 26, 1903 launched the scholarship program for the Filipinos now known as the *pensionado* program. It was to be the largest study program in the US for Filipinos before the Fulbright exchanges were established in 1948. The first batch of *pensionados*, totaling 100, were selected in

Pensionados, The Class of 1903. (Photo: AHC)

"Why are you crying, Carmen?" asked the old woman.

"I am not happy. I want to be pretty. Then every one will love me," said Carmen.

"Do not cry, my dear little girl," said the old woman. "You shall have what you want.

"Do what I tell you every day for one year.

84

A page from an early reader redesigned for Filipino pupils. (Reproduction courtesy Ige Ramos)

While bilingualism is found in elementary schools and secondary schools, the predominant language of instruction remains English at the tertiary level — although History and Government of the Philippines (3 units), Filipino Language and Literature (6-9 units) are now reserved for Filipino.

The Philippines still has the shortest number of years preparatory to college (6 years of elementary school and 4 years of secondary school). However, at the tertiary level, all courses are now 4 years long with some longer (engineering) and with some (medicine and law) demanding an undergraduate degree before one begins the professional courses.

College — like most in the US — demands a quota of units to attain degrees, while graduate courses are taught with a guided thesis or dissertation.

What has changed in the past fifty-five years since independence is the magnitude of the system, demanding more and more facilities and manpower.

Culturally, the content of learning has changed. the former emphasis on American literature, history and culture, in Filipino intellectual resources, its books and ideas have all adopted greater indigenous content.

A problem remains in providing adequate teacher-training outlets to offer youth fully competent instruction.

There is also an imbalance between country needs and educational output. There

1903 and left for the US the same year. Grantees were selected on the basis of individual merit. The selection criteria included "natural ability, mental and physical fitness and promise, and moral character." The first phase of the competition consisted of a written test. Those who got the "highest averages" were certified fit to the civil governor for the next level of screening. Eligible candidates came from the public schools; they were between ages 16 and 21.

Before being officially nominated for an award, a *pensionado* was required to sign an agreement stipulating that they would join the Philippine civil service immediately upon return to the Philippines – the period of service equal to the time the scholar spent in the US at government expense. The *pensionado* awards were allocated based roughly on school population and the "importance in industrial lines of the respective provinces." For example, in the first batch the biggest numbers came from Manila (5), Pangasinan (4), Cebu (4), Ilocos Sur (4), Cavite (3), Batangas (3), Bulacan (3), La Union (3), Tarlac (3) and Occidental Negros (3).

The *pensionado* program continued until the outbreak of World War II. As an immediate response by the colonial government to pressing development needs of the Philippines at that time, most awards were given in fields such as teacher education, fisheries, maritime studies, weather forecasting, and coast and geodetic engineering.

Pensionado Paulo Castillo, Jr., who hailed from Samar, went to Massachusetts Institute of Technology to study techniques of weather forecasting. He marveled about the many ways that the weather service could contribute to national progress. Writing enthusiastically from the United States, he related to his countrymen how American farmers, merchants and exporters used accurate weather forecasting to promote their business. "By relying on constant weather reports," Castillo excitedly told his Filipino friends, American farmers and businessmen would know "when to put on sale certain goods, when to transport certain perishable products, or even when to start selling umbrellas."

are too many business and liberal arts graduates, and too many lawyers. Too many nurses and doctors wind up overseas. There may be too many first degree engineers, but not enough technicians. There is a shortage of well trained vocational graduates. IT specialists trained at an advanced level are insufficient. And there are too many teachers poorly trained in science, mathematics, IT and increasingly in English.

It would interesting to ask the Thomasites and the first Department of Public Instruction organizers and implementers, was it worth it?

Objectively, most Filipinos without axes to grind would say: what was left as a legacy was positive, even great; what we have done with that legacy is our responsibility. Given the constraints, we did not optimize the legacy. But with political will, the legacy has given us a base to repair and to build on.

Governor-General W. Cameron Forbes fielding a ball at Teachers Camp, Baguio. Below, the Iloilo High School team, circa 1909. (Photos: AHC)

The new education system brought with it more than methods and topics of learning. New sports arrived. In a squatterless era of ample and available land, baseball grew initially into a popular pastime. Rizal Memorial Stadium was opened in 1934. The first home run hit out of the park? ...none other than Babe Ruth, visiting with the US All Stars.

Freedom of the Press: a US Legacy

By Raul Locsin

If the US brought nothing else but its concept of what a free press should be, it would have done enough in its close to five decades of colonial association with the Philippines.

In this part of the world, the Philippine press is the most free, far surpassing its model — the American press.

There were some gaps over the last one hundred years, but they were more of temporary aberrations. The more serious were brought about by war and domestic turbulence.

The Japanese occupation from 1942 to 1945 stifled the press. It again blossomed with greater dynamism after liberation and independence from the US on July 4, 1946.

On September 21, 1972, when Philippine President Ferdinand E. Marcos declared martial law, the press was silenced again from whence it had to limp back to today's free-wheeling circus.

Even before the August 1983 assassination of opposition leader Benigno Aquino Jr., the Philippine press began to undergo a sort of renaissance — that of going back to normalcy. It was by no means as free as it would have like to have been, but freer somewhat since the imposition of martial law.

The year 1984 saw the birth of quite a number of newspapers and magazines which, although limited in circulation, began publishing dissenting views.

But to many who exercised the profession this was merely an illusion — there was yet no real freedom of the press, not in the sense that it used to be known. At its best, the situation resulted from the indulgence of a government that, since the assassination, had been beleaguered on all fronts.

If there was at all a semblance of a free press, it was because some tested the limits of their journalistic freedom. When the government lifted martial rule it did not restore the foundations and the environment on which the freedom of expression is ensured.

• • •

Freedom of the press in the Philippines is guaranteed in the Bill of Rights of the Philippine Constitution by a provision not unlike the First Amendment of the US Constitution.

The Philippine Constitution drew much of its substance from the American Charter in the establishment of what was then the Philippine Commonwealth during America's first real colonial adventure.

An early newsroom in operation. (Photo: AmCham Journal)

Subsequent amendments to the Philippine organic law may have altered its political structures but have kept intact the intent of the provision on press freedom which, as in the US Constitution, makes the press the only organized business accorded Constitutional protection.

In spite of this, to paraphrase an American statesman, eternal vigilance is still the price of liberty. For lack of vigilance had once deluded the Philippines as a nation into thinking that a temporary surrender of its civil rights, among them the freedom of the press, was essential to the myth of national interest that would be dictators use as a lure to the citizen.

• • •

The turn of the nineteenth century was then the golden age of colonialism. In the Far East the British were in Pakistan, India, Burma and Malaysia and North Borneo.

In the southeast, nearer east, the French controlled Indo-China — Vietnam, Laos and Cambodia; and down south the Dutch were in Indonesia. Even tiny Portugal had Goa in India, Macao in China, and the eastern half of Timor Island in the Indonesian archipelago. Somehow, the European colonial adventure, except for the social and lingual vestiges of their respective civilizations, left little of useful value to natives who were now seeking their own national identities. There were forms of government and the manner of governing which kept the civil service in each country intact and functional when the foreign links were dismantled. But these had become pitifully inadequate and irrelevant to nations suddenly in control of their own destiny. There was too much to catch up on and so little time to match the demands of social and economic development. For the nations of Southeast Asia this meant different concepts, new tools, novel and faster ways of doing things. There was now the need to meet the imperatives of an exploding population, spawned in poverty and ignorance, sapped by war and disease, and abused by exploitation. But somehow things were taking too long to achieve with the social and governmental infrastructure inherited from the white man.

Thus the region's development was marked by the surrender of some values for other values. And very often the adoption of new, untried values meant the dismantling of cherished traditional ones. This sometimes even meant the eradication of a whole way of life, of lifestyles and beliefs bred in an era. No matter how tragic or blissful, these were an outgrowth of their own time, willed by their own cultures and not something desperately brought into being by technology, nuclear blasts, space travel, computers and such.

New values, because they are untested, and are not yet culturally acceptable, are most often force-fed. And the political and social machinery to feed these values must of necessity have the strength if not the tyranny to ram down these values.

It thus became fashionable in the region to polarize power in the hands of a select

LXXX

THE MANILA TIMES.

~~~

Published every morning except Monday and every afternoon except Sunday.

Business offices and Editorial Rooms, 95, 98 and 99 Escolta (formerly 29).

Subscription price, Morning or Evening edition:—

In the Philippine Archipelago and United States of America.

Per month $ 1 00 gold or $ 2.00 Mex.
3 months $ 2 50 gold or $ 5.00 Mex.
6 months $ 5 00 gold or $10.00 Mex.
Per year $10 00 gold or $20.00 Mex.

All subscriptions payable strictly in advance.

Subscriptions price for Europe and other foreign countries: (No foreign subscriptions booked for less than three months, and all foreign subscriptions strictly in advance.)

3 months $ 6.00 Mex.
6 months $12.00 Mex.
1 year $24.00 Mex.

Single copies 10 cents (or one nickle).

Cable Address: TIMES, Manila.

Telephones: Business 44.
Editorial 20.

This paper is kept on file at L. P. Fisher's Advertising Agency, Merchants Exchange Building, San Francisco, California, where contracts for advertising can be made for it.

[Entered at the Manila Post Office as second class matter]

Geo. C. SELLNER, Business Manager.
Wm. N. SWARTHOUT, Managing Editor.
Wm. SMITH, Assistant Editor.

Reproduction of The Manila Times rate sheet, ca. 1910 (Photo: AmCham)

few. The strongman came into his own in Southeast Asia. And the rationale for the acquisition of power was that urgent national needs could not be met by systems of government which vacillate on human rights, require great debate, checks and balances, and consensus to crystallize policy or its implementation. If checks and balances are demanded, they can be allowed to exist only in acquiescent conformity with national interests. Governments, if they are to keep their stability, can no longer procrastinate on the needs of a long deprived populace; needs made more acute by aspirations measured against the outlines of the highly industrialized countries.

• • •

For the nine years of martial law the Philippine press exercised self-censorship as its contribution to the call for national development, mostly out of fear, oftentimes by acquiescence. Thus, it unwittingly helped allow a political regime to perpetuate the fiction that it was pre-empting revolution to "correct" inequities and injustices spawned by the concentration of wealth and power in the hands of a feudal few. It carried the myth to defuse anarchy in the streets and provide food, clothing, shelter, and economic well-being to every man, woman and child in a "new society."

Shorn of its rhetoric, however, the new society resulted in the concentration of greater wealth and power in the hands of a new, favored elite and in the perpetration of violence and degradation on a people which had survived in an economic milieu of negative growth.

The process of change not only ensured the continuance of a political dynasty presided over by Ferdinand Marcos, his family and cronies, but for almost two decades also dismantled great institutions, replacing them with substitutions controlled by a new set of overlords.

Although the Philippine Constitution did indeed provide the same Bill of Rights as those in the American Charter, subsequent amendments to the organic law after the declaration of martial law indirectly neutralized the protection of the citizen from his own government.

For one, the President and those acting pursuant to his orders during and after his tenure were not accountable to the people for their acts. For another, Amendment No. 6 to the Philippine Constitution provided: "Whenever in the judgment of the President, there exists a grave emergency or a threat or imminence thereof or whenever the interim Batasang Pambansa or the regular National Assembly fails or is unable to act adequately on any matter, for any reason that in his judgment requires immediate action, he may, in order to meet the exigency, issue the necessary decrees, orders or letters of instructions, which shall form part of the law of the land."

From Amendment No. 6 emanated the various decrees which exerted influence on how the Philippine journalist should conduct his affairs. Consider two decrees — Nos. 1834 and 1835 — both issued on January 16, 1981, the day martial law was officially "lifted." The first increased the penalties for rebellion, sedition and related crimes and the other codified the various laws on anti-subversion and increased the penalties for membership in subversive organizations. In both decrees the maximum penalty was death.

Hidden in the verbiage were amendments to the Revised Penal Code which among others, imposed the penalty of death on those "...who, without taking any direct part in the crime of sedition, should incite others to the accomplishment of any of the acts which constitute sedition, by means of speeches, proclamations, writings, emblems, cartoons, banners, or other representations tending to the same end or upon any person or persons who shall utter seditious words of speeches, write, publish or circulate scurrilous libels against the government of the Philippines, or any of the duly constituted authorities thereof…"

Likewise, death could also be imposed "…upon any person who having control and management of printing, broadcast or television facilities, or any form of mass communication shall use or allow the use of such facilities for the purpose of mounting sustained propaganda assaults against the government or any of its duly constituted authorities which tend to destabilize the government or undermine or destroy the faith and loyalty of the citizenry thereto."

The decrees also effectively put a damper on the right of the people to peaceably assemble and seek redress of grievances. It further provided for the sequestration of property and equipment used in what the state interprets as subversion.

On the strength of these decrees, after martial law was lifted, two newspapers were sequestered, their staff arrested and detained, also by virtue of another decree which authorized the president to issue search, commitment or detention orders which he alone and only he could rescind.

• • •

Above, then President Sergio Osmeña during the late 1940s. Below, broadcasters at work. (Photos: AHC)

With the full return of democracy after the EDSA revolution in 1986, the Philippine press surged back to health. But so did its deficiencies. Even with all its vices and more, it undeniably underlines the fact that only in an atmosphere of freedom and democracy that a real press can exist, and conversely, no freedom and democracy can survive without a free press.

Today, as of latest count, there are seven national dailies, 19 provincial dailies, 79 provincial weeklies not to mention the myriad of magazines of assorted publication frequencies. Each of these is a voice in the broad marketplace of ideas; and like it or not, part of our inheritance from the unique experience of US colonization.

US Cultural Influence

by Luis Guerrero Nakpil

Damian Domingo's "Indio de Manila", circa late 19th century. (The Edward E. Ayer Collection, The Newberry Library, Chicago)

The notion of the enthusiastic adoption of American culture by a country like the Philippines that has struggled so long for its own identity is puzzling. First of all, it should be pointed out that in a world that is dominated by only one super power in terms of military, industrial, financial, scientific, technological and cultural aspects of human endeavor, cultural influence is inevitable. All nations and peoples participate in Americanization. American culture is being spread throughout the world. McDonald's in Paris, Pepsi in Moscow, Madonna in London, Backstreet Boys in Bangkok, CNN in Sadam Hussein's living room; these are the vivid images that describe the extent of Americanization.

In Europe, American culture was, and sometimes still is, viewed with a combination of humor and disdain. Their vast resources of history and tradition confer a certain superiority. Others, both European and Asian, are willing to admit that there is something to admire about the core values and cultural elements of the US, but they all share a niggling doubt about how their own cultures are being eroded. This is not the case in the Philippines.

With the exception of a very small sector, Filipinos have a genuine admiration for the US. They eagerly adopt American ideas.

There are two reasons that make US culture so attractive. The first is that the culture itself is so vibrant. It is a culture that mixes many different ideas from all over the world.

The second reason is peculiar only to Filipinos and is part of their sociological baggage. The Philippines was a colony of Spain for more than three hundred years. Filipinos became steeped in European culture, religion, and ideas. In the last quarter of the 19th Century, the upper classes had accumulated enough wealth to transform themselves from Asian Pacific islanders to European gentlemen.

The Spaniards viewed all this development with deep suspicion. While they had made concessions to allow a certain degree of social mobility and commerce, they were always wary of any stirrings for independence. Filipinos had to be kept in their place. For example, it was forbidden for a Filipino (or *Indio*) to tuck his shirt into his trousers (see picture at left). Even when he had the money to buy a suit complete with silk tie, top hat and cane, the Filipino risked being publicly scolded if he were to dare to wear his shirt inside his pants. This act of social discrimination is, in fact, how the national formal wear, the *barong tagalog,* evolved. Filipinos took the European dress shirt, embellished it with pleats and embroidery, discarded the coat and kept only the trousers of their suits.

Nevertheless, the *barong tagalog* was considered an indignity by most members of the elite. They despised the fact that they had been forced to appear ridiculous, and had wanted to be recognized as men of equal if not better quality. The so-called *ilustrado* class went so far as to go to Spain and then to France for their education and to prove their worth. They did this with resounding success by excelling in literature and the arts, winning gold and silver medals in painting (in Madrid and in Paris), publishing novels (in Spain and Germany), contributing scientific research papers to German universities, and lobbying for reforms with Spanish liberals. The *ilustrados* made a big unwelcome, dangerous splash.

In the meantime, Spanish intellectuals like Sinibaldo de Mas were writing confidential papers advising the government to discourage the teaching of the Spanish language and to curtail foreign travel in order to lessen the possibility of exposing the native population to liberal ideas. It was this intransigent Spanish attitude of preserving complete control with the most oppressive methods that finally compelled Filipino intellectuals to start searching for an alternative model for the embryonic Philippine state. They looked far and wide. Visits were made to Japan, Germany, France, Britain, and even the US.

It was precisely because of the democratic principles espoused in the US Constitution that the Philippine revolutionaries started negotiating with the US government for aid in their war against the Spaniards. Apolinario Mabini, a top

Filming Apocalypse Then

by Bobby Greenwood

"Apocalypse"?

Yeah, I remember it, sometimes not fondly, mind you. We started to call it "Apocalypse When" and that turned into "Apocalypse Never". Well, we were used to shooting a film in three or four weeks — a couple of months was already a long shoot. None of us ever dreamed of two years!

The list of Oscar winners is, of course, really impressive. And the budget — for that time — was incredible. In the days when US$ 500,000 was big, a budget of US$ 7,000,000 was mind-boggling. And that was just the start of it. It wound up at over US$ 40 million.

We learn pretty quickly around here. One of the first things we learned was that telling the truth was a really quick way of getting fired. The casualty rate, in the beginning, was pretty high — a production manager, two assistant directors, the leading man — sort of

scary if you cavort with the lower echelons.

I'll give you an example. The film used three PBR speed boats from the Vietnam War era. One was a real PBR with Mercury engines — swift, stop-on-a-dime, swivel turn radius capability — the real McCoy. They called that the "A" boat. The "B" boat was a real PBR but without Mercury engines, just little ones to move it around. That was supposed work by the dock or riverbanks. The "C" boat was a mock-up, its only reason for being was for the helicopter that was supposed to pick it up and put it in the river. To handle this small fleet, they had

Francis Ford Coppola with a script coordinator on the set of "Apocalypse Now" (Photo: Greenwood collection)

Fashion was an interesting cultural influence, particularly given the climate. Above, Thomasites and local teachers training in Baguio. (Photo: AHC)

advisor to President Aguinaldo, had even stated that the new Philippine national language should be English. It would be, in his opinion, the best way of unifying the archipelago and imbibing the virtues of the new world.

When the Americans arrived in 1898, they were received as allies and mentors. Despite the Philippine-American War, which played itself out horribly, the US government formulated an enlightened policy of cultural assimilation. The Manifest Destiny of "Rough Rider" Theodore Roosevelt was tempered by the social consciousness of Mark Twain such that annexation included educational, social, and economic elements. They would create Filipinos, as Stanley Karnow's brilliant book is titled, *"In Our Image"*.

By 1901, when then President Emilio Aguinaldo was captured in the isolated east coast town of Palanan, the Filipinos girded themselves for a regime of oppression and

a "marine coodinator" (MC).

So the first marine coordinator told them they couldn't tow the mock-up by sea as it would break up, it had to be transported by land. They tried to tow it. It started to break up and they fired that marine coordinator.

The second coordinator told them they couldn't reinforce the mock-up as it would be too heavy for the chopper to pick up. They reinforced it, the chopper dropped it (nearly hitting the camera crew). They fired the marine coordinator.

Now, we are in Olongapo and the "A" boat is in Baler or somewhere. The third MC told director Francis Ford Coppola that the "B" boat wasn't fast enough for the shot he wanted and would have to wait for the "A" boat. They tried it anyway, the thing wasn't fast enough and they fired that marine coordinator.

A.D. Flowers, special effects expert, preparing to blow something up. (Photo: Greenwood collection)

The fourth and final MC was a great guy and smart, a local hire that made good. Pete Cooper handled most things from then on. Big Pete could charm anyone. Don't misunderstand, he really did get things done – quickly and well. But he was also the world's number one slinger of bull. He told them anything they wanted to hear and then got the job done when no one was looking. Now that's the way to deal with Hollywood.

To be fair, the production did have some wonderful people working on it. A.D. Flowers was the special effects man. Everyone loved watching him running around in a beat up straw hat planting his charges and taking such delight in blowing things up. He had also done "Tora, Tora, Tora," so we were really impressed – but not surprised.

The camera crew was from Italy. Vittorio Storraro was director of photography. That crew did incredible things. They also cooked and served fabulous meals. They were nice enough to invite a lot of us to join them.

Gombi the Tiger was a delight to behold. He was trained naturally, but was still a tiger. One shot was very carefully planned. In the film it was supposed to look as if Gombi was chasing one of the leading men. The head

a guerilla war. Instead they got the "Thomasites". A shipload of idealistic, high-minded school teachers aboard the US Army transport ship "SS Thomas" came to share the blessings of American schooling not only with the children of the elite, but with everyone else, too. English, the new language of power and pelf, would not be kept exclusive to the rulers. It would be taught in free public schools along with reading, writing, arithmetic, and democracy. As for the elite, their children were selected to go to the US.

Painting and sculpture in the Philippines were initially less affected by Americanization. The Filipinos had had a direct link to Europe, and remained largely unimpressed by US artwork. Up to that time, few could blame them. After all, impressionist painters like Juan Luna and Felix Resurreccion Hidalgo had won important prizes in Paris at about the same time John Singer Sargent had gone there and returned to the US relatively unnoticed. It was a time when these awards were still the internationally recognized measure of talent. Even the young Pablo Ruiz Picasso had considered joining them.

Much of the art scene was dominated by Luna's and Hidalgo's spiritual heirs like Fabian dela Rosa, Fernando Amorsolo, Irineo Miranda, Jorge Pineda, and Toribio Herrera. Unlike the two *ilustrados,* these artists did not make any references to their social or political context. Instead, they concentrated on neutral landscapes of idyllic

Juan Luna's "Parisian Life,"
Paris, 1892. (GSIS collection)

stunt man was supposed to grab a pig by the hind legs and throw him in a cage — the pig was only rented as the owner didn't want to sell him.

The tiger, some distance away, would hear the squeal of the pig and run in front of the camera toward the sound. No one realized quite how swift a tiger can leap. Stuntman and tiger went for the pig, grabbing it simultaneously. Gombi dragged both about ten yards before the stuntman could let go of the pig. He was left on the road, while Gombi disappeared into the undergrowth with his prize.

Things got pretty chaotic. The stuntman's wife thought the tiger had her husband and started to scream. Monty Cox, the tiger's owner and trainer, was yelling at her not to scare the tiger. We finally got the tiger back, after *his* lunch. No harm done — except to the pig and an unhappy farmer (who received compensation, if not *lechon*).

To add insult to injury, the tiger also ran behind the camera so they never got the shot either. So it goes.

Gombi the Tiger on his way to a lechon lunch. (Photo: Greenwood collection)

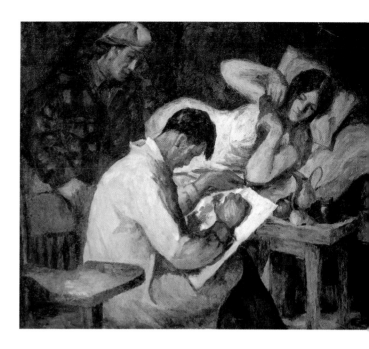

perfection and extraordinary beauty. They revolved around the University of the Philippines School of Fine Arts and their technical skills could only have been acquired previously in Europe.

It was not until Victor Edades made his debut exhibit at the Philippine Colombian Club in 1928, that modernist painting challenged the academic styles of the original *ilustrado* artists and their followers. Educated in the US, Edades inspired Carlos Francisco and Galo B. Ocampo to join him in becoming the first three artists who adopted the modernist style in the Philippines. They started bringing the realities of the street into the salons of art. Soon, they were joined by the "Thirteen Moderns" (Diosdado Lorenzo, Vicente Manansala, Cesar Legaspi, Anita Magsaysay-Ho, and Hernando Ocampo to name some of them). Even though Edades was pivotal in bringing modern art to the Philippines, no one can deny that the concepts of abstractionism, cubism, expressionism, and surrealism were not developed in America. Filipino painters bypassed America and made a beeline for Europe once again.

Literature was slowly but completely taken over. Having learned the language from Americans, Filipino writers drew all their techniques and attitudes from the US. Poets, essayists, novelists, and playwrights continued to produce highly refined, immensely entertaining work in Spanish for an already small readership (only 3% to 5% of the population in 1898 were literate in Castellano) that dwindled into near oblivion by the 1940s. Jose Rizal's landmark novels in Spanish were followed by poetry and essays by Fernando Ma. Guerrero, Cecilio Apostol, Jesus Balmori, and Claro M. Recto. Others who wrote in Tagalog (the dominant dialect that would be recognized in a modified version as the national language only in 1937), like Gabriel Beato Francisco, Lope K. Santos, and Valeriano Pena Hernandez, were energized by their defiance of America.

Unfortunately the same impulse was switched on in writers of other regions with different Filipino dialects (Vicente Sotto, Florentino Borromeo, Buenaventura Rodriguez in Cebu; Cornelio Hilado, Miguela Montelibano, Valente Cristobal in Iloilo; and a host of others from the Ilocos, Pampanga, Bicol, Pangasinan, Leyte-Samar). The overall effect was a reactionary movement that eventually doomed the potency of their work to forms and themes that shunned innovation and experimentation. What started out as a way to preserve their culture only served to alienate them from a larger public and, worse, sapped their energy.

In the meantime, English was being taught on a nationwide scale by US-sponsored egalitarian education. While different regions clung to their own dialects, by the 1940s only one language dominated the entire country: English.

continued on page 67

American Influence on Philippine Theater

By Joy Virata

When the US declared sovereignty over the Philippines, theater had already been an important part of Filipino life and culture for centuries.

Out of a mélange of religious and semi-religious rituals and celebrations and theatrical forms, and a deliberate effort by Spanish colonizers (aware of the influence of theater on Filipinos) to use theater to bring about religious conversion and control, there evolved various forms of theatrical entertainment — the *Sinakulo* (the most enduring of the religious plays) and the *Komedya* ("a play in verse introduced… from Spain in the 16th century and institutionalized in the 19th century," according to Nicanor Tiongson in his essay on Philippine Theater).

American influence on Filipino theater began to be felt towards the third decade of the 20th century. Film began to replace theater as common entertainment and by the 1930s American Vaudeville had invaded the country, but took on a distinct Filipino flavor by becoming *Bodabil* — like its American counterpart a hodge-podge of musical revues, circus acts, and stand up comedy.

By the end of the 1930s theater began to replace American movies as entertainment and during the Japanese occupation *Bodabil* productions were about the only source of public entertainment.

After the war two groups in Manila began to stage plays regularly – the Manila Theater Guild (MTG) and The Barangay Theater Guild. Both performed modern works of American and English playwrights.

The turn of political feeling in the late 1960s saw the shift to Tagalog as the preferred language of communication and instruction — and therefore the preferred language in the arts.

American movies may have changed Filipino entertainment tastes, but deep within the Filipino psyche there remains that original, instinctive love for the theatrical — a love that makes him one of the best performers in the world.

The UP Dramatic Club, in a late 1950s production. During regular seasons, the club performed plays from the classic "Antigone" to the modern "A Streetcar Named Desire." Held on the UP campus in a theater now named for the club's founder, playwright Wilfrido Ma. Guerrero (who also directed most of the plays), actors were students and alumni. A few years later it became a travelling company and performed only in Tagalog. (Photo: courtesy of Joy Virata)

The Philippines' Gift to Broadway

She began as the little girl with the whiny voice, "Birch Tree, it's everybody's milk!" But under her mother's constant control, and the tutelage of some seasoned theater directors, Lea Salonga grew into one of the world's top theater actresses. She is most famous for her award winning performances in both London and New York as the lead in the hit musical "Miss Saigon". A talented singer as well, she has recorded several albums, both locally and abroad.

Right, Lea Salonga in an early Philippine Repertory production of "Annie." Far right, as Kim, the Vietnamese girl who falls for an American soldier in "Miss Saigon." (Photo, above: Reproduced from "Tuklas Sining," courtesy Alice Guillermo; right: Courtesy Chase International)

Poster from the film "Madaling Araw" a popular kundiman song (Reproduced from "Tuklas Sining", courtesy Alice Guillermo)

As early as 1925, Filipino writers were churning out short stories (Paz Marquez Benitez, "Dead Stars") of considerable merit. Jose Villa Panganiban published his collection of short stories "Stealer of Hearts" in 1927. The internationally renowned Jose Garcia Villa had as many as 600 stories to chose from to publish "Philippine Short Stories: Best 25 of 1928." The linguistic landslide became an avalanche as succeeding generations continued throughout the 1930s and well into the 1970s to write plays novels, and poetry of outstanding quality and energy.

Music, perhaps even more than literature, was truly and inexorably Americanized. Indigenous Filipino music traces its own roots as far back as the Pre-Hispanic era, which was recognized by Frances Densmore (in 1904) who conjectured that Philippine tribal music "could be one of the oldest forms of musical expression in the world." Much of this was ignored by the Spanish friars who sought to impose their religion and its music on the population. It was in music that the Spaniards laid the foundations for the quick success of the Americans. They had given the Philippines the European diatonic scale and filled it with receptive ears for Western music. Mostly church-inspired and quaintly medieval, Spanish popular music did have elements of Moorish animation. Unlike most Asians, who have only six notes or fewer in their ears, the hispanized Filipinos were not merely acquainted with the octave, but they had also started composing operattas, ballads, marches, and hymns before and after the Americans arrived. Sentimental *kundiman* and spectacular

U.S. Influence on Philippine Art

Alice Guillermo

Vicente Manansala's "Jeepneys" – 1951 (Photo: The Ateneo Art Gallery)

US influence on Philippine art since the turn of the 20th century has been profound.

The American colonial period also gave rise to cultural forms that melded indigenous styles with existing Spanish colonial strains and US cultural norms of the times.

Under Spanish rule, the Catholic Church was the sole patron of the arts. Later, the landed gentry and merchant elite emerged, commissioning portraits — celebrating their new prosperity.

The US administration set up the School of Fine Arts, within the University of the Phililippines in 1908. Though administered by the US colonial government, it was European in orientation. Artists such as Fernando Amorsolo and Fabian de la Rosa trained in Europe under Filipino expatriate artists Luna and Hidalgo. However, the European influence was not sustained for long.

zarzuela by Nicanor Abelardo, Juan Hernandez, Rodolfo Corejo were performed all over the country.

Initial exposure to American music came from campfire songs, military marches, and ditties of the Philippine-American War, as well as the early music books introduced by the teaching Thomasites. Soon Filipinos became completely enthralled by the lively, sensual beat that they heard from American gramophones. As they were to discover only much later, these deeply evocative rhythms and beats found their roots in black music. This epitomizes the real value of American culture. It has an ability to absorb the wonders on one culture, filtering them only slightly, then combining them with elements from yet other cultures, and finally with the advent of gramophones and radio, disseminating the end-product over the entire planet.

In the realm of radio and television, the Philippines is thoroughly American. This has everything to do with the fact that the US invented these media and established the framework of their content. Even as broadcasts are made in the national language, they remain very much simulations of programing from the US in sound and style of content.

Today, young Filipinos have foresworn their *barong tagalog* and dress like inner city African-Americans. They remain unaware that, like the *barong tagalog,* this jailhouse chic of loose clothing, no belts, and shaven heads (covered by ski-caps)

Frederico Elizalde, pioneer Filipino Jazz musician. (Photo: Ritchie Quirino collection)

Amorsolo

Fernando Amorsolo, acknowledged as one of the most prolific Filipino painters, reached his peak in the 1930s, shedding the ponderous tones of the European academy.

With his technique of backlighting — the warm tropical sunlight serving as background to the human tableau — Amorsolo became the premier artist of paintings portraying rural folk, pretty barrio lasses and stalwart young men, steeped in their feudal virtues — this despite the fact that this period was marked by bloody peasant uprising in the countryside — one of the several contradictions of Amorsolo's art. Alejandro Roces recently wrote "it was not till the coming of Fernando Amorsolo that Philippine scenes would be painted with a Philippine light. In short, it was Amorsolo who first captured the exact illumination of the Philippine sun." This technique is most evident in "Sunday Morning Going to Town."

Fernando Amorsolo's "Sunday Morning Going to Town", 1958. (Reproduction courtesy of The Ayala Museum Collection)

Amorsolo's work in the 1930s came during the preparation for commonwealth status and self-government. In a sense, his art constituted a shift in the colonial imaging of Filipinos overseas. The St. Louis Exposition in 1904 had conveyed a strong impression of ethnic "otherness" with exhibits of Igorot and Maranao villages, thus an implied justification of the colonial project as a mission *civilisatrice*. But Amorsolo's subjects were Christianized lowland Filipinos, in idyllic agricultural settings. They went about their tasks in harmony with Christian virtues. Besides the popular genre and rural landscapes, Amorsolo also received lucrative commissions to do official portraits, as can be seen from his portraits of successive American governor-generals.

evolved out of the petty criminality, prevailing poverty, and relentless discrimination of the African-American experience. Filipinos listen to rappers and identify closely with the "lyrics" of astounding vulgarity, menacing rage, and disturbing relevance.

American culture is a genuinely global culture mostly because of its inclusive nature and only partly due to its pervasive technology. At its core, it lays claim on all the world's culture, drawing mainly from the creativity and originality of the European migrations and little by little from its exposure to subsequent immigrant waves from Africa, South America, and Asia. Seemingly unconcerned with the issue of a genuine cultural identity, American artists live and work in an atmosphere of unhindered freedom that encourages their talents and reflects the primacy of their country's democratic system. This is the environment that the US created and fostered in the Philippines and in the end remains an invaluable contribution to its national culture.

Vicente Manansala "Still Life with Green Guitar", 1952 (Photo: The Ateneo Art Gallery)

Hernando Ocampo's "Beefsteak", 1953 (Reproduction courtesy Ateneo Art Gallery)

Ocampo and Manansala

Direct influence from the US came as a result of the Great Depression. The mass lay-off of workers and long bread lines had important effects on American culture and art. From this new mass culture sprang proletarian art with expressions in literature, the visual arts, and music. Proletarian art in the United States had its effect on the Philippines. This was despite the fact that the Philippines remained a predominantly agricultural, feudal, plantation economy. The fledgling industrial sector had no working class to speak of.

Many modernist artists took the side of proletarian art following the devastation of World War II. Among them were Vicente Manansala, Hernando R. Ocampo, and Cesar Legaspi. In their works, proletarian art dealt with the tragedies of war and its social toll.

By Patis Tesoro

The arrival of the Thomasites in 1901 not only brought the benefits of education into the country, their coming also inspired a revolution in dress for women, in terms of practicality and freedom of movement.

The then popular American "Gibson Girl" look, consisting of wasp waist, big bustled skirt and billowing sleeves, personified by the "leg-of Mutton" sleeves worn by the Thomasite ladies, was avidly copied by the Filipinas and integrated into the local fashion scene. *(Photo courtesy Tom Carter)*

Changes in style came about with the shorter Camisa sleeves, allowing for more freedom of movement and comfort, where the modest and prim Maria Clara blouse — which barely showed the wrist — was restrictive. *(Photo courtesy Tom Carter)*

The Panuelo (neckerchief), which covered the back of the nape, was placed lower providing more comfort to the wearer in the intense tropical heat. Note also the Westernized crimped hairstyle. *(Photo courtesy Patis Tesoro)*

The traditional eight-piece traje de mestiza, consisting of anaguas (half-slip), camison (chemise), saya (skirt), tapiz (overskirt), serpentina (train), baro (blouse) and panulelo (neckerchief) became a work of art in the hands of our master sewers, weavers, beaders, and embroiderers. But it also evolved into a simpler one-piece dress called the balintawak.

Reportedly first worn in high society by Mrs. Claro M. Recto in 1935, it rapidly became in vogue especially for local fiestas and picnics. The American emphasis on comfort and adaptability for work is best exemplified in this mode of dress. *(Photo courtesy Patis Tesoro)*

In the 1920s the rage in America and Europe was the low waisted chemise, quickly adopted by the fashion-conscious Filipinas. *(Photo left: AHC; Photo, right, courtesy Patis Tesoro)*

The modern terno is the equivalent of this period piece from the 1930s. *(Photo courtesy Patis Tesoro)*

Franchise Frenzy: US and Filipino Taste Buds — not the wiser!

By Ted Lerner

It is a technological wonder of the modern world, a feat so extraordinary that our ancestors would look at us as if we were completely nuts if we tried to explain it to them. And yet, we take it utterly for granted.

No, we're not talking about lightning fast computers, jet airplanes or artificial hearts. We're talking cheeseburgers. Yes cheeseburgers, that great American mechanical invention that swept the world during the 1950s. Now, we know a good cheeseburger is pretty much orgasmic. But what is so ultra special as to warrant a printed page?

Walk into a McDonald's in Phoenix, Arizona and order a Quarter Pounder with cheese. You know how it's going to taste because you've eaten approximately 6000 already, and you're not even middle aged. And it sure goes down well. Then two days later you find yourself in Tarlac, Philippines. You spot the famous golden arches and instantly get a craving for a Quarter Pounder with cheese. And darn if it doesn't taste exactly like the one you ate in Phoenix. Then a few days after that on a trip to Shanghai, China you again stumble upon the golden arches. And again you get that craving for some good hot grease. Again it tastes just like the other two you scarfed recently.

The technological wonder is how a fast food cheeseburger in Phoenix, Arizona can taste exactly the same as its counterpart in Tarlac, Philippines and Shanghai, China is truly a mind-boggling accomplishment of business and technical know-how.

Welcome to "franchise frenzy," a US phenomenon epitomizing globalization, and which has swept across the Philippines. It is a cultural phenomenon. And it has become one of the Filipinos favorite means to satisfy hunger.

Visitors expecting to see the exotic Philippines would surely be disappointed by the proliferation of American fast food chains dotting the landscape. One can almost predict what they must be saying; just another case of American imperialistic kitsch mowing down indigenous cultures. Well, the critics might want to think again. It may be the case in other countries, but not in the Philippines. One only has to consider the long intertwined history between the Philippines and the United States to realize that things American like the burger and fries and the ice cream soda do not really feel out of place in this country. In the Philippines the fast food seems more culturally benign because of its history.

One thing the anti-everything neo-liberals of the world fail to mention is that these imperialist monsters do a pretty darn good job of feeding the world. Most of them can't afford more than a Big Mac per meal anyway.

And in terms of business, one could hardly pick a better model than the franchise. We already mentioned consistency of product, but there is clearly more. The health standards at most fast food franchises are well above local norms. They keep their places spotless. They give it to you fast. They always carry change. They readily replace your meal when there is a complaint.

Those are some reasons why Filipinos have readily accepted fast food franchises. Another reason could be that eating at McDonald's or Kenny Rogers Roasters or Wendy's is a way for Filipinos to feel good, a touch of the "love" part in the incessant "love-hate" relationship with the former colonizer.

It would be simple to say Filipinos prefer foreign imports. But in the world of fast food it's not that simple. The roaring success of homegrown Jollibee is testament enough to that. And it's not like just any American fast food joint can open up and automatically be a success. Several have gone under in the recent past.

For the Philippines, franchised fast food started back in the 1960s with A&W — which pioneered US fast food in Asia. It was the late 1970s before McDonald's found its way, after powerhouses like Kentucky Fried Chicken, and Shakey's, originally a subdivision of San Miguel. By the 1980s, Pizza Hut, 7-11 outlets and Wendy's came around, while the 1990s saw Burger King try its hand. Forty years after inception, American fast food franchises had successfully penetrated the Philippine market — an insatiable appetite for US kitsch (don't forget the toys!).

In recent years, however, this frenzy of fast food franchises has spread it's market from ordinary chicken wings to "Buffalo" hot wings—with mostly second or third generation oligarchs capturing more upscale franchise names like TGIFriday's, Kenny Rogers Roasters, California Pizza Kitchen, Chilies and Outback Steakhouse. Popular with the middle class, these have even spawned local versions.

Franchise food seems to be a merger between excessive noise and giggling happiness. At the semi-upscale places they offer irreverent waiters with funny hats and buttons sticking out of every orifice, golden oldies rock 'n roll, brass railings and

Efren Reyes: The Magician   *By Ted Lerner*

Known as one of the fiercest and most fearless competitors in billiards, Efren Reyes is regarded by his peers worldwide as perhaps the most knowledgeable player to ever to break a rack.

Pool came naturally to him and by the time he was 12 years old, he was hustling games against US soldiers in Angeles City. He beat everyone he played, took their money and soon couldn't get a game with the GI's because they never beat him.

By the late 1970s Reyes was considered the best player in the Philippines. But he had trouble finding money games because was just too good. Reyes had to give even the best players "weight" – a handicap.

In the late '70s and early '80s he competed in several tournaments in Japan. Then in 1985 he made his move to the US in classic hustler fashion. His name was already known in the US, so he entered a pro tournament in Houston, Texas under the name of his friend Cesar Morales. By making side bets on "Morales", the Filipino contingent made a killing as their "unknown" boy swept the field.

In 1994 Reyes became the first non-American to win the US Open. Next year he won the first of two straight World 8-ball championships and was named Player of the Year on the US tour.

With his victory in the 1999 World 9-ball championships in Cardiff, Wales, his popularity at home went through the roof. *(Photo: AMF Puyat collection)*

oak wood decor and authentic looking antique kitsch from a bygone US era that try to build an American fantasy. If your father died that morning, and your children were thrown out of school, and your spouse stomped out of the house in disgust, and your neighbors ate your dog, it's still all "Have a Nice Day!".

Another similarity is that no matter where you eat, you're always eating corporate food prepared out of a manual. As we all know, it's a false sense of security — similar to the baby boomer generations of the '50s and '60s, the years fast food proliferated.

The biggest and most obvious difference between fast food and semi-upscale food is simply the food. In fact, success in the world of low down fast food comes down to who has the best tasting grease. Like people everywhere, Filipinos love hot grease. In the Philippines a day without hot grease is a day without satisfaction. It's just that those with money eat better quality grease than those broke. Which grease joint one chooses depends upon taste — but one word of advice. Make sure your grease is piping hot. The cardboard taste of a cold McDonald's fry is unmistakable. The grease is still on this page.

Bon Appetite!

A Most Unlikely National Sport — *By Ted Lerner*

(Photo: Alaska Milk Corporation)

If you didn't know the real score, basketball is perhaps the last sport you'd associate with Filipinos. Like everyone else in South East Asia, in the rest of Asia and, heck, like the rest of the planet, you'd think Filipinos would be into soccer. But Basketball? They're not exactly considered one of the planet's tallest races right? So what is it that makes Filipinos go positively bonkers over basketball?

Simply put; because the Philippines was a part of America and the US has never fully taken to soccer like the rest of the world and, perhaps more importantly, because Filipinos adore the game. And really, if you forget the height problem for the moment, the religious-like passion for basketball in the Philippines makes perfect sense. That other American import, baseball, used to be popular in the Philippines. But who can find space enough to put in so much as an infield when open spaces in Manila are as rare as elephants walking down Roxas Blvd.?

So the sport of the Filipino masses became basketball. The Philippines became home to one of the first professional leagues outside America.

The Philippine Basketball Association (PBA) has been in existence nearly three decades. And it is easily the number one organized professional sport in the Philippines. For over a generation, the PBA has played host to dozens of US imports, who couldn't quite make it to the NBA. While the PBA is the most popular league in the Philippines, other popular leagues have sprung up. The MBA, the PBL and even college leagues draw huge and enthusiastic crowds.

PART 2

AmCham History

Spanning the Decades: Colonial Frontier to Globalization

By Guy Sacerdoti

The seeds of AmCham were planted by the pioneers who saw the "Philippine Islands" as a frontier — three new territories which might someday graduate into Statehood.
Is this our Round Table? Possibly. This photo was taken after 1912 but before AmCham's 1920 incorporation.
(Photo: AHC)

When one says "AmCham Philippines", what image does it conjure? There're two really, one perception and one reality.

For today's businessman, or politician, or journalist, it usually means that large group of rather conservative people — half of them American, half Filipino — who meet once a month for an adequate lunch in a Makati City hotel with a guest speaker who speaks to an issue of the day.

Whether salaried employee, executive, or entrepreneur, the morning is tidied up at 11:45 for the drive to the venue. Then comes two hours of "networking"— what an awful word. Checking out what the competition is doing, flying the corporate flag, meeting new folks in town, and talking to people one hasn't seen for "ages" is all part of the fare. Confirming trips, golf outings, committee meetings, trying to decipher what's really (!) happening to the macro-economy and passing snide remarks about the latest political faux pas is also part of the personal agenda for a "working lunch"— power lunch a *non sequitur*.

But there are also glimpses and glances. It's a community of business people. There is both subtle and not so subtle lobbying. It could be a comment to a ranking official about the rumor of a possible change in an executive rule which might effect one of the 43 non-production cost categories determining margin, next year. Or it could be for help during the annual AmCham Thanksgiving Ball — proceeds to the AmCham Foundation.

But the reality of AmCham is much more. It is also a Chamber of Commerce. It is people working for a common denominator of freeing trade, easing investment, building opportunities for jobs as well as profit. It is a lobby with Washington and US policy. It commemorates the past and looks to the future. It is a 100-year-old institution that seeks fair play in business, and organizes position papers to do so— singularly, or with other chambers, both local and foreign. It is an organization that transcends specific US business interests. It is not merely a group that one "must" be a member of to affirm business credibility. But it remains a collegial group working together — via its numerous committees and central office — to further the common interest of fair business and free commerce.

OK, that's today.

Now picture this:

It is July 1902. That's right… July 1902. Think of a pioneer town near Tulsa, Oklahoma — its dust, its surrounding prairie, its horses, its wagons, its buildings, its saloons. The settlers are tough, working hard to make a living. The town's businessmen want their town to grow, bringing in more customers requiring greater services. They hope to emulate some of the institutions and culture back East. They band together to work with the fledgling territorial government and aim some day to bring their territory to statehood — which, by the way, Oklahoma did five years later.

Right…keep the image in your head.

• • •

Capt. Herbert L. Heath
AmCham President
1920-1921; 1924-1928
(Photo: AmCham)

July 1902, Manila, Philippine Islands, Colony of the United States of America:

It's 10am. It's raining, naturally. Or it's steaming, really. The horse-drawn calesa is sloshing up the street. A group of eight buddies — several from the same Oregon volunteer regiment who fought in the just-ended Philippine-American War — saunter into Clarke's place, a coffee shop on the Escolta. It's half parlor, half saloon really. They do this nearly every day, if they can, to talk business and anything else. For them they've been up long enough that for some, 10am could be lunch.

One is a former Captain, Herbert Lee Heath, who arrived as a company commander with the first US Volunteer Expedition against the Spanish. Several come from the port. One works finance, another adept at extracting donations from successful businessmen for those "down on their luck," as it were. Greetings are shared, coffee is poured — some of these men of business still massaging their temples from the night before. Biscuits and buns arrive from the small kitchen.

One of them complains, "I've been here nearly four years now. I fought for this place. There's a Government, sure, but I can't get approval to ship what I want where I want it. They say you can't build that, you can only build this. We gotta do something."

Another complains he needs permission to ship in goods the Spanish used to provide regularly. And another says, "You know, the insurrection has been put down. We're looking at maybe three new territories, maybe even states some day. We're at the US frontier. It's muggy and hot, but I like it. There's gold in them there hills," he chuckles.

They leave the bar with their coffee and when they reach a round table in the corner, they sit. Insurance broker Eddie Elser walks in, waves to the group and joins them. "So when are we going to set up a Chamber? The English have their Manila Chamber, the Spanish have theirs, even the Chinese are organizing. We've been talking for weeks. The Philippine Commission isn't helping."

The talk continues and the idea of an American Chamber of businessmen is broached, yet again. "What about really getting the others to join, too. We are all in this together. There are 40,000 Americans living here, and that's a lot of business right there."

The men of the First Colorado Infantry. Many stayed on to make their home in the Philippines, moving into business to make a living. (Photo: AHC)

The talk goes on and the coffee pours, buns consumed, and a couple of late arrivals sneak a shot of whisky — or two. "Let's talk to the others and see what happens."

"Meet here tomorrow?"

The Colonial Frontier (1902-1920)

And so members of the "Manila Coffee Club" sat at their first Round Table and started the first Amcham. It was not incorporated, because they felt it wasn't necessary. They were the frontiersmen. The Philippine Islands was a US Colony, after all. And there really shouldn't be a problem lobbying the US authorities.

Wrong!

The early administrations weren't heading the laissez faire route of the remaining mainland US territories. They were increasingly in competition with business and infrastructure. And they were making sweeping changes to develop local politicians along US democratic lines. Nothing like the way they had treated native American Indians. A Filipino advisor to the Governor-General and two Filipino observers to the US Congress were to be elected to take office in 1908. US-style education was beginning to spread throughout the archipelago with the arrival of the Thomasites.

The opportunities were vast and growing. But the only way to compete with government was to band together — regardless of nationality. Chauncey McGovern, who became publisher of the "Manila Monthly," lobbied to create an association of businessmen. In 1907, the Manila Merchants Association was founded; the small group meeting regularly at Clarke's (M.A. "Met" Clarke was its first president). After a year, membership (majority American) grew to about 250, rapidly outgrowing the coffee shop venue.

Urban planning was high on the American agenda. The US wanted a "new architecture" for the Philippines. In 1901, US Governor-General William Howard Taft appointed Arcadio Arellano as consulting architect. His first project was the Insular Ice Plant and Cold Storage, built in 1902. (Photo: Lico collection)

Now doesn't this sound familiar...

Nine years after the US assumed sovereignty, six years after the end of the Philippine-American War, after new seeds of democracy had been planted, after trade was opening and infrastructure growing, the Philippines was getting bad press abroad. It was driving away potential business, trade and investment. And yes, people complained about the lack of tourism — 1907 style.

Of the five Association committees at the time, the Publicity Committee was the largest. With the government supplying nearly a third of its P85,000 budget (the rest from member donations), the Merchants concentrated on the US, Japan and China for its investment "roadshow," stressing the burgeoning opportun- ities in agriculture and trade — distributing general information.

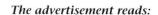

The advertisement reads:

"There is no drink as delicious or fortifying as Coca-Cola.

Try it and see – it relieves headaches and quenches your thirst."

Don't forget to phone Clarke's at Tel: 903!

Although Americans led many Merchants' projects (they remained the majority of the membership), members of the original AmCham group still met at Clarke's, at their "Round Table." Clarke himself fell onto hard times around 1911, after a typhoon wiped out his mining venture in Benguet, and his bank took over the restaurant, except for the table, which was bought by 14 Manila Coffee Club members.

But there was one major issue that led to the mass American exodus from the Merchants Association, and its rapid demise.

(continued on page 87)

"The Manila Hotel was to become the 'Waldorf' of Manila Society..." writes Beth Day Romulo. It was commissioned by William Howard Taft — America's first Governor General. It was designed and built by Daniel Burnham, America's top architect and city planner at the time. Ships would dock at nearby Legaspi Landing and Pan Am "Flying Boats" would taxi into the basin to moor near the seawall. All passengers made straight for this elegant address — "one of the finest hotels in the Far East." (Photo: Lico collection)

The American Community

Governor General W. Cameron Forbes (seventh from right, second row) meets with men and women of the American community at Malacañang, circa 1912. Couldn't have been terribly comfortable in all that finery. (Photo: AHC)

The drift of the Anglo-Saxon toward the West — dating from the sixth century when the Angles, Jutes and Saxons, three Teutonic tribes, conquered the aboriginal tribes of Britain — has never stopped. Without a doubt, this drift of people toward the West until the East has been reached is the greatest flow of people the world has ever witnessed. The flood has reached the coast of Asia and the present century will tell the story of whether the Oriental peoples will be overwhelmed, or the flood thrown back upon itself, to surge forward again and again.

The First Phase:

The first phase of the American Community in the Philippines covers that period of time from the beginning of the United States to the close of the Civil War. The Civil War wrecked American trade and prestige in the Pacific through the destruction of some nine hundred American ships by Confederate privateers. With the passing of the ships went American business firms. The only record of the American Community in the Philippines during this period of time is found on the gravestones of those who died there.

On a little mound of earth in Plaza Cervantes, in the financial district of Manila, stands a small marble monument, queer shaped, battered and patched with cement. It is the congregating place where the Filipino

A capsule history of the American Community from 1796 – 1921

(The following edited article was written by Capt. H.L. Heath, first AmCham President, and was published in the AmCham Journal in June 1921.)

The story of the American Community in the Philippines has been delegated to me to write. In the absence of ability, records, and space, brevity is strongly indicated; yet the full story of the American in the Philippines would take many words and the pen of a master, for in the history of the community there is a new epic of pioneering.

Early History of the American Trade and the Chamber

There is a misconception that Philippine-US trade only began after Admiral Dewey's victory over the Spanish fleet on Manila Bay in 1898. While AmCham considers its roots to date from

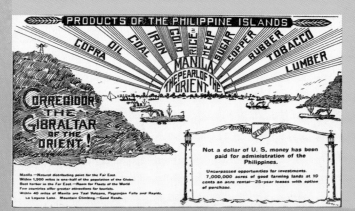

1902 — soon after US occupation of the Philippines — records clearly show there was in fact active trade between the port of Manila and the US dating back to 1796, when the Philippines was still under Spanish rule.

On October 3, 1796, a small trading ship, the "Astrea" out of Salem, Massachusetts, via Lisbon, dropped anchor in Manila Bay and loaded a cargo of 750,000 lbs. of sugar, 63,695 lbs. of pepper and 29,637 lbs. of indigo. Thus began US commercial history in the Philippines. From 1797 to 1858 there were 82 ships arriving in Salem from Manila — enough to indicate a reasonable trade between these two ports alone.

chauffeurs, waiting for their bosses, spend their time playing *dama (Ed. Note: a board game similar to checkers).*

The inscription reads:

"This monument is erected to perpetuate the memory of George W. Hubbell, Esq., United States Consul to this Island, who died May 3, 1831, aged 35 years. He was a native of Bridgeport, State of Connecticut, and son of Captain Ezekiel Hubbell."

Thousands of people pass daily within thirty feet of the monument and very few notice it, yet it is the only monument in Manila, erected in a public place, to the memory of an early American resident of the Philippines. *(Ed. Note: The monument is now located on the grounds of the U.S. Embassy.)*

In the Cemeterio del Norte (North Cemetery), on one of (its) main avenues, rests a little group of Americans, adventurous men and (their) wives who braved the conditions (for) the spread of American trade, commerce and prestige. Here are a few of their names, still decipherable not withstanding the ravages of time.

"Nathan L. Durand, of Medford, Connecticut, died 21st February,1835"

"Mrs. Mary Greene Sturgis, of Boston, Massachusetts, died 17th of September, 1837"

"Gilbert Watson, of Newberryport, Massachusetts, died 6th of November, 1847"

"Josiah Moore, of Malden, Massachusetts, died the 25th of March, 1845"

"John Munro, of New York, died the 5th of November, 1862"

Note that the final date coincides with

Built in 1909 under William E. Parsons, consulting architect for the Bureau of Public Works, Manila's original YMCA (above left) was pure California Mission Revival style adapted to the tropics. It had large windows and used translucent local capiz rather than glass to reduce solar heat. The "Y" was home to many who came to make their way in America's new frontier. (Photo: Lico collection)

Those venturing to the frontier included the couple above, a Thomasite teacher who came to inculcate "the American way", and a mining engineer to seek fortune in the mountains of northern Cordillera. (Photo: AHC)

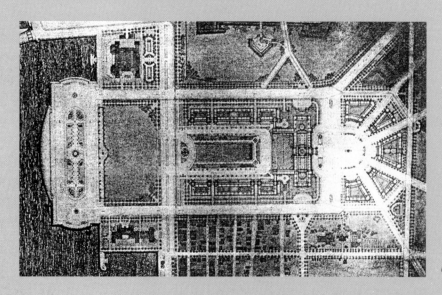

(Plan reproduction: Lico collection)

The Luneta was always a popular gathering place for Manila residents. Brass bands would play along the promenade, as can be seen in this 1910 photograph, above.

As with the central plan for Washington D.C., the US plan for Manila (lower left) was designed with government buildings arranged in a formal pattern around a rectangular mall. Architect and urban planner Daniel Burnham (below) also provided a site for the Manila Hotel, the Army Navy Club, the Philippine General Hospital and the Post Office. (Photos: AHC)

the Civil War and you can, no doubt, picture the sorrow of the rest of this isolated American Community in Manila as it witnessed the destruction of the merchant fleet and the passing of its high hopes and ambitions. With the destruction of the American merchant marine, business was no longer possible and the community disappeared.

The Second Phase:

The second phase of the American Community in the Philippines is found in that period from the termination of the Civil War to the occupation of the Philippines by American troops in 1898. It represents the period when an effort was made to re-establish trade with the few American ships left and its record is found on the gravestones in the British cemetery at San Pedro, Macati (sic). *(Ed. Note: The area is now Olympia Village –located between J.P.Rizal Avenue and the Pasig River, near the Makati Municipal Hall. All known remains were transferred to Manila Memorial Park in 1969.)* Here are some of the inscriptions:

"William D. Huntington, of Salem, Mass., died March 12th, 1868"

""J.C. Bramhall, died May 7th, 1868"

"L.S. Crockett, of Scarsport, Maine, died July 25th, 1876"

"Fred Campbell Eaton, of Cambridge, Mass., died April 21st, 1876"

"J.W. Killman, of Stockton, Maine, died November 14th, 1878"

"Francis Oakey, of New York, died November 17, 1880"

"A.D. Field, of Chelsea, Massachusetts, died October 26th, 1882"

"Julius G. Voight, United States Consul in Manila, for five years, died April 7, 1888"

"Henry Grafton Chapman, of Boston, Mass. Died March 14th, 1883"

"Robert Fisher, of Chelsea, Mass, died April 25, 1893"

"Theresa L. Frost of Portsmouth, New Hampshire, died July 13th, 1894"

These came and made their contribution to the epic of American pioneering in the Orient. Their troubles can be summed up in the statement that when American troops arrived in 1898 there was no American Community to greet them.

The Third Phase:

The genesis of the third phase of the American Community is found in the Spanish-American War, the Philippine Insurrection, and the institution of American business enterprise since.

In the beginning the community was made up almost entirely of American soldiers, officers and men, adventurous spirits and legitimate descendants of the people who pioneered Ohio, Kentucky, and other states of the Middle and Far West states.

The construction of Kennon Road from 1901-1905 created new access to mountainous Baguio, which was later officially declared the summer capital of the colony. The De Dion cars were specifically built for this road. (Photo: AHC)

did the American in business have a real opportunity for the extension of his energy. The real development of the Philippines commenced when modern methods were instituted in the construction of general systems of communication and the connecting up of the localized systems of the Spanish regime. This forms the basis upon which the whole development of the Philippine Islands rests.

Do not think that the American participation in this development has been easy or that it has not been paid for. Scattered all over the Philippines are mounds of unmarked earth beneath which rest the bones of Americans who ventured a little too far; too far into the *bosque,* or too far into competition and politics.

The Fourth Phase:

The fourth phase of the American Community is its chastisement — "adventurers" and "carpetbaggers" alike — by the administration of Governor Harrison who, lent himself and the power of his office to all that was deterrent to American faith, precept and prestige. The "carpetbaggers" thus became "adventurers" for they were soon

The latter, seeing a big, undeveloped country, felt the urge of their forefathers to settle land and asked for their discharge and remained. Many of them accepted appointments to office under the civil administration instituted by Governor Taft; others distributed themselves over the country seeking various outlets for their abundant energy.

Not until the advent of W. Cameron Forbes, as Secretary of Commerce and Police,

More fancy hats and stiff suits — but better suited to the climate of Baguio where this photo was taken. Governor General William Cameron Forbes entertains guests at his Baguio home, called "Topside". (Photo: AHC)

The Elks Club (left), built in 1909 and the double wings of the Army Navy Club (center), built in 1911, stand at the far side of the Luneta – opposite the Manila Hotel in this 1912 photo. The Urdaneta Monument is seen in the right foreground. A tranquil scene, very different from that of today. (Photo: AHC)

absorbed into the business life of the community.

Soon after the amalgamation of the two elements of the community had taken place, an effort was made to bring it into unity. However, the various groups constituting it had been isolated so long that unity on the basis of business interests was impossible.

(However) the group idea had proven satisfactory and had been evidenced in forceful and satisfactory ways (socially) for there are three physical monuments to (such) group energy in the city of Manila: the *Masonic Temple, the Army Navy Club, and the Elks Club.*

Under the muddled and meddling administration of (Governor) Harrison the American Community would have ceased to progress, and probably to exist, had it not been for World War (I). Impartiality of administration was shown by greater partiality than ever.

The racial line was drawn to an alarming degree and the two races gradually drew apart until there was left but a shred of cordiality and respect (that had been) generated by over a decade of work for the betterment of the country and its people.

The lust for power was rampant. Political leaders usurped the exercise of sovereignty delegated by the people of the United States to Governor Harrison. They grew ruthless in the use of authority and one day attacked an Act of the Congress of the United States, in its application to the Philippines.

(They) attempted to force compliance on the part of Americans, and American-controlled organizations, to the mandates of the political oligarchy opposing the Act. Then, once more, the American Community shed its docile aspect, kicked its dormant sensibilities out of the window and waxed indignant.

Out of the ruck *(Ed. note: mess)* came the American Chamber of Commerce of the Philippine Islands, founded twenty-two years after Admiral Dewey broke down Spanish power. The work of putting the Filipino people on the map of the world had commenced.

(The Chamber) was organized with a larger membership and a greater capital than any other American Chamber outside the homeland. It represents every phase of American business and interest in the Philippines.

It proposes to be heard on every subject affecting the business or political life of the community. It proposes in all matters: first, to suggest a remedy; second, to ask for its application; third, to demand its application; and fourth to fight for its application, if the other processes are not successful.

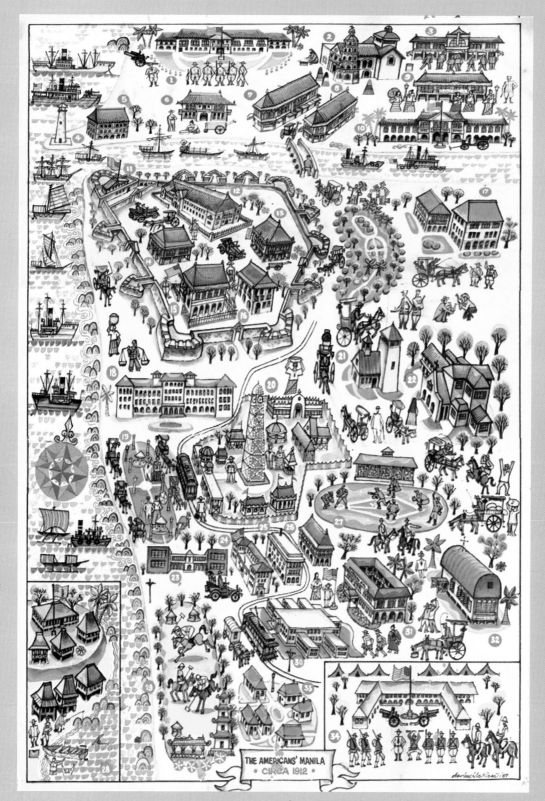

Originally commissioned for and published in *The Manila Americans (1901-1964)*, by Lewis E. Gleeck, Jr. — these maps are with the American Historical Collection, at the Ateneo de Manila University. They were created by artist Da Vinci la Rosa, based on the data provided by Gleeck. There are three in the series — 1912, 1938 and 1964 – and, while taking great architectural and geographical artistic liberty, they nonetheless graphically depict the growth of the American community and business in Manila through the years. The two other maps in the series are reproduced on pages 92 and 106.

MANILA – 1912

The community centers around Intramuros, Ermita and Malate; Pasay, Santa Mesa and Santa Ana are the distant suburbs. The districts of San Pedro de Makati and Guadalupe were "the provinces" then.

Now picture this:

It's now June, 1920.

Life has changed dramatically for at least ten of the "pioneers" who sat down at that first Clarke's round table for coffee and buns 18 years before. Their entrepreneurial instincts made their businesses flourish. Capt. Heath is now a known expert in hemp and maguey, and exports abaca. Others control several cigar and tobacco companies. Some have rapidly expanding shipping companies. Still others have started highly successful trading firms.

There is now also a group of former government officials turned businessmen — including a former Director of Posts, a provincial Treasurer, Customs stenographer and officer in the US Governor-General's Office. There are also at least eight former military men turned entrepreneur, some engaging in banking, publishing and coconut farming.

They are all members of the Manila Merchants Association. But with offices now scattered about an ever-expanding Manila, meetings are becoming rare. The five directors have proposals delivered to their offices for action.

Now something of a shock...

The US has proposed to extend US coastwise shipping laws to the Philippines. Manila's trade is growing rapidly, and changing Manila from an international to a US domestic port means only US registered ships can move goods.

The directors call a meeting and unanimously agree — including the US directors — to lobby *against* the proposal.

But the majority of the membership, still American, are in an uproar. First, they are insulted by the board's pre-emptive decision. And besides, when they think about it, it's probably good for the US business community.

So the Americans resign the Association en masse. Letters flash back and forth. Meetings are held. Heath jumps to the fore and pushes for a formal AmCham to protect and lobby US business interests.

He finds widespread support and the decision is made. Incorporate an American Chamber of Commerce of the Philippine Islands — not to confuse the new group with any other chamber, foreign or local.

Although AmCham's by-laws limit the number of active corporate membership to 125, membership rapidly reaches 1,200 — although only the Active Members can vote.

An early postcard of an estero in the Binondo District of Manila. These esteros — or canals — traversed old Manila providing avenues for commerce. The city was often referred to as the Venice of the East. (Photo: AHC)

An Incorporated Business Lobby (1920-1941)

The irony is, of course, that after all the fuss and fanfare about the coastwise project — which led to AmCham's incorporation and the disintegration of the Merchants Association — the proposal was dropped by Washington.

The point, however, is that the loosely organized AmCham that sat at the Round Table would have evolved quickly into a formal organization in any case.

Several factors were at play.

First and foremost, F.B. Harrison's tenure as Governor-General from 1913-1921 brought a tumultuous response from the American business community. The Jones Act of 1916 had promised independence, and Harrison took it upon himself to act as "Constitutional Monarch" over a "government of Filipinos."

For many of the early business pioneers and entrepreneurs, that was anathema to their motivation. Remember, many had arrived with Dewey to fight ("takeover" is more like it) against the Spanish. Still others arrived to subdue "the insurrection" during the Philippine-American War.

They built their businesses from scratch and, after 10-15 years of struggle, were finally basking in success. Some had become outright millionaires. Business was growing quickly. Mines up near Baguio, sugar plantations in the Visayas, coconut plantations in Mindanao were all sprouting. Trade in equipment and supplies surged, both inter-island and internationally. There was an increased worry among a critically influential faction of the US business community that political realities would soon effect their corporations. They felt they needed a formal institution to protect what they had accomplished and the future of their businesses.

Second, the American community had grown substantially and new companies mushroomed. New entrepreneurs arrived, many acknowledging the political realities of the day. Many of AmCham's incorporators felt it important to lobby this newer crowd to present a united front in both maintaining business growth and in negotiating with the authorities, whether the now active Filipino legislature or the Governor-General's office.

June 1921 – First issue of "American Chamber of Commerce Journal" The editor was H. Edmund Bullis. "What would the Philippine Islands be like without coconut trees?"

The Sanitary Steam Laundry – established by Mr. Thomas Wolfe, a Chamber member – was a large and going concern in 1913...

Ad extolling the benefits of being a member of the American Chamber of Commerce

Charles Mason Cotterman, AmCham president 1922-24

Also, the incorporators wanted a better and more formal access to Washington. This was via both direct lobbying with the US Congress, and through the support of the COCUSA (the Chambers of Commerce of the United States of America). In fact, one of the early moves of the Philippines' AmCham was to help fund the construction of COCUSA's Washington headquarters.

Thus AmCham was bound to take on a more formal visage.

Heath, who was president while organizing its incorporation, was elected president in 1921. But he resigned later that year for an extended home leave through 1924, during which he helped solidify AmCham's relations with Washington.

Harrison's replacement, General Wood, took over as Governor-General in 1921. AmCham, working to build its relations with the Executive, offered to help staff positions if needed. According to Walter Robb, who edited the AmCham Journal from 1924 through 1941, it was "one of the best decisions the Chamber ever made" (before WWII).

Heath's replacement, Charles Cotterman, was as effective in people skills as he was an effective businessman. He had instant access to the Governor-General, and was appointed as Director of the Philippine National Bank.

Cotterman was one of those early stalwarts — he arrived in 1900 as Director of Posts — who was firmly against independence. But Robb writes that he maintained the trust nonetheless of Philippine political party leaders, Manuel Quezon and Sergio Osmena. One reason was a rescue plan for some P50 million owed by sugar centrals. He basically restructured the loans to be paid out of operations rather than sell the

... offering ship to shore service – with a smile. (Photos courtesy Peter Wallace)

Mayon Volcano, Albay

assets to a US syndicate. The lands remained in Filipino hands while the money remained in circulation.

Heath returned in 1924 and was re-elected AmCham president from 1924-27. He led an AmCham mission to New York City in 1924, opening an AmCham branch.

There was still a strong sentiment within the Chamber against granting independence, with the US Congress asked to make the Philippines a formal Territory. The argument was that Congress could not give up sovereignty of US-controlled land without a mandate of the then 48 States. Heath promoted the argument in a resolution to Congress, where it was stillborn.

That more-or-less ended moves by AmCham's anti-independence faction — the "end of an era," as Robb writes.

By this time AmCham had on many occasions and in documents emphasized it would never meddle in political affairs, but promote economic, trade and business policies that aided its members. During the Depression-laden 1930s, it did just that. Paul Meyers was elected president 7 times, with H.M. Cavender — who was the first Manila Hotel manager — elected in 1934 and 1935.

Business was dull and growth mediocre, so AmCham promoted trade policies. It also argued against an onerous sales tax that applied only to foreign businesses.

Pagsanjan Falls, Laguna

But most importantly, it finally accepted and supported the political developments of the Quezon-led Commonwealth and its 1935 Constitution. Towards the end of the pre-war period, the economy was on an upswing, and again expanding trade was the mantra. Relations with the new government were definitely moving forward, and many individual friendships began in the new Philippine political firmament. AmCham members were preparing to grow and prosper in a new environment.

Independence was just around the corner. But what a corner it turned out to be.

The AmCham Journal of April 1922 describes an idyllic Philippines that even then did not get the attention of the world's travelers: "The Newspapermen's Section of the American Chamber of Commerce has started a movement having as its objective the attraction of a larger number of tourists to the Philipppine Islands than have in the past come to this Archipelago.

Japan, the Dutch East Indies, Manchuria and other sections of the Far East are carrying on an active propaganda having as its object the attraction of the tourist traffic.

In the opinion of the writer... the attractions of the Philippines are equal, or even superior, to those of Japan, China and the Dutch East Indies. The scenery in various parts of the islands cannot be surpassed anywhere. Between the Islands is a magnificent system of natural ocean waterways traversed by steamers. Baguio is a mountain resort having few rivals in the world. Manila itself is replete with interest, with its churches, public buildings, institutions, aquarium, Luneta, sunken gardens, etc., etc. It boasts the finest hotel in the Far East. Why these attractions and advantages have not been emphasized sufficiently in the past is something that must arouse wonder. However, there is no reason why they should remain unadvertised in the future. If the government, the chambers of commerce, the newspapers and periodicals, and the people will pull together, the Philippines can easily be made one of the world's greatest meccas of tourist traffic."
(Photos: AHC)

(continued on page 22)

JAMES C. ROCKWELL – Early Vice President and General Manager of MERALCO, the Manila Electric Rail and Light Company. (Photo: AmCham Journal, October 1922)

Portrait

Why "Rockwell"? . . . meet Mr. James C. Rockwell

OK, figure this out.

When people around Manila say "Rockwell," they think of an urban subdivision of high rise residences, office buildings and a shopping mall tucked away between the Pasig River and downtown Makati City. Now how does this relate to a railroad engineer who helped build the Wabash?

James Rockwell was born in Scranton, Pennsylvania in 1881. He graduated from Cornell in 1904, and started working on the Chicago and Northwestern, Wabash, and other railroads in the US. He began in management on the Syracuse urban rail system briefly before moving on to Charleston, West Virginia, where he ran the Interurban Railway Company in 1908.

In 1911, he was offered the position of manager of Meralco's railway department. By 1922, he was vice president and general manager of the entire company.

Aside from being an active member of AmCham, Rockwell was the first Commodore of the Manila Yacht Club and was also member of the Rotary, Manila Golf, Elks, Army and Navy Club, and Manila Polo Club.

Meralco's Makati thermal power plant was named after him. And once the property was returned to the Lopez family after the EDSA Revolt of 1986, the family decided to convert the antiquated facility into its current real estate venture.

He's probably smiling.

Chambers of Commerce of the USA — COCUSA

Since 1912 COCUSA has been the voice of business in Washington, D.C. Ann Crittenden wrote in AmCham's Business Journal in December, 1982, "It is the largest business lobbying group in business-minded America. Secure in its stately headquarters in Lafayette Park, directly opposite the White House, the United States Chamber of Commerce seems impregnable…At a hint from the Chamber, its membership…can deluge Capitol Hill with thousands of letters and tie up the phones in legislators offices for hours."

"The influence of the Chamber goes well beyond Washington…" It is in fact the world's largest nonprofit business federation and currently represents 3,000,000 businesses, 830 business associations, 3,000 state and local US Chambers, and 93 American Chambers of Commerce in 81 countries.

The American Chamber of Commerce of the Philippines is one of those 81. In fact, one of the first actions taken by the incorporators in 1920 was to support the formation of COCUSA, even donating funds for the building of its Washington, D.C. headquarters.

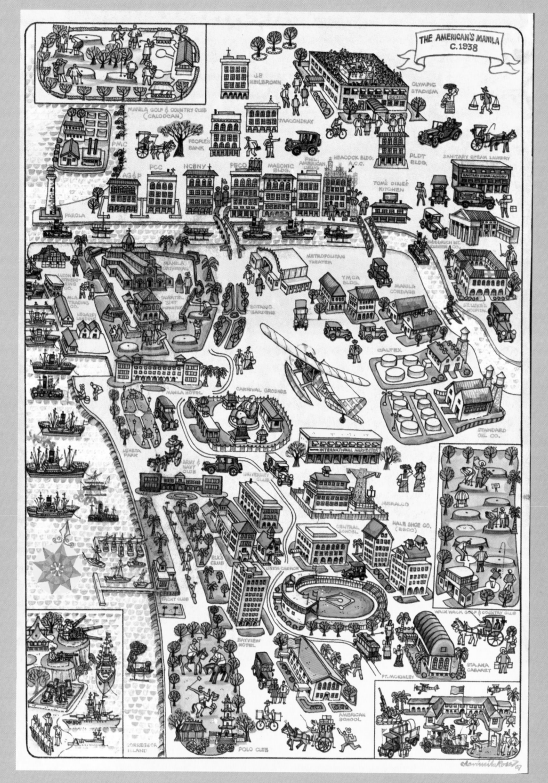

MANILA – 1938

Artist Da Vinci la Rosa again offers his interpretation of Manila during the Commonwealth era. The principal points of American community interest at the time are labeled. Gleeck calls attention to the movement of the bulk of community activity away from Intramuros to areas both south and north of the Pasig River. There is an expansion of successful American businesses. Note the insets of Manila Golf and Country Club, then in Caloocan, and the Wack-Wack Golf and Country Club, located in Mandaluyong, a suburb like Santa Ana, and the change in Fort William McKinley and Corregidor from 1912.

AmCham Membership Card, circa 1933

This American Chamber membership card was issued as a courtesy to H.E. Ambassador Frank Murphy, Governor General of the Philippines (1933-1935) for the duration of his stay. It was donated to the AmCham office by Mr. And Mrs. Leo Larkin. Mr. Larkin (a resident of over 52 years and former member of AmCham) states "the card is credible testimony that Frank Murphy had license to grace the halls of AmCham in days of yore."

John Manning: "Mr. MANTRADE"

*John Manning
AmCham President*

Jack and his mother, Cora Coulter Manning, were interned for more than three years in concentration camps in Manila and Los Baños by the Japanese. This photo was taken shortly after their liberation from Sto. Tomas in 1945. (Photo: AHC)

John Lordan "Jack" Manning had serious ties to the Philippines.

His father was an Irish immigrant who joined the 13th Minnesota Volunteers, fighting on Leyte during the Philippine-American War, remaining to become Insular Treasurer during the administrations of Governor-Generals Harrison and Forbes. In 1921, the elder Manning drowned in the Ozaana River in the Caribbean.

Twelve year old Jack and his widowed mother moved to Oklahoma, where Jack graduated from Oklahoma University in 1930. He transferred to New York City to stay with a close family friend, Julius Reese, who sent the 25 year old Jack back to Manila in 1934 to work with the Manila Trading and Supply Co. (Mantrade), the Ford dealership for the Philippines. As service manager his salary was P400 a month; enough to buy a car at P50 a month, pay his monthly rent of P125 at the YMCA — and even buy 2 white suits.

Mantrade was growing and Manning was promoted to sales manager. In 1940, with the prospect of war, Jack sent his wife and son home. His mother, in Manila, refused to leave.

Manning was imprisoned in Santo Tomas Internment Camp. However, the Japanese authorities let his mother stay at home until early 1944 when she then joined him. By 1943, the camp was overcrowded and the Japanese ordered abler men to Los Baños to build

another camp. Manning's mother remained in Sto. Tomas until he rejoined her, just prior to liberation, due to her illness.

He stayed in Manila (after learning his wife had remarried) and rehabilitated the company. Manning leased Mantrade's four buildings at the port to the US Army, reconstructed company financial records, secured 90-day loans — and Mantrade was back off the ground. Personnel, scattered during the war, began to return. He built work sheds, imported 30 truck chassis to make buses — helping get basic infrastructure back on track.

He also became first secretary of AmCham for P500 a month. After a year, he was sent home for a rest and medical check-up while two colleagues replaced him in the interim.

Manning remarried in 1948 to Carlyn Truax, a model and professional dancer, and built a home in Makati's newly created Forbes Park subdivision.

He became President of Mantrade upon Reese's death, a position he held until the company was sold in 1968.

Remaining active with the American Chamber of Commerce, Manning was President twice (1952, 1958). He also served on the Boards of the American Association Philippines, the Rotary Club, Manila Polo Club, American School, was active with Elks Lodge No. 761. B.P.O.E. and their Cerebral Palsy Project, St. Luke's Hospital, the Salvation Army, and the William J. Shaw Foundation. He was a founder of the American Historical Collection, served on the vestry of Holy Trinity Church, and worked with several organizations devoted to the care of crippled and disabled children.

He was a man with keen Irish wit and solid Philippine roots — a storyteller come full circle.

Hi Jinks at the High Commissioners' Residence — 1940

Ralph Graves, the stepson of Francis Sayre, first US High Commissioner in Manila, writes on life at the High Commissioners' residence.

"My family — my stepfather, my mother, my brother and I — were the first to live here. When my stepfather, Francis Sayer, arrived as High Commissioner in October, 1939, the building was not quite ready for occupancy. In my parents' opinion it was *never* ready for occupancy.

"Designed by some architect who had never lived in the tropics, it looked more like a Federal Prison than an embassy. It was built on landfill, and the entire landscaping consisted of a scattered handful of scrubby trees. When it rained — and we quickly learned that it rained often in Manila — the water poured under those tall French doors. I can still remember the horde of houseboys in their starched red, white and blue uniforms piling sheets and towels against the doors.

"But my younger brother and I loved the Embassy, which in those days was also the Residence. It was the first home I had ever seen with a private, self-operating elevator. When I brought my girlfriend over to the Embassy, the only place I could take her for privacy and intimacy, away from the eyes of all the houseboys, was inside the elevator. I could make it stop between floors. In those far-off innocent days, I am sorry to confess that nothing very wicked happened in the elevator, but both my girl and I thought it was romantic.

"My younger brother, Bill, enjoyed a different aspect of the Embassy. He was crazy about darts that he made out of matchsticks, needles and paper. He would stand on one of the little ballroom balconies and throw his darts up towards the ceiling and watch them turn in the air, zoom down and land far below on the parquet floor. Later a friend taught him how to make a dart-launcher out of a spring clothespin. Then he would stand down on the floor and fire his darts way up into the ceiling, where a number of them stuck in the plaster. They were impossible for the houseboys to reach, but since they were also hard to see from the floor level, nobody ever bothered about them."

Graves studied at Brent School, Baguio and upon graduation went on to college in the US. War broke out and he went into the

Bottom right and left: Two views of the front and back façade of the building originally designed as the Residence and offices of the American High Commissioner built by the Marsman Building Corporation for the sum of $374,704.53. The building was once termed the "most perfect on American soil". The flag pole clearly seen in the photo still flies the flag today. Made of non-welded steel, it was shipped directly from Washington.
(Photo: AmCham Journal)

The Embassy Ballroom, 1940.
(Photo: AmCham Journal)

Number One Son to the Rescue

"The year 1940-41 was the best of my life. I was 16, and I was a senior at Brent School in Baguio, and when I was in Manila, I was the High Commissioner's son — a role I had then learned to enjoy."

"My father was a modest man. Even though his car had the license plate 'U.S. 1' and flew the High Commissioners flag on the fender, my father would never let his chauffeur use the siren; he thought it much too flashy and imperialistic.

"Now can you imagine… you are the High Commissioner's chauffeur — a delightful old man named Ambrosio — and have finally reached the very peak of your profession: you are driving 'Number One' car of the 'Number One' government official in the entire country. The flag, the 'U.S. 1' license plate, the siren — but the boss won't let you use the siren!

"To Ambrosio's rescue came Number One Son. When on school vacation in Manila, my father would let me borrow the 'U.S. 1' Cadillac at night to take my school friends to the movies. I had no inhibitions about the siren. Seven or eight of us piled in the car and Ambrosio went screaming down what was then Dewey Boulevard with the siren at full blast all the way — and a huge happy smile on his face."

armed forces. He returned to Manila in late 1944 as an Army Air Force sergeant and was "horrified" by the devastation. He made his way to his former home, through rubble-strewn streets and, with much effort, was finally able to convince the American soldiers on guard to let him inside the building.

"Much of the building was in rubble, but the ballroom was in surprisingly good shape. In spite of all the bombs and the shocks, the big vaulted ceiling had survived…and way up there in the ceiling, where only a real insider would think to look, two of my brother's darts still hung there in the plaster."

Now picture this:

Let's stop for a moment and go back in our chronology.

It's May 1, 1898. Commodore George Dewey arrives in Manila Bay and approaches an obsolete Spanish fleet. News that a British ship will soon arrive to protect British "interests" reaches several members of the Manila Chamber of Commerce, all British. They gather along the Bay riding *calesas*, bringing lounge chairs and some snacks. After setting up well out of way of Spanish positions, Dewey gives his famous command, "Grindley, you may fire when ready." They watch the three-hour show. The Spanish fleet is now history. "Hear hear. Quite a spectacle!" The British pack up and go home.

Fast Forward:

It's December 8, 1941. Three hours after the Japanese have decimated the US Pacific Fleet at Pearl Harbor, the bombs start falling on Baguio. The incredible news reaches Robert Hendry, for only two months editor of AmCham's Journal. He rushes out to the printer to check the status of the December issue. The last few days have been hectic indeed, putting the finishing touches on what would be the last Journal for four years. The cover had the official "Keep 'em Flying" emblem on it. Distribution is completed December 10. The bombs are already falling. Within a week Manila is declared an open city. Hendry is stuck. After the Japanese bring him to the Sto. Tomas Internment Camp, they grill him for hours about the emblem on the cover, thinking it an "insidious, super-secret organization." General Douglas MacArthur slips out of the island fortress of Corregidor, weaves his way through the Japanese-controlled archipelago, and arrives in Australia with his famous words, "I shall return."

AmCham Journal Issue of December 1941, the last issue prior to the war, with the "Keep 'em Flying" emblem. The Japanese interrogated editor Robert Hendry for hours about the emblem on the cover, thinking it an "insidious, super-secret organization." Below, Manila under siege. (Photo: AHC)

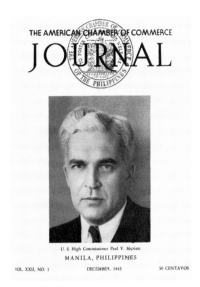

THE AMERICAN CHAMBER OF COMMERCE

JOURNAL

U. S. High Commissioner Paul V. McNutt
MANILA, PHILIPPINES

VOL. XXII, NO. 1   DECEMBER, 1945   50 CENTAVOS

AmCham Journal Issue of December 1945, the first issue after the war.

War & Reconstruction (1941 - 1954)

Quite a contrast.

Many AmCham members were among the hundreds interned at the Sto. Tomas camp, including Samuel Gaches, who was AmCham president since 1939. Life was hard. But the membership there worked together to ease things as much as they could and several, who had done business in better times with the Japanese, lobbied to ensure it didn't become more of a prison than it was.

Liberation of the Camp occurred in early February, 1945. On the 17th, AmCham held its first meeting — at Sto.Tomas. Fighting was still going on around the city. It was a struggle to begin again. Promissory notes covered initial expenses, which including an office opposite the camp on España. Rent was P1,000 a month. Pre-war Board members attended meetings during March, with AmCham's office becoming a distribution center for radio messages, and acting as an unofficial post office.

Paul McNutt, the US High Commissioner, suggested independence might have to be delayed (it wasn't), and the press asked AmCham to comment. On March 31, Gaches proposed and the AmCham Board approved a statement saying the Chamber would have nothing to do with politics, and that it would work only for "the commercial and industrial rehabilitation of the Philippines." AmCham would strive to help reopen financial institutions, get transportation moving to increase supplies, lower prices, and recreate normal distribution through the private sector, rather than use government agencies.

The first post-war Journal, December 1945, screamed "Give Us Imports," and spoke of widespread black markets. Gaches died of a heart attack a month later, and on January 25, 1946, 22 active AmCham members held the first post-war annual general meeting.

AmCham was beginning to get its act back together. But yet another AmCham era was at its end.

Just as Dewey and the Philippine-American War brought with it troops and officers who stayed on to become the entrepreneurs to help build the Colony and AmCham, so too did MacArthur and his liberation army bring with them a new generation of Americans who would fall in love with an independent Philippines and stay on to help rehabilitate the economy and reinvigorate AmCham.

Rehabilitation was long and hard. But several US Congressional Acts on trade and rehabilitation preceded the formal July 4, 1946 return of sovereignty. War "surplus" was transferred.

Reconstruction was a major infrastructural challenge. (Photo: AHC)

The Board of Directors of the American Chamber of Commerce present a plaque to J.A. Parrish, AmCham president 1951 "in recognition of distinguished service to the American Chamber" and "valuable contributuion to the American business community." Presentation was held at the Manila Club. Left to right: Mrs. Virginia Gonder, Frank C. Bennett, D. O. Gunn, J. L. Manning, J. A. Parrish, J. H. Carpenter, Ewald E. Selph and Harry Stevenson.
(Photo: AmCham)

AmCham was reorganizing as well. The need to rebuild infrastructure provided ample opportunities for businesses ranging from finance to construction to local manufacturing. And AmCham worked hard to help, advise, cajole and lobby the new government on issues such as trade, shipping, quotas and tariffs — to ensure that new laws would not be a detriment to economic development.

But the most important post-war AmCham initiative was the establishment of an information clearing house for businesses offering services or looking for opportunities. It was, in fact, Hendry's idea which he proposed during that first Sto. Tomas AmCham meeting, and he was given the task of organizing it.

The period ended with unprecedented growth for the Philippines and a brewing debate that would last another 20 years. The Laurel-Langley Agreement was signed by the US in December 1954, and passed both Philippine Houses in May 1955. It basically revised the 1946 Bell Trade Act that gave "parity" to US firms doing business in the Philippines in terms of rights and owning property. For AmCham it also meant "parry"— as accusations emerged that the "colonial economy" had really not changed.

1920-1939

1939-1960

1960-1988

1989-present

AmCham Seals

Tom Carter (AmCham historian) writes "Analogically, the present AmCham was born in 1920, but like all living things, life begins prior to birth; in this case AmCham's (original founding) being 1902.

"In remembrance and honor (of this) the...seal, stamp or logo (of) the Chamber will, in all honesty, exhibit the 1902 date also."

Up to July 1939 the wording on the seal read "American Chamber of Commerce of the Philippine Islands." In anticipation of Philippine Independence the design was amended to read "American Chamber of Commerce of the Philippines" in August 1939. At the same time the eagle on the seal took on a very stiff, square look. A return to the more regal, spread-winged eagle came about in 1960. The current seal, with the two important Chamber dates, came into use in 1989.

Chick Parsons: A Hero Larger than Life

Charles "Chick" Parsons (Photo: AHC)

Books have been written about the man. The definitive film has yet to be made. Charles "Chick" Parsons was as much about MacArthur's famous "return" as MacArthur was himself.

It was he who set the stage. And it was the guerilla infrastructure he helped establish that convinced a skeptical US President Franklin Delano Roosevelt to go for the Battle of the Leyte Gulf in October 1944 instead of bypassing the Philippines entirely for a debatable invasion of Formosa (today's Taiwan). Although Philippine history tends to emphasize the landing, it was the concurrent sea battle that decimated the Japanese carrier and destroyer fleet around the Visayas and signaled the death knell to Japanese maritime control in Asia.

It wasn't the big boats that cemented Parsons' fame, however. It was the submarine. Shuttling back and forth between Australia and Mindanao, Parsons ran a 19-month series of escapades across the archipelago that armed underground battalions, coordinated guerilla spy networks, and fomented havoc through currency manipulation.

Carlos P. Romulo, "Mr. UN," long-time Philippine foreign minister and UN ambassador, energetic journalist to the core, story-teller *par excellance*, and the man carrying the typewriter in that classic Leyte photo (and monument), wanted dearly to write of his friend's life. With the kind permission of his widow Beth Day Romulo, we edit from their original proposal for a work still begging to be "in progress."

The working title is: "The Man Who Fooled An Army."

At the headquarters of the U.S.Navy Department in Washington, D.C, on an early fall day in 1942, a small, sunburned, southern American, who had recently escaped with his family from the Japanese occupied Philippines, was asking for permission to return to the islands, as a spy.

A Commander in the American Naval Reserve, Parsons had been a successful businessman in Manila prior to Pearl Harbor (shipping, stevedoring and molasses) and an active and popular figure in pre-war Manila society. Through his shipping connections, an Honorary Consul for Panama, he had succeeded in convincing the Japanese that he was Panamanian and had thus escaped internment. But now, with his family safely out, he wanted to go back.

His reason? "I know they are there" he kept saying, "the guerrillas – Filipinos and Americans who went into the hills and the jungles when the Japanese came in. If we can contact them, organize and equip them, they will be ready to assist MacArthur when he returns. It could cut the war short by months, maybe years."

Parsons was persuasive. He not only had the bold idea of arming guerrilla units in occupied territory. He also had worked out a five part plan. First he would go in alone to contact the different guerrilla leaders…. Second… an intelligence network could be set up throughout the islands to feed information back …radio stations and coast watching stations could be set up to supply observation of all Japanese movement. Offloading onto small native craft from a submarine, he could bring in ammunition, arms, food – whatever was most needed –

from Australia — to the guerrillas. Last but not least, the operation would be a morale booster for the civilian population as well as the guerrillas — sustaining them with the knowledge that eventually the islands would be liberated.

The Navy brass reluctantly approved Parson's plan but warned him it would have to be cleared with MacArthur. A cable was sent to Australia, the cryptic reply was "Send Parsons immediately. MacArthur."

Beginning alone, Parsons built up the Spy Squadron unit (known as SPYRON) which, before the war ended had succeeded in supplying a guerrilla army of over 100,000 Filipinos and Americans who had escaped Bataan or internment. It was the largest secret army ever to welcome an invasion in the history of the world.

In many ways The Bamboo Project was a vest-pocket operation, between MacArthur and Parsons. When Parsons returned from a trip to the Philippines, he called on the General's residence. "Jean would ask me to join them for lunch or supper, then excuse herself and we would go over, verbally, what I had done and make plans for the next trip."

Some of their projects were wildly successful. Eminently effective…was the plan to counterfeit Japanese occupation currency and flood the island with this "Mickey Mouse" money to make the currency worthless. Assigned to bring samples of the bills, ink and paper to Australia for counterfeiting, Parsons brought back the actual plates.

Slipping into the islands by rubber boat from a submarine, Parsons brought arms, food and most important — hope from the outside world. For the children, there were special chocolate bars heavily laced with vitamin supplements. . . . After his first trip Parsons came back to Australia with so many requests and orders that he convinced the Navy to provide him with their largest cargo-carrying submarine for his return. He carried everything from arms to a set of false teeth for the guerrilla commander who had lost so much weight in prison camp his mouth had changed size. He also brought in a copper still so that the guerrillas could brew their own booze from coconuts.

Parsons' near misses were legion. He was fired on more often by nervous friends than by the enemy. But after one abortive attempt to pose as a priest, he never wore a disguise and never carried arms. He relied on superior stamina to outrun and out-swim the enemy. With his small stature, deep sunburn, knowledge of Spanish and Filipino dialects, he was easily lost in a crowd.

The crowd, however, will never loose him.

Members of the First Cavalry Tank Corps with internee Bernard Herzog, who was traveling in the Philippines as a tourist when he was taken prisoner by the Japanese and interned at the Sto. Tomas Internment Camp in Manila. (Photo: AHC)

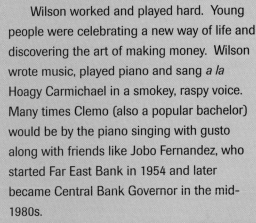

Portrait

From Savannah to Manila:
Those Who Stayed

Wilson and cohorts partying in the 50s

Claude Marion Wilson, Jr. belonged to that American breed who stayed. Whether they stayed like those patrons of Clarke's in the early 1900s, or stayed after Liberation in 1945, they found opportunity and capitalized on it.

Born in Savannah, Georgia, Claude served in the Quartermaster Corp during WWII. He was discharged from the army in 1949 and chose Manila as his home. His contemporaries became the business legends of an era — as much as Captain Heath's were half a century earlier. Lou Sheff, Ray Lehman, Jack Manning, Chuck Butler, Henry Brimo, Cappi Capotosto, Freddie Clemo were among them. So too were the controversial — Harry Stonehill and Bob Brooks.

With Manila destroyed by the vanquished Japanese Army and the liberating American forces, Claude found opportunities in reconstruction. He imported everything from GI sheets and other building materials to ladies dresses.

Just like Dewey's "frontier" businessmen, being young and brash was the order of the day. Fun loving, yet hardworking, these entrepreneurs dominated both the social and economic scene. Some called them latter day carpetbaggers, but others saw them more as saviors.

Wilson organized other companies after a time — he distributed Olivetti typewriters and calculators, manufactured sewing machines, and marketed appliances on installment.

Wilson worked and played hard. Young people were celebrating a new way of life and discovering the art of making money. Wilson wrote music, played piano and sang *a la* Hoagy Carmichael in a smokey, raspy voice. Many times Clemo (also a popular bachelor) would be by the piano singing with gusto along with friends like Jobo Fernandez, who started Far East Bank in 1954 and later became Central Bank Governor in the mid-1980s.

Weekends were spent at the Manila Yacht Club racing in vintage "Dragons". His other serious hobby was chess, which he played Saturday afternoons with friend Ray Lyon. He was also a budding amateur magician.

Wilson joined the Manila Theater Guild (MTG), an amateur theater group (the precursor of Repertory Philippines) producing shows at the Army & Navy Club. As an unpaid actor he moved on to Hollywood movies filmed in the Philippines. He was often hired as the odd General or Colonel or the GI lover who left his Filipina lady love at the pier. In later years he graduated from being the lover to playing the father — which upset him a little. His wife, Isabel, who later was appointed Philippine Ambassador to Spain, was always amazed at how much he was paid for playing those minor roles.

Wilson served as an AmCham Director and Chairman of Republicans Abroad Philippines. He was Vice President of the Harvard Business School of the Philippines and President of the Harvard Club of the Philippines. He died in Manila in 1983, a man who arrived in adversity and built a future — like many others of his era.

The Wilson Family
(Photo: Wilson collection)

Now picture this:

It's July again, now 1955.

AmCham President Paul Parrette is mingling with the VIP crowd at President Ramon Magsaysay's July 4 Philippine Independence Day celebration. It's a crowded affair at Malacañang. Congressmen are politicking. Some spit-and-polish military elite are immersed in a corner cabal with US Bases' brass. Top businessmen from Manila and the provinces are hobnobbing with their favored legislators. Magsaysay is holding court with several cabinet secretaries and a group of foreign ambassadors. They are talking about Indonesian President Sukarno's highly successful Bandung Conference a few months before and the possibilities of a nationalist, "non-aligned movement" forming, countering an ever-intensifying Cold War between the Soviets and Americans.

Then Vice President Richard M. Nixon talking with Sen. Claro M. Recto on a visit to the Philippines. (Photo: AHC)

Parrette passes a group of Liberal Party senators and overhears one of them lambasting the newly passed Laurel-Langley Agreement between the US and the Philippines.

"My friend, come and join us!" says a smiling Senator Claro Recto, extending his hand. "We were just discussing our new 'reciprocal parity' with your country. You have economic rights here, we now have the same possibilities there," chortles the 65 year-old legal luminary.

"I am happy that you think it fair," says Parrette with his pleasant, relaxed smile only half hiding his sarcasm. "I'm glad my government didn't cut your sugar quota, and slowed the application of tariffs to Philippine exports.

"But we're not government, you know. We're businessmen. And I'm really worried that nationalizing the retail sector, for example, is going to hurt you as much as it hurts our members in the Chamber," Parrette adds.

"Ahhhh, but not only can you bring in goods duty free, but you sell them freely, *di ba*?" the long-time nationalist retorts. "You, the bastion of world capitalism, produce so much so cheaply that it's almost 'dumping.' It's like Godzilla versus Bambi!" and the group breaks out in laughter.

"Seriously," the respected orator continues, "how can our manufacturers and industrialists challenge you in the marketplace. We can't let your members compete with our fledgling businesses. That's why we set bans on your members producing competing goods. And we will continue to do so despite Laurel-Langley," nodding heads all around.

Paul R. Parrette, AmCham President 1954-1956 (Photo: AmCham)

"But Senator," retorts Parrette diplomatically. "Don't you think Filipinos should have a choice in quality? And besides, local productive capacity can't possibly satisfy growing demand. Don't forget, the economy is doing quite well."

"Thank you for your confidence," and the chuckles return. But Recto's visage is becoming stern. "But I'll tell you something, my friend. Things are changing across the world. The new nations will continue to break through the yoke of colonialism. We have a modicum of political independence, perhaps. But your Bases remain, and we remain stuck in a colonial economy. So, yes, we will protect our businesses. It was good seeing you again."

THE AMERICAN CHAMBER OF COMMERCE

JOURNAL

OF THE PHILIPPINES

Published monthly by the American Chamber of Commerce of the Philippines
Elks Club Building, Manila, Philippines—Telephone No. 3-75-04
Member, Philippine National Committee, International Chamber of Commerce
Member, Chamber of Commerce of the United States

A. V. H. Hartendorp
Editor and Manager

Entered as second class matter at the Manila Post Office on May 15, 1921, and on December 10, 1945
Paul H. Wood, President; Newland Baldwin, Vice-President; Mario S. Rubio, Treasurer;
Harold D. Carl, Earl Carroll, J. P. Cotton, J. L. Manning, R. J. Manciel, E. E. Selph;
Stanley N. Fisher, Executive Vice-President; I. T. Salmo, Secretary

Vol. XXXIV   January, 1958   No. 1

Contents

50 CENTAVOS THE COPY

AmCham Journal, January 1958. For the entire decade of the 50s the Journal had no cover page; whether this was due to some post-war shortage of suitable paper or to place the emphasis on content is unknown, but it did focus attention on the "business of business".

Frequently derided as an "AmBoy," President Ramon Magsaysay (right) was nonetheless a populist leader. He died in a 1957 plane crash. Here he sits with "Mr. UN" Carlos P. Romulo. (Photo courtesy Beth Day Romulo)

Parity vs. Nationalism (1954-1968)

Recto was right. It was an unprecedented period of nationalism around the world, with nations in Africa, Asia and South America asserting their independence against the remnants of colonialism.

And in terms of business, the fight against colonialism became a fight against unfettered capitalism and, in particular, foreign capitalism. Non-aligned or not, the drift was towards interference, intervention and regulation of foreign capital and investment. In certain domestic sectors and some restricted foreign ones, the Soviet or Chinese socialist model of government ownership was followed.

Southeast Asia was becoming the next "front" against communist expansion. And the Philippines was in a quandary. It too wanted, needed, to assert its independence — not just to Filipinos, but to the growing number of new nations around the globe. It wanted badly to prove that it too should be considered non-aligned. But the political reality was that the newly independent nations looked down upon Manila for its alliance — politically and militarily — with the US.

So the government took its nationalism to the economy. Protectionism became the name of the game. And despite the parity assured by the Laurel-Langley Agreement, the government closed off entire business sectors to foreign (mostly US) participation. Even specific products which foreign-owned companies manufactured locally were banned in the domestic market.

AmCham had to adapt to a far more sophisticated and diplomatic posture in lobbying for free trade, market access and level competition. The US still clearly dominated foreign investment, and AmCham positions were still sought out by congressional committees on a plethora of trade and investment issues. But on the proactive front, it had to develop a more refined tack.

For example, in 1956, AmCham President Paul Wood presided over the creation of sector-specific committees to monitor proposed legislation effecting members, writing position papers as a lobbying technique — these committees still exist. And as the 1950s came to a close, AmCham began to take a polite, yet adversarial role in attacking nationalist legislative — and executive — tendencies.

Despite Laurel-Langley — and "parity" — restrictions were proposed on everything from equity, labor, management, foreign exchange, retail and wholesale trade, both exports and imports, taxes and in law.

AmCham saw things worsen during the first part of the 1960s. It argued against a capital gains tax that would stifle foreign inflows, resulting in less take for the government in the end. It also began criticizing statements by President Diosdado Macapagal rhetorically welcoming foreign capital on one hand, while legislating restrictions on the other.

But the low point came after the US Congress, in 1962, turned down Philippine War Damages claims. Macapagal cancelled a state visit to Washington. And while the US finally approved a revised version, it was during the interim that the Philippine President changed the nation's Independence Day from July 4, 1946 to June 12, 1898.

By 1965, AmCham was still pushing for its input on new legislation. But more importantly, it had studied and assessed just how badly nationalist restrictions had stunted — not just growth — but the deepening of the manufacturing and industrial base in general. Effects of that thin industrial veneer remain.

1965 was an election year — an extremely violent, expensive and vitriolic election year. New President...Ferdinand Marcos.

Marcos initially tried to assuage US business fears by addressing each particular issue separately. Great politics. He would make enough individuals happy to dilute and thus weaken the common denominator. That's how he usually dealt with organizations, and AmCham was no different.

But he allowed, even encouraged, debate on what would happen once the Laurel-Langley Agreement expired in 1974. What would happen to US citizens' "property" or equity or other assets? And how would this effect US companies?

January, 1966
One Peso

AmCham Journal, January 1966. Described as a "striking aerial photograph of the Luneta...taken when new work on the area was in progress," the photo shows the Quirino grandstand still under construction; at center right is the Rizal Monument. Lower left is the Manila Hotel, top center is the Manila City Hall. The first large building to the left, above center, is the Shurdut Building, housing AmCham. (Original photo courtesy of Teodoro Valencia.)

President Diosdado Macapagal (right) took a much more nationalistic stance towards protectionism, as was the trend of the early 1960s. (Photo courtesy Beth Day Romulo)

Portrait
William Quasha: Legal Luminary

William "Bill" Quasha
(Photo: AHC)

William H. Quasha was the only American, actually the only foreigner, ever licensed to practice law in the Philippines after Independence. That alone would make him a rarity, but his legacy is far larger. The Boy Scouts, American Legion and St. Luke's Medical Center all bear the Quasha imprint.

Part of the wave of Americans washed ashore during WWII, Quasha landed as part of Gen. Douglas MacArthur's staff in Leyte. Then a Lt. Col., he was assigned Asst. Enemy Property Custodian during liberation. Released from the army, he returned to Manila in early 1946 and was admitted to the Philippine Bar after applying to the Supreme Court.

A New York lawyer since 1936, Quasha was actively involved with the Episcopal Church. When the Philippine church was in Ermita, the Quashas, with Carlyn and Jack Manning, worked towards moving the church to its current Makati site. It was Quasha's idea to construct a 20-storey building with the church on top, commenting, "We'd all be closer to God." But the idea was rejected in favor of a Cathedral complex.

He taught law at Sto. Tomas University and was active with the Rotary Club of Manila, the Army-Navy Club, the Elks Lodge, Republicans Abroad and member of the National Executive Board of the Boy Scouts of the Philippines for 25 years. He was Chancellor of the Episcopal Church from 1965 until his death on May 12, 1995.

It was his close relationship with the Church that led him to St. Luke's Hospital. In 1975, St. Luke's was having financial problems, and Bishop Benito Cabanban, then head of the Episcopal Church in the Philippines, enlisted Quasha's help in rehabilitating the hospital. Quasha was given a free hand.

Today, St. Luke's is probably one of the best-equipped hospitals in Southeast Asia, with its onsite college: the William Quasha - St. Luke's College of Medicine.

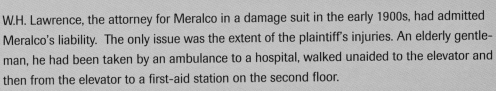

The "Magical, Mystery" Room

W.H. Lawrence, the attorney for Meralco in a damage suit in the early 1900s, had admitted Meralco's liability. The only issue was the extent of the plaintiff's injuries. An elderly gentleman, he had been taken by an ambulance to a hospital, walked unaided to the elevator and then from the elevator to a first-aid station on the second floor.

In cross-examination, Lawrence asked the gentleman:

"How did you get from the ambulance to the room where the doctor bandaged you?"

"I don't know, Señor."

The adjustor assured Lawrence that his report had been correct and suggested that the interpreter might be at fault, so he tried again:

"You remember that the ambulance stopped at the door of the hospital?"

"Yes, Señor."

"Was the room where the doctor bandaged you on the ground floor or upstairs?"

"Upstairs, Señor."

"Well, how did you get upstairs to that room?"

"Truly, Señor, I don't know; I went into a little room and the door was closed, and when the door was opened I was upstairs, and to this day I can't understand it."

(Photo: AHC)

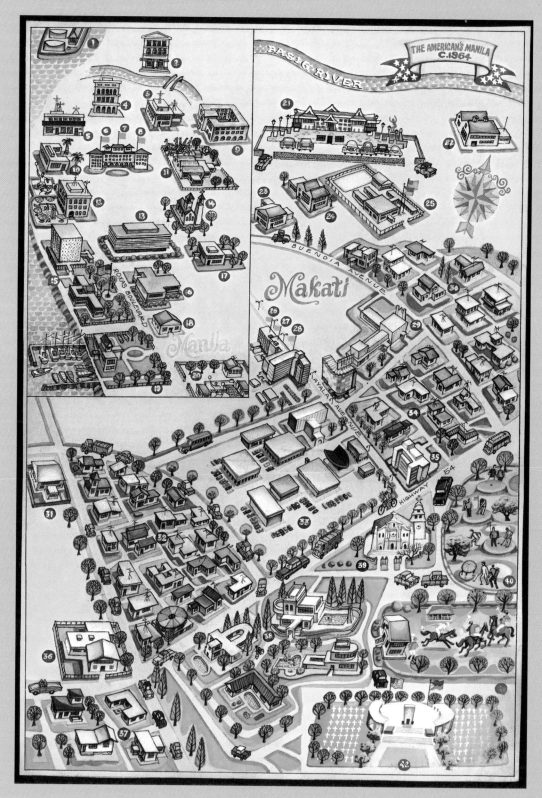

MANILA / MAKATI - 1964

Da Vinci de la Rosa captured the changed lifestyle in his 1964 illustration. The architecture of the new American School probably best typified the change — slick, modern, suburban. The Americans, for the greater part, now lived in new villages (gated communities), and their way of life, shared by their Filipino neighbors, was that of modern American suburbia.

Stanley Phillips:
The Son-in-Law with a Heart

Stanley Phillips (Photo: American Association Philippines)

Most remember Stan with a beautifully tailor made shirt, perfect accessory to his tailored suit — and always on the phone. When one mentions his name the anecdotes pour in.

The tales of the ladders on fire trucks which only reach a certain height — "I know, because my friend Stan sold all of them and he told me."

Widowed in 1958, "he broke out in a rash of blondes." Another regales with tales of wonderful parties at the house by the sea.

Another laughs recalling Stan and friends started that breakfast club now known as AmCham Kapihan: "He yelled when he saw me, 'Kid, get in here...' " (The man was then in his sixties). "I was so charmed I went in and never left."

Stan Phillips was a great deal more than these tales. Active in both business and civic work, Phillips worked constantly to improve the lives of those less fortunate.

He was for many years President and guiding light of the American Association of the Philippines — a charity formed to take care of Americans in trouble in the Philippines. These efforts extended to Amerasians. He once said, "if they have one drop of American blood, they belong to us."

He was a member of the Rotary, Masons, Kiwanis, Elks and, of course, AmCham. Possibly the work closest to his heart was the Elks Cerebral Palsy, which he joined in the mid-sixties and headed after John Manning resigned in 1986.

In 1996, together with William Quasha, he received an award from the American Chamber of Commerce. This was presented by former US Secretary of State George Shultz and then AmCham President William Tiffany. The award was given in part for his "development work of financing and opening the Cerebral Palsy clinic."

The award also mentioned the AAP as overseeing body of the American Historical Committee:

"Without this historical entity, which has a library of over 10,000 volumes of American/ Philippines history — and the priceless efforts of private researchers and writers, the important collection representing what America has meant to this land would have long ago disappeared behind the veil of time."

His father-in-law, Joseph Shurdut, brought Stan to Manila in 1949. Shurdut first arrived in the Philippines in 1919 as a young soldier. He worked for the Pacific Commercial Company for several years and then went into business for himself as the Shurdut Mill Supply Company. Interned during WWII, he returned to the US in 1945 to convince firms to invest in his adopted country. The first steamer carrying merchandise to the Philippines after WWII had on board both J.M. Shurdut and machinery that would rehabilitate coconut oil mills, sugar centrals, and sawmills.

A successful businessman in his own right, the one thing people remember about Phillips is that he was always *there* for people. Need to find someone? Call Stan. Have a problem? Call Stan? Know someone in trouble? Call Stan. Which probably explains why he was always on the phone.

Now picture this:

It's 1968 — and the world is in chaos.

The US is transfixed by the half million troops now fighting in Vietnam, a 90 minute plane ride from Manila. January's Tet Offensive has failed with huge losses for the North Vietnamese regulars and Viet Cong. But the vulnerability of the South and its US defenders has been made abundantly clear. Network film crews air shocking newsreels daily. Lyndon Johnson announces he will not seek re-election in November. Robert Kennedy is shot after winning the California Democratic primary in June and the phoenix-like Republican Richard Nixon becomes the leading candidate for US President. Martin Luthur King is assassinated in April. US ghetto riots heat the summer, most destructively in the Los Angeles Watts district. Jimi Hendrix reigns on both sides of the Atlantic, and Haight-Ashbury is in full LSD psychedelia.

In Europe, French students are rioting on the Left Bank. Russia invades Czechoslovakia. NATO and the Soviet bloc glare at each other over the barbed wire of the Berlin Wall. Communist rebel groups are proliferating in South America. The Arab world is still reeling from the shock of last year's devastating defeat after attacking Israel. Chaos indeed.

Outside Indochina, Southeast Asia is trying to build a semblance of stability. Singapore, thrown out of the Malaysian Federation three years earlier, is building a staunch anti-communist city-state. Five-year-old Malaysia is trying to balance its multi-ethnic population within a parliamentary framework. The Kingdom of Thailand hosts US bases, and parliamentary politics are dominated by military influence. And Indonesia's General Suharto is tightening his sure-handed grip on power 30 months after a communist-inspired putsch against the military.

World business is not in disarray, but is at an epiphany. Twenty years after the Marshall Plan and "MacArthur's plan," West Germany and Japan are back on top of their respective regional economies. Western Europe's industrial capacity is back, and exports are rising. "Made in Japan" is not as derisive as it used to be, and its companies are looking for off-shore production sites for intermediate raw materials.

• • •

The Philippine Civil Action Group was sent to South Vietnam to assist on civic projects. Photo shows Lori Ferguson, Bobby Greenwood, and Rolf Beyer during filming of a documentary on PhilCAG-V with members of the group including Fidel Ramos (far left). (Photo: Greenwood collection)

It's Sunday morning, early June, 1968. The highly respected former University of the Philippines Business School dean Cesar E. A. Virata is playing golf with Roberto "Bobby" Ongpin, the man who replaced him as consultant with the renowned audit and consulting firm SGV. Walking down the fairway, he muses on the whirlwind he's been through the past 17 months.

It is barely six months since President Ferdinand Marcos began calling him Chairman of the governors heading the newly created Board of Investments. And now Marcos has just elevated Virata to Cabinet rank.

He thinks of his father Enrique, eminent mathematician and former UP president, a government-appointed post. He thinks of his grandfather, General Baldomero Aguinaldo, signatory of the 1897 Constitution, co-exile in Hong Kong with Emilio Aguinaldo in 1898, Secretary of War and Public Works in the 1898 and 1899 revolutionary governments, and commanding general of Southern Luzon rebel forces in the Philippine-American War in 1900.

It was February 1967 that Marcos, at a simple 8 pm dinner at the Palace, asked Virata to join the Presidential Economic Staff as Deputy Director. His task — consolidate the various investment bills pending in the legislature and make the Investment Act of 1967 happen. Congress wasn't a problem, but the Senate, liaising with the nationalist Senator Jose "Pepe" Diokno, was a challenge. Incentive and equity limitations, what constituted "Pioneer" and "Non-pioneer" industries and other issues dominated negotiations.

Marcos also put Virata as head of the Philippine side working out what to do when Laurel-Langley expired in 1974. At the time, he is still UP Dean, and teaches in Cebu on Saturdays. Then Virata learns that Marcos has named him President of the Philippine National Bank as well.

Now, with Cabinet rank, he must consolidate. He effectively ushers in a new era. Little does Virata then know that he would eventually become the nation's longest serving Finance Minister and only Prime Minister, retaining respect and credibility despite Marcos' excesses.

Then Finance Minister (eventually Prime Minister) Cesar EA Virata and US Ambassador William Sullivan, 1974. (Photo: AHC)

Joint-Venture Era (1968 - 1990)

For the next 20 years, the joint-venture was the name of the game. It made sense, balancing the need for capital inflows, investment, and technology transfer, while satisfying the middle ground nationalists.

For AmCham, it ushered in an extremely confusing and, at times, disruptive era.

Initially, the joint-venture did make sense, and in 1969 AmCham loudly encouraged its members to look at joint-ventures as a way of moving beyond parity and the expiration of Laurel-Langley. The Board of Investments (BOI) was the hub for coordinating regulations, limitations and restrictions into an understandable and hopefully cohesive whole. Also, it was somewhere an investor could lobby, proposing a tit for tat — incentive for limitation.

In those early days, however, there was much confusion, and AmCham was the voice of reasoned rationality in discussions with the BOI.

But as Virata was promoted to the Department of Finance in 1970 to cope with the first of several financial crises he would face over the next 16 years, it became clear that the nationalist fringe was, if anything, intensifying. The new Maoist-oriented National Democratic Front and its then miniscule armed wing, the New People's Army, had infiltrated a growing leftist student movement. And Marcos was using the dissent as an excuse to perpetuate his rule — he would have to step down in 1973 after his second term.

AmCham could do little but watch the politics from the sidelines. But quietly it agreed that things were getting out of hand, and a stronger rule of law was needed. Martial Law was not quite what AmCham members had in mind, but the early stability it established was widely welcomed.

For US companies, it was evident that long-held dominance in certain economic sectors was ending. And this meant some hard decisions about existing investments

The 1,000th Ford Taunus rolls off the assembly line. (Photo: Manning collection)

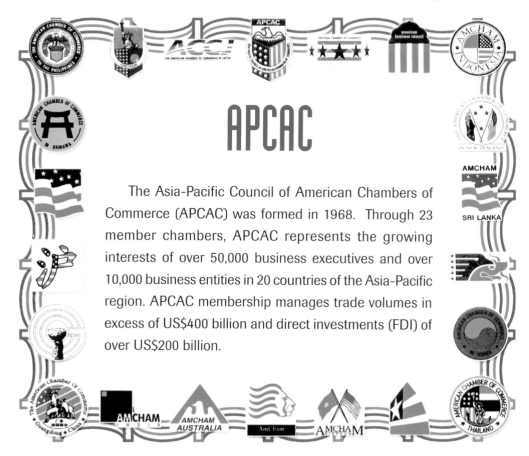

APCAC

The Asia-Pacific Council of American Chambers of Commerce (APCAC) was formed in 1968. Through 23 member chambers, APCAC represents the growing interests of over 50,000 business executives and over 10,000 business entities in 20 countries of the Asia-Pacific region. APCAC membership manages trade volumes in excess of US$400 billion and direct investments (FDI) of over US$200 billion.

AMCHAM JOURNAL
THE AMERICAN CHAMBER OF COMMERCE OF THE PHILIPPINES, INC.

SPECIAL ISSUE: THE LAST FIVE YEARS   OCTOBER 1977

AmCham Journal, October 1977. The Journal took on a new, streamlined look in the 70s, complete with a new Journal logo on the masthead. The issue focused on a review of the five years of Marcos' "New Society" with its two-fold objective: "to restore order out of near chaos and to reconstruct society so that a more equitable distribution of wealth could be effected."

AmCham members meet with President Ferdinand Marcos in the early 1980s. Relations during the immediate post martial law period were cordial if cool. (Photo: AmCham)

and how best to package them — to maximize business and trade within the context of minority equity and greater competition from other foreign investors.

Gone were the days of "this is our Philippine company." Now it was a shared venture with mixed boards and mixed management. There were no more American companies running things the American way. Everything had to be massaged to accommodate the local environment, from finance to labor.

If anything, the early joint-venture period favored Japanese and European investors, who the government wanted for variety as much as fresh capital — and who were arriving fresh as first time investors. AmCham members had to readjust to the new realities post-Laurel-Langley.

Marcos had other plans as well. He liked the Japanese *zaibatsu* (financial/industrial combines) that served Japan so well in rebuilding industry and creating the export dynamo of the 1960s/70s. And he wanted to mimic that in the Philippines. Unfortunately, Japan's "country and culture first" attitude did not jive with the Philippines personality-oriented "me first" approach. Marcos' experiment by the late 1970s degenerated into personal corruption and cronyism.

By 1974, with Laurel-Langley expired, AmCham members began taking those hard decisions — divesting land holdings, scrounging for viable partners, or simply leaving. Benguet and Lepanto mining diluted. Esso left. Mobil sold a portion of its refinery. Long-entrenched trading firms like Mantrade also divested.

Utilities PLDT and Meralco found equity structures overhauled, with US ownership sidelined into tradeable "B" shares, and local "A" shares forced out of the jailed or exiled former Opposition oligarchs into the grasp of Marcos' crony capitalists. A slew of smaller service companies opted out as well, such as North American Van Lines, although many shifted to agency, partner, or affiliate arrangements, satisfying the law without disrupting business presence — and retaining at least a piece of the business pie.

With Marcos' ruling by decree, preferential tariffs and political pressure subsumed entire industries — from cigarette manufacturing to coconut oil refining. The initial, quite rapid 6%-7% GNP growth during the mid-1970s overheated into crisis after the second oil shock in 1979, and by that time the indebted crony edifice began to crumble.

President Ronald Reagan's Secretary of State George Schultz presenting Stan Philips a plaque at an AmCham luncheon. (Photo: AmCham)

During this period AmCham began to change as well. While the Proctor & Gambles and Del Montes remained, the membership too shifted into joint-venture mode. The dominance of investment boards, restrictions on foreign equity, and the ensuing splinter-like investments made by US multinationals with local partners expanded throughout the region.

As ASEAN (the Association of Southeast Asian Nations) grew in stature, so too did local AmChams see the need for cooperation among themselves. APCAC — the Asia Pacific Council of American Chambers — became an effective lobby with Washington. It was also a way to build lobbying strategies with individual governments competing for foreign investment and capital.

However, the Philippines stood apart. The non-stop political — and economic — crises during the 1980s lost the country virtually the entire decade of rapid growth, experienced by the rest of ASEAN. AmCham often found itself in sensitive, sometimes precarious positions that it handled with political aplomb, even with its commitment to avoid politics.

Safety in numbers helped.

As the political pressure on Marcos mounted, AmCham was occasionally approached by local chambers to take stands that could be construed as political. Joint foreign chamber positions were published, while cooperation with influential groups like the Makati Business Club grew.

The initial euphoria after the "People Power" revolt of 1986 soon evaporated as the loose political coalition began to dissolve. And each time investors were growing keen on the country, yet another coup attempt shelved plans.

But AmCham was looking forward. Despite the political uncertainty during the latter part of the 1980s, it saw the beginnings of an influx of outsourcing firms supplying a myriad of companies.

People like Virata were speaking of competitive reforms as early as the 1980s. But then, nothing could be done. Now something could. Reform and deregulation was something AmCham had supported for years. Now it was becoming the mantra for growth — globalization.

AmCham Business Journal, February 1981 – The theme for this issue was "Foreign Investments and Martial Law – the political risk factor and the need for protection."

Phil Gielczyk: The Big Man — in Action

Phil Gielczyk
(Photos: AmCham)

Phil Gielczyk was one of those Peace Corps types who just had to stay. He arrived in the Philippines in 1973 and later became Regional Director for the Visayas and Mindanao and then Associate Director until 1982, when he got smart and set up his own consulting firm, Gielczyk and Associates. He was company President and Managing Director until his death on April 15, 2002.

Gielczyk joined AmCham in 1981. He was a Director (1987-1990); Second Vice-President (1990-1991); and again Director (1992-1994). From October 1994 up to his departure for medical treatment early in 2002, he served concurrently as Director and Treasurer of the Board.

His dedication extended beyond AmCham. Phil had an impact on both Philippine and US business affairs. From 1984, he worked for the US-ASEAN Business Council, a non-profit, private sector body with its main objective being the promotion of trade and investment between the US and member nations of ASEAN. The Council's Regional Director since 1999, his duties included managing trade and over 100 investment missions. He was also included as an official member of both President Corazon Aquino's and President Fidel Ramos' official visits to the US.

Among his many "achievements", Phil helped start the "Kapihan sa AmCham" in 1990. Originally a "coffee club" like the first AmCham group at Clarke's, the Kapihan today raises funds for worthy causes, with an annual turnover of funds to charities chosen by participants.

Now picture this:

It is a cloudy, low pressure day in June, 1991. It is 2 pm. Philippine Economic Newsletter (PEN) Director Guy Sacerdoti is working on a paper for some Makati Business Club colleagues about competitiveness. He is proposing a study that will frankly assess which Philippine business sectors have the best chance to compete in the world market. He plans to present it at PEN's next quarterly "Critical Issues" gathering of foreign, multinational and local CEOs.

If there is no cost-effectiveness and little room for realizing potential, then drop it. Sub-contracting garments is out, for example, while outsourcing animation is in. An empirical SWOT analysis makes sense. If the Philippines has tuna and no tin, and Thailand has tin but no tuna, why beat each other's brains out over the US canned tuna market?

Suddenly, as is wont to happen each day about 2:30, the lights go out. A string of truck batteries kicks in via a UPS — uninterrupted power supply — allowing the former journalist, consultant and author the chance to finish up a paragraph on his computer and save the file. The blackouts have been battering business the better part of a year now, sometimes up to 8 hours a day. So he doesn't flinch.

He decides to leave his Malate home for the yacht club across Roxas Boulevard to check on his sailboat. There's a typhoon nearby and the mooring lines need to be checked. But as he walks out onto his office terrace, he notices something strange. It's pretty dark for a mid-afternoon.

It's snowing! Or at least it looks like it. It's getting thicker, cutting visibility and beginning to leave some accumulation. He turns on his 12 volt TV. Well, there it is. Mt. Pinatubo has finally erupted.

Volcanologists have said the pressure inside could produce the largest eruption of the century. The ash could settle as far away as Singapore. And it is expected to tint the earth's upper atmosphere for a couple of years. It is not really the kind of image the Philippines wants when its leaders speak of the need for globalization, deregulation and reform.

It's been 18 months since the last failed coup attempt. And a new president will be elected a year from now. It's make it or break it time for Manila. Economic performance is about what it was ten years ago. Confidence is at a low. Recession is hitting the US. There is even talk that the Philippine Senate won't be able to garner enough votes to ratify the just negotiated Treaty on the US Bases.

Sacerdoti steps out into the snow that won't melt. There's symbolism there, he thinks. Only he's not quite sure just what it is.

Mt. Pinatubo erupts, changing the landscape of Central Luzon and adding an exclamation point to the US Bases departure. (Photo: Greenwood collection)

Reform & Globalization (1990 – present)

AmCham Journal, February 1995. "Tourism" was the theme, focusing on the U.S. Embassy advisory to Americans of the dangers they face in coming to the Philippines. The AmCham strongly refuted this announcement stating there was in fact "a vast improvement in the overall security situation under then President Ramos" — further noting that "criminality exists in any country and common sense is advised."

This section should really begin around 1987, as it did for the rest of the region. The Philippines actually helped usher in the Information Age with its "People Power" revolt in February 1986. It was the first developing news story broadcast live worldwide, circumventing any possible attempt of the government to control news flow. Although IT was still a pronoun, desktop publishing had started and personal computers were proliferating — changing the entire concept of an office, workflow and, most of all, competition.

With productivity (i.e. efficiency) on the rise, the region began melding together as a single market — multi-language packaging was becoming the norm. It had to. Computers were overhauling distribution structures, particularly at the ports. Air cargo became the mainstay of several regional airlines' profits, and the big cargo carriers began eyeing the region. The business and economic advantages of a wider, more efficient market led business lobbies throughout Asia to push for greater competition via reform and de-regulation.

Purely domestic industry would still scream for protection. But those with a less parochial market could see only negative results from distributive isolation. So they began to argue in favor of deregulation to attract greater capital and investment to reach the regional economies of scale to compete.

Unfortunately for the Philippines, political stability remained elusive until the early 1990s, so many of the needed legislative reforms remained on the composite congressional shelf. Manila suffered nearly a decade of infrastructural neglect, and it was clearly beginning to show with its daily power outages.

During this period AmCham began to reassume a stronger pro-active lobbying stance on issues. And it could do this because government ears were becoming more receptive — particularly due to two changes in trend.

Even during the joint-venture period, multinationals would look for the wizened "old Asia Hand" to join their team. Long-time residents, these people knew the

As the 1990s brought about the need for reform and globalization, AmCham too sought alliances on common stands with other chambers in the country. Here President Corazon Aquino addresses a joint-Chamber luncheon. (Photo: AmCham)

Another joint-Chamber session, this time with then Senator (now President) Gloria Macapagal-Arroyo. (Photo: AmCham)

cultural and national traits of a country better than some of its own citizens, and they were an asset in massaging things through the system.

But in the era of high speed (and high stress) growth, competition for foreign capital and investment meant that the supply-demand equation was shifting. Whereas before a company would shop around for an offshore investment site conducive for growth, now a company would be courted by several countries to attract its investment.

The result was different type of businessman — yet again — streaming into the region. Not colonial frontiersmen, not WWII carpetbaggers, nor joint-venture "roll-up-the-sleeves" partners, these were "the suits".

They came as the 1990s began from the central — not regional — office, looking for the established, efficiently managed operation that needed capital to expand, to leap towards the next technological level, or to widen exports. In several cases with multinationals, they arrived to consolidate or reorganize regional presence. It was a rationalization of component production — cereals out of Malaysia, coffee out of the Philippines, milk products out of Indonesia would be one example. The market was the region…minimum.

US President Bill Clinton's Secretary of State Warren Christopher with then AmCham President Carlos Contreras in 1995. (Photo: AmCham)

The second trend was outsourcing. Productive expertise in the region matured during the growth spurt of the 1980s to the point that many manufacturers in North Asia, the US and Europe were looking for plain subcontractors to process raw materials, build components or even assemble modular products. Investors here need not be residents at all, or even onsite. They could act as production auditors, visiting only when needed.

AmCham Journal, January 2000. Despite the fact that the millennium actually began in 2001, the cover stated, "we celebrate its birth a year in advance."

The era of globalization — for all its good, and bad — was upon us.

For AmCham, it meant adaptation. One of its major strides was the July 1992 establishment of an American desk at the Dept of Trade and Industry's Board of Investments. Directly under AmCham's Board — actually an extension of the Board — the American Desk advises potential new investors, advocates policies conducive to expanded trade and investment, and helps in problem resolution for established US firms.

In an expanded, globally competitive environment, AmCham is more attuned to the original concept of the early 1900s Manila Merchants Association — developing position papers and lobbying in concert with other chambers, both foreign and domestic, for greater impact.

And as the new millennium — and AmCham's centennial — mark further changes, AmCham lobbies for a "level playing field." Issues range from intellectual property rights to the sanctity of contracts. But AmCham's main desire is to have the Philippines compete successfully with its Asean neighbors for investment capital — in an Asian era with China clearly the current star attraction for foreign investment.

Since the 1920s AmCham worked to create a school for expatriate children. First it was known as The American School, later the International School Manila. Today, it's new campus projects a true international character within a Philippine context.

Original campus, Donada Street, Pasay City (top); new campus, Fort Bonifacio, Taguig. (Photos: International School Manila)

Now picture this:

Early May, 2002, Makati City, Metro-Manila, Republic of the Philippines.

It's 10am. It's raining, naturally. Or it's steaming, really. Jeepneys, taxis, and just too many cars splash down Paseo de Roxas in front of Greenbelt shopping plaza.

"BBBBaaaaaeeeeiiiigggghhhhh!" goes the buzzer at the front door of the second floor office at Corinthian Plaza.

Four American buddies — two women, two men — collectively in the Philippines for over 100 years, saunter into the large meeting area around the corner from the reception area. They gather around the coffee machine. A button is touched — caffe latte appears. Another and it's hot cocoa. A third is some temple-rubbing espresso. The fourth has a diet soft drink in hand.

They move to the old Round Table in the corner and sit. At first it is more banter than anything else — shenanigans at the Senate, the US-Philippine military exercises against terrorists in the south, who's in town, who's just been through. And then down to business.

"So where are we on the book?"

"It'll be ready for the bi-centennial." Laughter.

"We've got copy for 395 pages according to our designer — without pix!"

"That's OK. I'm doing a slash and burn edit. And we'll make it a good read. A hundred years is a lot of history."

The four gaze at the shiny, if scratched, round plaque inlaid at the center of the table. They glance at each other, then at the table — the classic pregnant pause before something profound.

One thinks of what it must have been like drinking coffee (laced with whiskey?) at Clarke's. Another wonders how it, like she, survived the devastation of WWII. The third is thinking of Gombi the Tiger.

But it's the fourth who chooses to speak.

"You *do* know the story of where and how we found it?"

Grins… smiles… then laughter… and laughter… and laughter.

Ahh, history…some things never change. (See below.)

AmCham Journal, July 2002. One hundred years of AmCham in the Philippines; the brass plaque imbedded in the Chamber's old round table cites the historical roots of the Chamber. (Photo: AHC)

Opposite page: Many more round tables a hundred years on. (Photo: AmCham)

Portrait
Gordon Westley - The Balikbayan

When asked what AmCham positions A. Gordon Westly held during his years with the chamber, his widow Charing answers simply, "I think all of them."

Westly was actually born of Norwegian parents in 1923 on the Pampanga Sugar Mill central. His father learned the business while in Hawaii. Schooled on the Baguio campus of Brent, he went to Harvard as an undergraduate just prior to WWII. With Norway under Nazi control, he left university to join Canada's Royal Air Force, eventually flying missions out of England.

Returning to Harvard after the German defeat, he graduated and went on to Harvard Law School, still a Norwegian citizen. He was naturalized only after winning his degree. But by then he was keen on returning to Manila, and Dole hired him to help run its pineapple business. Westly moved to Jardine Davis Co. in the 1970s, and in 1983 he transferred to

Edward Keller Co, where he remained until his retirement in 1996.

Westly was the consummate AmCham stalwart – over a decade as chairman of the Publications Committee, serving as president and briefly as executive vice president (the executive director's position today). A man of great humor, a lover of softball (which he played avidly at Manila Polo Club), he epitomized the lasting lure of the Philippines to anyone born and bred during those years. A true balikbayan businessman.

Bobby Greenwood: Tough, Funny, Cool

Bobby Greenwood

Trying to tell the story of Bobby (Barbara) Greenwood is like trying to work a 2,000 piece jigsaw puzzle. She lost her private battle with cancer in May 2002 — not telling anyone of her diagnosis lest they feel pity and start to tread softly in her presence. This was not a lady to tread softly — she let her feelings and opinions be known — but never in a hurtful way; she just called " 'em as I see 'em!" Her sense of humor was legendary and she was a master of "one-liners".

She was project chair of this AmCham Centennial Book, and true to form, she was working up to the very end; signing documents in her hospital room two days before she died peacefully, at her home.

Bobby was in her own words "mid-West bred, corn-fed," having been born and raised in Ohio. Her father was active in local politics, which would account for her own strong interest in the workings of government — both US and Philippine.

She studied Journalism and Drama at Bowling Green University prior to setting off into a world where both were to be her life's work. She came to the Philippines in 1962 and almost immediately became involved in work on Hollywood and Philippine films — full features and documentaries — forming her own film production company.

She worked extensively with writer-director Lamberto Avellana and stars like Vic Salayan. She was particularly proud of her documentary on the work of PhilCAG-V; the Philippine Civil Action Group-Vietnam in the 1960s. She loved the Philippines to the core, becoming a Filipino citizen in 1975.

As Producer, Director, Production Coordinator, Script Supervisor, Scriptwriter and Actress, she worked with some of the best…Martin Sheen and Marlon Brando to name just two. As Location Coordinator for Francis Ford Coppola's "Apocalypse Now" she had countless adventures — she loved to talk of the antics of Gombi the Tiger.

When the Philippines' reputation as Hollywood East began to wane in the 1980s, Greenwood's journalist background returned to the fore. She wrote for "What's On" and "Expat" for many years, continuing when the two publications merged. She initiated the "Inquiring Photographer" feature — accosting people with provocative questions, taking their "snaps" while they thought how to answer. Bobby did much freelance writing — including the AmCham Journal where her "Commentary" column was a favorite. She also wrote her fair share of letters to daily papers promoting principles of civility.

Her friendships "ran wide and deep" as a friend said, and she was generous to a fault; whatever she had she shared with many less fortunate. She had numerous friends worldwide who marveled at her capacity for giving and "being there" for them. The AmCham, Kapihan, American Legion, American Association, the American Women's Club, and many other organizations — and individuals — with whom she worked all carry her mark in their histories.

But, as long as Corregidor stands — and the sound equipment holds out — she remains with us; her voice is that of the nurse in the Malinta Tunnel's "sound and light show."

(Photo: AmCham)

Kapihan Sa AmCham

. . .

From *Chamber Notes* – AmCham Journal December, 1922
"The Ten O'Clock Coffee Club, which meets every morning around Clarke's old Round Table, has moved its headquarters from the main dining room to the Director's room, where it enjoys greater privacy and also the breezes that come in from the Bay."

. . .

The banner reads, "KAPIHAN sa AMCHAM – 1990", but it would appear that the Kapihan sa AmCham – in principal – goes way back to the earliest days of the Chamber. However, from Tom Carter's writings, the Ten O'Clock Coffee Club was a more structured group. Other differences are the fact the present Kapihan only meets on Fridays, – and it meets at "about 7:30am", reflecting a big change in working hours.

The Kapihan sa AmCham evolved from a similar group that met at the Intercon's old Jeepney Coffee Shop (with jeepney bodies as booths). Long time residents Stan Phillips and Phil Gielczyk – sadly no longer with us – met there mulling over morning headlines and talking while "waiting for the traffic to clear." In 1990 they moved the meetings to the Elk's Club, five floors above the

Chamber, inviting friends to join them. The Kapihan sa AmCham are freewheeling, with topics ranging from current events, issues, and personalities in the news…to the sassiest jokes, often led by the late Bobby Greenwood – storyteller par excellence.

Originally, raffles were held, with each attendee bringing a raffle item. Now, each member contributes P 200 – faithfully deposited in a bank account. At the Christmas Kapihan, the funds are distributed to selected charities. Beneficiaries have included the Chosen Children Foundation, American Association of the Philippines (AAP), Philippine American Guardian Association (PAGA), the AmCham Foundation and the Cerebral Palsy Foundation.

Moving on... and on... and on

By Leslie Ann Murray

AmCham as an institution has been just about as transient as its members. Tracking the moves of Chamber premises from its beginnings to the present take the reader on a virtual tour of "old" Manila and "old" Makati.

Clarke's Manila Coffee Club on the Escolta was AmCham's frontier in more ways than one. Official records show that the Chamber's early locations were at the heart of the business district — near the Pasig River and the Port of Manila — following the traditional pattern of early trade and commerce:

December 1921 – 2 Calle Pinpin, Sta. Cruz
May 1923 – 14 Calle Pinpin, Sta. Cruz
Mid- 1936 – 180 David Street, Sta. Cruz
Mid – 1939 – 7th Floor, Heacock Building, Dasmariñas Street, Binondo

With the outbreak of WWII in December, 1941, Chamber operations ceased. After liberation, and during the chaotic times of reconstruction, the Chamber was again on the move and racked up a total of six transfers between February 1945 and April 1949 alone:

February 1945 – 348 España, opposite Sto. Tomas University (Internment Camp)
May 1945 – People's Bank Building, Dasmariñas Street, Binondo
mid-1945 – Gibbs Building, Dasmarinas Street, Binondo
May 1946 – Trade and Commerce Building, Juan Luna Street, Binondo
July 1947 – 512 Insular Life Building, Plaza Cervantes, Binondo
April 1949 – 4th Floor, El Hogar Filipino Building, Juan Luna Street, Binondo

424 San Luis St. (now T. M. Kalaw), on the south side of Luneta. The building, AmCham's home from 1951-54, remains today nestled among high rises. (Photo: AmCham)

AmCham Branches

The first AmCham branch outside Manila was organized in Iloilo in 1922, but was short-lived. It wasn't until 1987 that J. Marsh Thomson, then AmCham Executive Director, pushed for the establishment of regional chambers. Cebu was set up in 1987, with Davao organized the following year.

AmCham's spacious setting after World War II, and its dedicated staff below. (Photos: AmCham)

A.V.H. Hartendorp's article in the AmCham Journal of July 1955 notes that immediately post-World War II a "makeshift" office was set up at 348 España — opposite the gates of Sto. Tomas University. Due to the near complete devastation of the city in 1945, there was little housing space available and so a number of the "prisoners" remained resident in nipa shacks on the grounds of Sto. Tomas for many months after the war. There was also little transportation available — and in any case, the roads were strewn with the rubble of war. Thus the opening of a Chamber office opposite the camp gates was a most practical solution to the business of getting back to business.

Hartendorp reports that "for a time the España office of the Chamber became a distributing center for messages received over the Press Wireless, Inc. system, which provided the only means of telegraphic communication during those months. The office also became an unofficial post office."

He continues, "...in May the Chamber moved to the Peoples Bank Building at 650 Dasmariñas" (subsequently Heacock's store), sharing the ground floor, one large room, with five or six other entities while the streets were still being cleared of the debris of war and the building itself was just beginning to be repaired.

..."The work of construction on the Peoples Bank Building forced the Chamber to move to the Gibbs Building next door, and from there, in May 1946 the Chamber moved to the eighth floor of the Trade and Commerce Building on Juan Luna, shortly after that building had been vacated by the US Army."

The Chamber continued its vagabond existence. In July 1947, the offices were moved "to a larger room on the fifth floor of the Insular Life Building on Plaza Cervantes." In 1949 the Chamber again moved, "to two large communicating rooms on the fourth floor of the El Holgar Filipino Building...along-side the Pasig River," writes Hartendorp. "The office of the Chamber President at that time, Mr. Frederic Stevens, was right next door, very convenient for all concerned."

At this point Hardendorp mentions the frequency of moves "over which the reader may raise an eyebrow...but this (narration)...effectively conveys some idea of the difficult circumstances under which the (Chamber) operated during the early years following the war. Moving about characterized almost every government as well as business office in Manila, not to mention families and individuals. In (these times) it was literally true that hundreds of thousands of people in Manila had virtually nowhere to lay their heads."

AmCham's 2002 quarters — still spacious, comfortable, a 'never say die' magical coffee machine and, of course, a just as magical staff. That's a pretty special table, too. (Photos: AmCham)

In February, 1951 the Chamber made its first move south of the Pasig. It transferred from El Hogar Filipino Building to 424 San Luis Street (now known as T.M. Kalaw), opposite the Luneta, taking the entire ground floor of this "new three story building", still standing at this writing. Hartendorp reports "These were the Chamber's first really adequate and comfortable post-war quarters."

On August 20, 1954 the Chamber transferred to the ground floor, west wing of the (old) Elks Club Building — what is now the Museo ng Pambata (Children's Museum) on Roxas Boulevard. It was indicative of things to come, as many businesses began moving south of the Pasig.

At the time, the American School (now International School Manila) was in Pasay. The Episcopal and Union Churches were in Ermita. And most all of the social clubs — the Army Navy Club, University Club, Casino Español, Manila Club, Manila Yacht Club — were in this area as well.

Clubs were the center of social life for the elite and were favorite gathering places. Many influential families then lived in Pasay or in old Parañaque (Tambo), along the shores of Manila Bay. These shores today face hectares of reclaimed land.

Into the Makati Business District and its own home. AmCham now works out of its 2nd floor offices at Corinthian Plaza. (Photo: AmCham)

When the American School re-located to Makati, there was a trickle of businesses that moved on to Ayala Avenue — then the only business address in Makati (Legaspi Village and Salcedo Village did not exist). But the Chamber remained in Ermita...or more precisely Intramuros, when it moved to the Shurdit Building in January, 1964. There were two more moves within this area: in December 1968, AmCham moved into the Delgado Building on Bonifacio Drive in the Port Area. And in July 1969 it moved to the 4th Floor, Erlanger & Galenger Building, Isaac Peral (now United Nations Avenue), Ermita.

But by the early 70s the trickle became a flood — and the Chamber went with the flow, opening their first office in the "new" business district on the 6th floor of the Security Bank Building on Ayala Avenue in September of 1973.

In 1977, Lewis Burridge, then chairman of APCAC (the Asia Pacific Council of American Chambers), was quoted as saying "...it has been the dream of every AmCham to have its own facilities."

In July 1977, the Chamber opened its doors at the 2nd floor, Corinthian Plaza.

The dream became a reality — and as Burridge pointed out at the time..."the dream has never been realized anywhere except in Manila."

AmCham's Permanent Home

It was during William (Bill) Mitchell's 1972-73 term as AmCham President that the idea of securing a permanent home for AmCham finally came to fruition. Members are forever grateful for his foresight — particularly as the cost of the Chamber's efficient 418 square meter home was a mere P1.5 million at the time.

Mitchell, a navigator in the US Army Air Corps during World War II, came to the Philippines in mid-1970 as Executive Vice-President and Managing Director of B.F. Goodrich Philippines, Inc., from Brazil.

Given the lapse of the Laurel-Langley Agreement in 1974, AmCham's move made sense in more ways than one.

Beyond the Chamber Doors: American Chamber Community Outreach

In addition to its focus on the "business of business" over the past 100 years, the American Chamber has also been associated with several charitable organizations that address various aspects and interests of the Filipino-American community here in the Philippines. These organizations include: The American Association of the Philippines (AAP), The American Chamber Foundation, Inc., The Filipino-American Memorial Endowment, Inc.(FAME), The Philippine-American Guardian Association (PAGA). And, though not directly involved, AmCham also works in close association with the American Women's Club of the Philippines (AWCP).

The American Association of the Philippines

"The American Association of the Philippines...was bred of an idea and born of a specific necessity..."

The American Association of the Philippines constitution says it is **"founded on the concept of community interest, welfare, and responsibility. It is non-commercial. It is non-political. Its purpose is the general welfare of United States citizens. ...the American Association invites the membership, cooperation and mutual assistance of United States citizens residing in the Philippines...."**

The key words are "community interest", a concept deeply ingrained in American life since the frontier days when neighbors "raised a barn" in mutual aid. The Americans in the Philippines in 1900s and into the 1930s were a close-knit community, existing with shared uncertainties in a new environment, who often met to discuss how to deal with unfamiliar problems. There was an unspoken agreement that no fellow-American could be allowed to be abandoned in a situation of need and such cases were handled by the American business community itself, informally and promptly. Over the years, it became a habit to rely on this community in cases of need of all kinds.

After World War II the community had to deal with destruction of property, displacement of people, and the adjustment to Philippine independence. These factors inalterably changed the prewar informality of the business community.

Cases of need that were neither diplomatic, commercial, nor military became the special concern of a new organization, the newly formed American Association of the Philippines. The Association preserved the early spirit of working together in community endeavor. The first general meeting, was held on January 27, 1949.

AMERICAN ASSOCIATION OF THE PHILIPPINES

George Washington's birthday was designated an annual American Association celebration, as was the Fourth of July "Hometown Picnic" in later years. These became the two major fund-raising activities of the AAP.

Fifty-three years later, the purpose of American Association remains the welfare of indigent Americans or those of proven American lineage, who have no access to Philippine welfare organizations nor any that cater to Americans in the US. Thus the AAP assists in cases of proven need to assure they have adequate food, medicine, shelter, educational or legal assistance, as needed.

Others beneficiaries include travelers in genuine need; those seeking repatriation, and Americans held in Philippine prisons. The Association also provides for burial of indigent Americans at the AAP burial plot at the North Cemetery, and maintains the American Teacher's plot, final resting place of the Thomasites, the first American teachers who came in 1901. In 1958 the AAP initiated its Rh Negative Blood Donor list, in response to the rarity of this blood type in Asia.

AAP sponsors English language classes and citizenship training. (Photo: AAP)

The AAP also holds "ownership in trust" of the American Historical Collection Library, located at the Ateneo de Manila University, Quezon City. It is comprised of thousands of rare or out of print volumes, items of personal memorabilia, and a large collection of historical photographs, concentrated mainly on the American period in Philippine history — from 1898 to 1946. Though not a circulating library, it is open daily for the use of researchers and general readers.

Former American Ambassador Henry A. Byroade once remarked that this was the only post he has served in, or indeed knew of, where such a group as the American Association exists "...to look after the welfare of United States citizens"...and, more lately, those of American lineage.

Compiled from articles by Frank Tenny (first Vice-President of AAP, 1948-49); ACCP Journal, April 1951, and Anne Miller (scriptwriter for Voice of America); The Bulletin, American Historical Collection – Vol.I, June 1972

American Chamber Foundation Philippines

The AmCham Foundation was established in 1985 as a civic arm of the American Chamber of Commerce of the Philippines, Inc., with the objective to inspire, promote and facilitate corporate social responsibility among AmCham members.

Acting as a resource mobilizer, the Foundation solicits cash and donations in kind from AmCham members. Private organizations with projects in the Foundation's areas of concern — youth assistance and disaster response — are then selected, funded and supported. Thus donations are monitored, ensuring proper usage and accountability. This offers members guidance and opportunities for giving, through informed and meaningful programs.

The Foundation supports the following programs:

Youth Development – the Scholarship Program, supporting the education of 150 high school, college and vocational students in Metro Manila and nearby provinces; the Leonard Benjamin Program, set up "to respond to the growing problem of street children in Metro Manila and the Philippines in general" by the late Leonard Benjamin.

(Photo: AmCham)

The programs provide Comprehensive Assistance for the provision of food, clothing, shelter, education, recreational facilities, case management, medical and dental services, psychosocial support or developmental activities — and Reproductive Health, comprised of seminars and training on adolescent sexuality and family planning.

The Special Education Program – A part of the Leonard Benjamin Program, is designed for children with special learning needs, with additional funding provided by Lincoln Foundation in the US. The Basic Computer Literacy Training Project , funded by General Electric Philippines, aims to provide the children with opportunities to broaden their horizons through computer lessons.

Disaster Response — In a country beset with numerous natural calamities, a disaster response program is essential. The AmCham Foundation has organized its Disaster Response Program to assist affected communities through the mobilization of resources from AmCham member companies. The Foundation also organizes disaster preparedness seminars, further highlighting the need for proactive action in times of disaster.

Book Distribution Program — Over 3 million new and second hand textbooks and reference materials from the United States have been distributed to public schools throughout the country.

In networking with related government agencies and civic organizations, the Foundation also organizes regular fund-raising activities to secure the needed financial support for its programs.

Filipino American Memorial Endowment, Inc. [FAME]

There are a good number of monuments dotting the Philippines dedicated to the valor and bravery of Filipino and American WWII veterans, both military and civilian. Many of these were built shortly after the war. Some came later.

Two grateful nations saluted their heroes in stone and metal. But forty years later, time and weather had taken their toll. There was the need to address the problem of maintaining these memorials.

On May 21, 1985, plans were made for the support of WWII memorials in the Philippines. The initiative was spearheaded by Alex Keller, then President and General Manager of Proctor & Gamble, spurred by a previous donation of display cases to the Pacific War Memorial Museum on Corregidor by his colleague, Louis Pritchett. Other concerned individuals joined the cause.

Thus the World War II Memorial Committee was established, under the auspices of the American Chamber of Commerce, and a committee was formed. Committee members were (aside from Keller) Matt Holiday, J. Marsh Thomson, Col. Edward Ramsey, Col. Lee Telesco, and Helena Benitez.

In May 1986, the Committee registered with the Securities and Exchange Commission as the Filipino-American Memorial Endowment, (FAME), Inc. Its mission: "to help preserve and maintain tangible reminders of the shared values for which Americans, Filipinos and their allies fought side-by-side and won, in World War II." It objective is "NOT to build new memorials, but to raise funds in order to maintain existing monuments dedicated to the memory of Filipino-American co-operation during World War II."

FAME continues to work with individuals, companies and veterans organizations, serving as the catalyst for the maintenance and refurbishment needed to keep these Filipino-American monuments as fitting memorials. FAME is solely supported by donations.

FAME's on-going project during the AmCham Centennial is the repair and replacement of numerous kilometer markers along the route of the Bataan Death March from Km. 0 at Mariveles, Bataan to Capas, Tarlac.

Philippine American Guardian Association

"The American Guardian Association was organized for the purpose of caring for those American-Filipino children in the Philippine Islands who have been either abandoned by their parents or are without proper protectors.

"The credit for initiating the movement belongs to Lieutenant-Colonel Gordon Johnston,…a member of the Mission to the Philippines…Its purpose is properly to care for these children, give them a fair start in the world, prepare them for the struggles of life, and replace as far as possible the care and protection which should have been given by their parents." (from the 1922 introduction to the book *Good Cooking and Health in the Tropics* — signed by Leonard Wood, Governor-General of the Philippine Islands.)

"…these children have not had a fair chance in life, and also… they are a peculiar charge on us because they were brought into existence by American fathers who, through death, misfortune, or other reason, failed to provide the protection and care to which every child is entitled…" (Leonard Wood)

This holds true today and is the basis for eighty years of service to the many "unfortunate children" and their mothers in need of a "helping hand". However, in 1974 it was felt necessary to change the name of the Association to "The Philippine-American Guardian Association, Inc." (PAGA) to reflect the shift to more Filipino leadership and support of the Associations programs.

PAGA is a non-sectarian, non-political organization and continues to be dedicated to the protection and care of indigent Amerasian children in the Philippines. The Philippine judicial courts often assign to the Association children who are in need of care while their families are experiencing problems.

The services rendered by PAGA vary — some are "core" services; others are "support" services. The core services include:

Educational Assistance – providing assistance in the form of tuition, school supplies, uniforms, transportation and lunch money. Those who are ineligible for standard high school courses are encouraged to enroll in vocational high school courses.

Medical Assistance – providing free hospitalization, medicines and dental treatment. Medical assistance is also extended to parents who may need treatment in order to carry on their parental obligations.

Supplementary Food Assistance – providing additional food supplies to those children in need, in order to enable them to carry on with their schooling.

With unemployment being a common problem with PAGA-supported families, PAGA lends assistance through the Job Referral program to employable mothers — and their children.

PAGA "support" services include Counseling, Referrals, Consultative, Liaison and Legal Aid Services.

The overall aim is "to restore disjointed human relationships and help insure the well-being and future of children who are caught in often seemingly hopeless situations."

American-Filipino children at summer camp sponsored by PAGA. (Photo: PAGA)

PART 3

Corporate Sponsors

AmCham's "Pioneer" Companies

Date Incorporated

Mobil Philippines, Inc.	1892
(Exxon Mobil Petroleum & Chemicals Holdings, Inc.)	
Connell Bros. Co.(Pilipinas) Inc.	1898
Citibank, N.A.	1902
Otis Elevator Co., (Phils.), Inc.	1908
Singer Philippines, Inc.	1910
American Express International, Inc.	1916
American President Lines, Ltd.	1916
National Cash Register Corp.	1916
(AT & T Commercial Services, Inc.)	
Goodyear Philippines, Inc.	1919
Caltex Philippines, Inc.	1921
Colgate-Palmolive Philippines, Inc.	1926
Del Monte Philippines, Inc.	1926
(Del Monte Fresh Produce, Inc.)	
Globe-Mackay Cable & Radio Corp.	1928
(Globe Telecom, Inc.)	
Sterling Products International, Inc	1928
(GlaxoSmithKline Philippines, Inc.)	
Burroughs Corporation	1929
(Unisys Philippines)	
Kodak Philippines, Ltd.	1929
General Electric Philippines, Inc.	1935
Procter and Gamble Philippines, Inc.	1935
Watson Business Machines	1937
(IBM Philippines, Inc.)	
Abbott Laboratories (Philippines), Inc.	1937
Bank of America NT & SA	1946
Philam Insurance Co., Inc.	1947
Northwest Airlines, Inc.	1947
Pepsi Cola Products, Inc.	1949

That list on the preceding page is an interesting one for several reasons. Aside from the three that have already celebrated their centennial, most on the list are corporate names representing brands that have become a part of our lives. How those products developed and how they first came to the Philippines are mini-histories in themselves.

Many arrived in the new US colony in the early 1900s mimicking strategies of the old "West." First, scout out the new territory to find out what the potential market is. Early arrivals never imagined a large Filipino market. Mostly, they thought of catering to the growing yet still small number of US residents. But they soon realized this was not the "frontier" they were used to.

Import the product first to supply consumers or other companies, then if demand kept up, think about production locally. Sure, there were the plantations and logging companies (what a mess some of them made). But the vast majority soon understood that the market would rapidly turn Filipino, rather than simple export or satisfying the American community.

Business arrogance quickly shifted as eventual independence was accepted and the economy grew, giving Filipinos a rapid growth in per capita income (the total "capita" was of course much smaller then, so growth could be spread much more easily).

Companies saw the potential for nurturing these markets and step by step, built up a presence. What was Manila just prior to WWII? "Despite the thunderheads mounting to the north, the Manila of 1941 was truly the Pearl of the Orient, a city whose rising prosperity made even the thought of total war impossible for the average person to comprehend. Although a paternal Uncle Sam had ordered all diplomatic and military families back to the States, and many businessmen followed that lead, few thought such action really necessary." So writes CBS correspondent William Dunn in his book *Pacific Microphone*.

Reconstruction after the war brought with it as much opportunity as company hardship. Those who wrote of their corporate histories on the following pages are very much a part of Philippine history as well.

Intel was founded in 1965. One co-founder, Robert Noyce, said, "Do not be encumbered by history. Go off and do something wonderful." This has been the company's guiding rule; Intel created the world's first microprocessor in 1971.

No one anticipated the future products that this technology would inspire. As a rule, if a device uses electricity and can be "programmed" or "customized," there is a chip inside.

Some chips are more complex than others. The most sophisticated, the microprocessor, is also the most complex manufactured product on earth. It takes the cleanest environment on earth to make them.

Made of silicon, the second most abundant element on earth, microprocessors are made in a "cleanroom" — a room vastly cleaner than a hospital operating room. An incredible amount of technology is required to achieve — and maintain — such cleanliness. The air in the room is filtered about "ten times a minute" to prevent airborne particles from damaging the chips. As a chip is smaller than a ten-centavo piece, the smallest speck of dust assumes the size of a boulder and can cause irreparable damage to the chip.

People working in cleanrooms wear special uniforms called "bunny suits", made from a non-linting, anti-static fabric. Suiting up is an involved process that requires about 46 different steps that must be followed

Intel Philippines' headquarters

every time the wearer enters and leaves a cleanroom.

There is growing number of uses for microprocessors: the cellular phone and fax machine, traffic light controllers and interactive toys, your hard drive, car ignition, and hospital equipment. It has been predicted, "You will be wearing them, woven into your clothes, in your sneakers. They will be all over the place."

Intel Philippines was established in Makati in 1974 and its assembly and test facilities in both Makati and Cavite opened in 1977. Intel has invested more than US$ 1 billion in the country; training and employing thousands of Filipinos and winning numerous local and regional awards for personnel development.

With a workforce now numbering almost 6,000, Intel continues to play a key role in the evolution of the country's PC industry as the documented leading company in the Philippines in terms of value-added export revenues since 1995.

Intel Philippines prides itself on creating a safe work environment and maintains it through various targeted programs. In 2002, it achieved 13,5 million work hours without a lost-time injury.

Leading the community in reducing, reusing and recycling, Intel ensures that waste products from their factories are disposed of in a safe, environmentally friendly way.

Intel employees actively

contribute to its host communities through the Intel Involved Program, organizing projects such as free medical-dental missions for indigents; science, math and computer training; Intel Science and Math Excellence Awards; tree planting; Christmas outreach and Computer Quiz.

Intel's Teach to the Future program, started in January 2002, trains teachers on the effective use of computer technology in classroom instruction. The goal is to graduate 20,000 teachers under this program.

Intel sponsors the annual National Science Fair, encouraging student's interest in engineering, science and technology. Since 1998, high school winners of the Fair have won major awards in the annual Intel International Science and Engineering Fair, considered the Olympics of Science Fairs.

Corporate social responsibility is a global strategic objective of Intel Corporation and the Philippine upholds this objective.

President Gloria Macapagal-Arroyo visiting Intel's facility in 2002

One of the first advertisements for Ford was a statement by founder Henry Ford about his Model T. "You can buy a Ford in any color — as long as it's black."

Of course, that was in the early 1900s — things have changed a lot since.

Absent from the country for many years, Ford Motor Company reentered the Philippines in 1988 with a 22-hectare manufacturing plant in Santa Rosa, Laguna at a cost of about US$ 3 million.

But management denied they had ever been away, pointing out that Ford is, and was, the largest purchaser of automotive components from the Philippines; accounting for about 20 percent of the total Philippine automotive exports.

Ford has been a part of the Philippine scene since 1917. Julius Reese bought Manila Trading & Supply Company (more familiarly known as Mantrade) from Cleveland-Akron Bag Co., which traded cotton goods and engines aside from making bags. Reese described his company as a "sari-sari store." In 1917, he acquired the import business of E.C. McCullough & Co., and with it, the agency of the Ford Motor Company.

Within a few years, all other lines were dropped and the Ford Agency became the focus. The *Manila Bulletin* described Reese as "one of the great architects of...the economy of the Philippines."

The firm held office on the ground floor of what is now the Perez-Samanillo building in Escolta. With expansion Reese moved the company lock, stock and ink to the Port Area where it thrived until World War II.

At the outbreak of war, the United States Armed Forces in the Far East (USAFFE) commandeered everything — buildings, vehicle inventories, spare parts and supplies, service shops, equipment and personnel. That lasted until January 2,1942, when Manila was declared an "open city."

The Japanese seized buildings and equipment, the US staff were interned and other employees scattered. By Liberation, company assets were totally destroyed and liabilities amounted to about US$ 1.5 million.

Relying on his excellent credit rating, Mr. Reese reorganized Mantrade. Connections with the Ford Motor Company were re-established and on July 30, 1945, the first post-war letter of credit was opened for a Ford shipment to the Philippines. With generous assistance from the Ford Motor Co., despite critical material shortages in the US, the company rehabilitated itself.

In 1954, under import controls, Mantrade began construction on a new assembly plant in the Port Area. Julius Reese died that year and his protégé, John (Jack) Manning became president. The plant covered four city blocks with a floor area of 21,902

square meters. It was then one of the largest plants in the world devoted to selling and servicing trucks and automobiles.

In 1967 Ford Philippines Inc, a 100% Ford Motor Company-owned firm, acquired the Sucat, Muntinlupa assembly plant from Manila Trading & Supply. Their product lineup included such models as the LTD, Taunus, Cortina, Escort and the F and D series trucks.

Their selling point then was "we don't sell what we have; we do what you want." This was borne out by the fact that the assembly plant in Sucat produced a fleet of white Laser Hatchbacks for the detailmen of a drug firm, low side Fiera pickups for

the government's electrification program; Fieras for the Philippine Long Distance Telephone Company and an Econovan fitted out as an ambulance — remarkable flexibility.

In 1974 construction began on a Stamping Plant in the Bataan Export Processing Zone, Mariveles. The plant provided stampings for the entire region — Australia, Taiwan and Singapore; even shipping to England and West Germany. It closed down in 1985.

Originally the "old tin Lizzie" Model T was designed to allow anyone and everyone to own a car. Now, new models built here cater to high-end markets with luxurious premium, sporty utility vehicles and

vans as well as the luxury Lynx coming off the assembly line.

It is good to know that Ford intends to be rooted here. "We are in Asia for the long term," said former President Terry Emrick, "including the Philippines. We will continue to manufacture here, provide employment, develop world-class and highly competitive suppliers and as a whole, be a good corporate citizen of this country."

Ads from AmCham Journal circa 1923

Northwest Airlines, Inc.

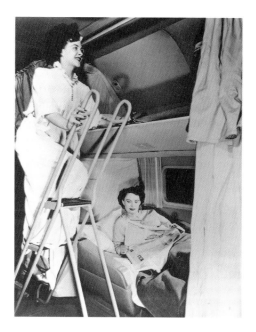

In the 1950s, the Northwest Boeing 377 "Stratocruisers" featured sleeping births for passengers on the trans-Pacific flights.

The Manila Hotel — that once gracious and elegant hotel situated amongst palms trees at the edge of old Manila-by-the-bay — was the site of the first Northwest Airlines office in Manila; a stones throw from the landing site of its now defunct predecessor that landed its Flying Clippers at the hotel dock.

The airline has been flying to Manila for 55 years and is now the world's fourth largest airline. Starting from humble beginnings on October 1, 1926, by providing a mail service between the "twin cites" Minneapolis/St. Paul and Chicago, the airline initiated passenger service a year later and has gone from strength the strength, with several "firsts" to its credit.

Northwest pioneered the "Great Circle Route" route over the north Pacific in 1947. This move stemmed from the fact that during WWII Northwest had been given the assignment of setting up a military air bridge to Alaska and the Aleutian Islands via Canada and the North Pacific. The expertise gained in this cold weather flying during the war provided the impetus for providing shorter, faster commercial flights to Asia.

By flying this northerly route, the flight distance between New York and Japan was reduced by 2,000 miles. However, at least 12 "survey flights" were flown on this route prior to the historic "first" passenger flight; their purpose being to set up the

maintenance bases, electric generating plants, radio bases, as well as housing for staff, should they be needed as alternate airports for the long haul.

On July 15, 1947 the airline flew its first trans-Pacific commercial flights into war-torn Asia to Tokyo, Seoul, Shanghai and Manila using a DC-4 aircraft.

At that time, with a speed of about 200 mph and limited fuel capacity, the aircraft had to stop in Anchorage, Shemya — and Tokyo — to refuel and change crews to complete the trip to Manila. Thus, in 1947, it took about 39 hours to travel from New York to Tokyo; today this flight takes just over 13 hours. In 1947, on the Minneapolis/St. Paul leg there was seating for only 24 passengers. However, on the inter-Asia legs there was room for 32 passengers because once the plane had crossed the Pacific, it carried less fuel, therefore, it could carry more passengers.

In 1947, Northwest's three flights per week could accommodate a maximum of 72 passengers; by 1997 Northwest was carrying 18,000 per week to Asia.

On July 14, 1947, the original DC-4 aircraft, *The Manila,* was christened on US soil, in Minnesota, with water from Manila Bay, signifying the "coming together" of America and Asia. That same year, the airline held inaugural ceremonies in three other U.S. cities — New York,

Seattle and Washington, D.C. — to promote its "Great Circle Route". At the event in New York, a Northwest vice-president walked directly under the nose of the DC-4 at the exact moment of the christening — and was drenched by Manila Bay water; providing an excellent "photo-op" for press photographers.

The early days of flying provided a very different level of customer service due to the more leisurely pace of travel, as well as the uniqueness of it. The cabin crew had time to tailor the food service, cooking eggs to individual order, and sometimes holding contests in flight to see who could invent the most original hors d' oeuvres. There are tales of flight crews baking cakes and making fudge en route as special treats for passengers, and it is said that one Captain on the Orient Division flights was a gourmet cook who brought his own food for everyone. With only 24 passengers, this was likely quite feasible — and must have provided the co-pilot the opportunity to log some extra hours while the captain cooked. While customer satisfaction and service remain a cornerstone of Northwest Airlines' on board product — especially its World Business Class luxurious seats, with a 60 inch seat pitch — fudge and cakes made en route aren't on the menu.

With its world headquarters in Minneapolis/St. Paul and over 47,000 employees, Northwest serves more than 400 cities in over 80 countries

on six continents. Its US system covers 49 states and the District of Columbia. Northwest has more than 1,700 daily flights and operates more than 130 nonstop flights between the US and Asia each week.

Above: Inaugural ceremonies for the first trans-Pacific flight to Manila. Below: Crew of The Manila, July 15, 1947; Northwest's first commercial flight from the US to Tokyo, Seoul, Shanghai and Manila.

Philippine Geothermal, Inc. - UNOCAL

Philippine Geothermal, a US firm and wholly-owned subsidiary of Unocal Corporation, was a pioneer in the Philippines..

The Union Oil Company of California (Unocal) was founded October 17, 1890 when the oil industry was only 30 years old and the first gasoline-powered automobile had yet to appear in the western US. The original co-founders, Lyman Steward, Thomas Bard and Wallace Hardison were true entrepreneurs, working to expand the uses for fuel oil in factories, steamships and railroads; sending their own mechanics and technicians to convert power or heating systems to oil instead of coal, to demonstrate fuel oil's superiority.

In 1891, Union Oil opened the first petroleum research laboratory west of the Mississippi. That rudimentary lab began a long tradition of research that served the company well.

As the world went to war in the late 1930s, Union beefed up production and refining, pouring out fuels to support the Allies. In the booming postwar era Union expanded in all directions; discovering the first natural gas in Alaska and the first oil in Australia; taking a lead position in offshore development in the Gulf of Mexico. It built a thriving chemicals business, and developed a revolutionary refining technology — Unicracking — that became the most widely used

in the world.

Over the next 25 years, Union, amongst other achievements, became the world's largest geothermal energy producer.

Geothermal energy is derived from natural heat within the earth. In effect, the earth serves as a boiler in which geothermal fluids can achieve the high temperatures and pressures necessary for commercial development. Typically, these fluids occur in reservoirs at depths of up to 9,800 feet (3,000 meters) and can be recovered by drilling wells. Surface facilities convert ("flash") a portion of the fluid into steam, used to power turbines for generating electricity.

Here Philippine Geothermal Inc., under a service contract with the National Power Corporation, developed geothermal resources at the Tiwi and Mak-Ban contract areas in Albay and Laguna, providing energy capable of producing an aggregate 756 MW of electricity to NPC's power plants. The Tiwi and Mak-Ban generating units produce 15% of the electricity requirements for Luzon's 40 million residents and save the Philippine government an estimated US$ 100 million yearly by replacing fossil-fuel generation; they have performed reliably for more than 17 years.

From an environmental perspective, electricity generated through geothermal energy offers clear advantages over fossil fuels. Fossil-fired plants emit sulfur dioxide, nitrogen dioxide and ash to the atmosphere; geothermal emissions consist mostly of water. Fossil fuel plants also require cooling water from local sources; for geothermal plants, reservoir fluids satisfy the cooling requirements.

The company also works to be a good neighbor. On-site nurseries at Tiwi and Mak-Ban produce hardy native tree seedlings which are used in reforestation programs to enhance the watershed and prevent erosion. Also, at both Mak-Ban and Tiwi, PGI has drilled water wells and constructed domestic water distribution systems for local residents.

When Typhoon Rosing caused major damage to the Tiwi field and surrounding communities in 1995, PGI made available emergency services, manpower and equipment; roads and bridges were repaired; food, clothing and medical supplies were provided; and potable water supplies were restored.

PGI also sponsors community improvement programs in areas near its facilities. Projects have included road and school building and the creation of child care, pre-school and health and nutrition programs.

PGI employs about 650 Filipinos. Its senior employees, many of whom have completed advanced training in the US, are among the most highly qualified members of the geothermal industry worldwide.

The Mak-Ban geothermal project in Laguna.

San Roque Power Corporation is a special-purpose company incorporated in 1997 to operate the San Roque Multipurpose Project (SRMP), at a total cost of US$ 1.2 billion. The primary feature of the SRMP is a 200 meter high, 1.2 kilometer-long embankment dam on the Agno River spanning the municipalities of San Manuel and San Nicolas, Pangasinan, an agricultural province, 200 km north of Manila. Construction of the dam and other facilities began on March 6, 1998.

The dam impounds a reservoir with a surface area of about 12.8 square kilometers extending into the municipality of Itogon, Benguet, and provides many benefits to the residents and farmers of the affected provinces.

Constructed with a gated spillway, runoff collected during the wet season is stored for later release through water turbines to generate power and irrigate crops. With a rated capacity of 345 megawatts (MW), the plant can operate year-round at its dependable capacity of 85 MW for a minimum of eight hours a day — even during periods of extreme drought. Whenever surplus water is available, the SRMP can either provide extra peaking capacity (beyond 85 MW) or generate off-peak power, or a combination of the two. A recently completed 500 KV transmission line enables this benefit to provide electricity to Metro Manila residents and to those living in the islands south of Luzon.

Aside from providing electricity to the consumers, the dam irrigates up to 87,000 hectares of farmland per year covering areas in Pangasinan, Nueva Ecija and Tarlac. According to the National Irrigation Authority (NIA), more than 53,000 farmers will benefit from the SRMP's irrigation component. Reducing the perennial flooding of the Agno River, which affects at least 16 Pangasinan and Tarlac towns, is another benefit of this project.

The SRMP also serves to enhance the water quality of the Lower Agno River by serving as a settling basin and trapping sediments transported by the runoff of typhoons or the tailings generated by unregulated small-scale mining activities.

In early 2003, the SRMP will provide power, irrigation, flood control and enhance water quality benefits to the surrounding regions, which includes the Northwest Luzon Economic Growth Quadrangle.

At the height of construction in November 2001, the company employed over 5,000 people. This number includes those working for SRMP's Construction Contractor Raytheon Ebasco Overseas Limited. This number will gradually decrease as portions of the work are finished. Ultimately SRMP will have a staff of about 50 operating and maintenance personnel.

Financial and construction

contracts of the SRMP rely on the power purchase agreement (PPA) with the National Power Corporation (NPC), which incorporates a build-operate-transfer (BOT) approach. With NPC contributing funds for the non-power components, ownership of the dam and spillway will transfer to NPC upon construction completion. The San Roque Power Corporation will own and operate the power- generating facilities for 25 years, after which their ownership will transfer to NPC.

The San Roque Power Corporation is owned by corporate shareholders, namely: Sithe Philippines Holdings, Inc. — an indirect subsidiary of Sithe Energies, Inc. of New York, USA, Marubeni Corporation of Tokyo, Japan and a wholly-owned indirect subsidiary of the Kansai Electric Power Co., KPIC Singapore Pte. Ltd.

There are many "Horatio Alger" stories – stories of men who worked hard and had a dream and succeeded beyond anyone's wildest imaginings. One such person in the Philippines is Henry Sy, the Founder and Chairman of the SM Group of Companies.

He was born in China and, at the age of 12, followed his father to the Philippines. While working in his father's sari-sari store he went back to school, starting all over again in first grade.

Sy says, "My first business was shoes and the first store was on Carriedo Street."

An unlikely starting point for someone who changed the way the people of the Philippines shop. "…after liberation, I started a shoe business. I bought shoes by job lots from American shoe importers and sold them retail. The Americans trusted me with their merchandise even if I had nothing to back me up because I always paid on time."

He continues, "The store became very popular. One store grew to three stores. But shoes were mainly a cottage industry and supply was limited." Soon Sy was traveling to the US and Europe. While on these buying trips, "I observed the merchandising trends, and in ten years I saw the shopping center developments in the US from the East to West Coast. I knew this could happen in the Philippines."

In October 1958, Sy opened the first Shoemart on Rizal Avenue in downtown Manila. From this beginning, Sy conceptualized a chain of shoe stores, each characterized by a distinct merchandising layout.

In the sixties, the company expanded its shoe store chain and was one of the pioneers in the new urban centers, opening bigger shoe outlets in the Makati Commercial Center in 1963, and in Cubao in 1967.

It was during this time that James Rouse popularized the enclosed shopping center in the US and coined the term "mall." As part of the growing suburban communities, the malls served as a catalyst for growth and socioeconomic development.

In the 1970s, Shoemart made the shift from a shoe store to full line department store and a change in corporate identity; "Shoemart" became known as "SM Shoemart" and eventually "SM".

SM positioned itself for growth in the 1980s, diversifying into supermarket and appliance stores.

Late 1985 marked the opening of its first shopping mall.

SM emerged as a key player in the shopping center industry in the 1990s, giving rise to the "malling" phenomenon. In 1994, the group established SM Prime Holdings, a publicly listed company that owns and operates its chain of world-class super-malls.

Ask any Filipino where they spend their free time and more than likely 80% will say they spend their time at an SM store or mall. Not surprising, since leisure and entertainment are a catalyst for family fun, and shopping is a passion for most Filipinos.

With its department stores and shopping centers all over the country, totaling more than 1.8 million square meters, SM has become part of the lives of more than one million customers each day. They can shop, dine, see movies, or just have fun with family and friends.

And, to an American, the SM stores and malls evoke a sense of *déjà vu* since shopping malls, with their department stores and specialty shops, are a part of the American lifestyle too.

American brands fill the malls— Levis, Guess, Maybelline and MAC, Nike, Speedo, Apple and HP. Or want a meal? There's McDonald's, Wendy's, Pizza Hut and KFC, among other food outlets. Hollywood movies draw crowds at SM's cinemas.

On a weekend, you may catch a mini-concert with a visiting artist like Jim Brickman or 98 Degrees, or meet well-loved characters like Winnie the Pooh or the Power Puff Girls.

But it's not all about American goods; at SM's malls other well-known international brands are sold beside Filipino products, many of which got their initial start through SM marketing. The scene of the local and foreign mix—of Filipino traditions like fiestas in provincial SM malls being celebrated beside promotional tie-ins with Hollywood blockbuster movies—is what makes SM the acknowledged trendsetter and innovator it is today.

The SM department stores and supermalls were inspired by the American concept—incorporating appliance centers, and specialty shops for toys, home and lifestyle, personal care and hardware (SM is

the Philippine franchisee of US based ACE Hardware), as well as the leisure affiliates of food courts, bowling centers, and even ice skating rinks – and all adapted to the local lifestyle, forever changing the way Filipinos shop and find fun.

However, the real novelty in this tropical country are those SM ice skating rinks—and they have produced teams that have won in competitions in the US; an SM team recently placed third in the prestigious 2001 ISI world Championship in Ohio.

As its market evolves, and as it continues to grow, SM will have more stores and more malls. With the company's goal to open to mall a year, shoppers can look forward to more SM malls in the urban Metro Manila Area, as well as the three major regions in the Philippines— Luzon, Visayas, and Mindanao. See you at the mall!

A Manager of 3M once said, "We are in every industry there is." With more than 60,000 products and new ones being brought forward every year, that statement is easy to believe. It is entirely possible that many 3M products are used without our even being aware of their source.

The Minnesota Mining and Manufacturing Company was founded in 1902 in Two Harbors, Minnesota. The mining division may be lost in the mists of time, but the manufacturing has continued for a century.

3M began with the manufacture of sand paper and the company still produces millions of sheets every year. But in 1925, Dick Drew, a young researcher acting on his own initiative developed Scotch™ Masking tape. The tape was designed to help automobile painters to make two-tone paint applications. He took a prototype roll to a St. Paul auto painter. The painter carefully applied the masking tape along the edge of the color already painted and was just about to spray on the second color when the tape fell off! Angry, the man examined the 2-inch wide tape and saw that it had adhesive only along the outer edges. He told Drew, "Take this tape back to those Scotch bosses of yours and tell them to put more adhesive on it." Drew did, and the name stuck.

3M began manufacturing in Muntinlupa City in 1973. Original products were masking, cellophane, transparent and packaging tapes. The local distribution network includes Cebu, Bacolod and Davao.

It sells about 10,000 products including tapes, flexible adhesives, contact cements (ceramic and vinyl adhesives), floor finish chemicals, rubbing compounds, rubberized automotive underseal coating and traffic control materials.

Rosa Miller, who headed 3M in the Philippines for several years, once said: "Our growth comes from new products, as the company's focus is innovation." An example is Post-It™ pads. One of 3M's laboratory workers was developing a different adhesive. A co-worker sang in a choir and he wanted to be able to keep his place in the songbook when they took a break, but couldn't find a way to do so. The lab worker found the adhesive he was working on wasn't strong enough for his purposes, so he gave it to the choir singer. There it was found they could place it in a book, remove it and place it somewhere else, without damaging the book. Voila! Post-It™ notes.

3M also introduced health products like Steri-Strip™ (closes wounds with tape), disposable face masks; 3M™Scotchcast™ for broken limbs, an asthmatic inhaler that delivers accurate doses triggered by breathing, and about 10,000 other products.

Enhancing the communities in which they operate is one of 3M's core values. It works with Habitat for Humanity and the Virlanie Foundation, which currently operates 12 homes for over 300 children with histories of physical abuse, neglect and abandonment.

Wherever you go, whatever you do, 3M is with you.

Evolution of the 3M logo

1906

1950

1961

Abbott Laboratories grew from the vision of a single dedicated doctor whose desire was to improve people's healthcare by providing standardized and dependable medication. In 1888 — an era when most medication was individually prepared from formulas, prescribed by doctors, and therefore not always precisely the same at each mixing — this was a revolutionary step forward. Young Dr. Wallace Abbott of Chicago, Illinois, initiated this pharmaceutical revolution when he started making "active principle" granules...and pharmaceutical history.

Dr. Abbott's vision was not only for quality healthcare for his own country, but to spread such healthcare worldwide through the availability of these standardized pharmaceutical products around the globe. With this objective Abbott Laboratories has grown and touched the lives of people in over 130 countries, including the Philippines.

Very much a part of Philippine history, Abbott began as a distributor of pharmaceutical products in 1937 with Mr. Luiz Gomez Macias as the first General Manager.

After Liberation in 1945, when the country was reeling from the massive devastation caused by the war and with thousands injured and malnourished, Abbott was the first pharmaceutical company to the rescue, shipping 70 tons of medicines to the Philippines via US military vessels.

The company, reaffirming its faith in the economy of the country, rebuilt and expanded its Philippine operations to include investing in a state-of-the-art manufacturing facility in 1952; uplifting not only healthcare but morale by utilizing Filipino skills and talents in all facets of its operation and returning a people's pride and confidence in their future.

Consistent with its vision of providing total quality healthcare, Abbott Philippines today has diversified its business and expanded its operations to include product lines that encompass the areas of nutrition, hospital, pharmaceutical, consumer and diagnostics. Over the years, many Abbott products including Gain®, Cecon®, Iberet®, and Ensure® have become household names.

In 1999, Abbott International acquired Knoll Pharmaceuticals, the pharmaceutical business of BASF worldwide. In the Philippines, the integration of Knoll Pharmaceuticals into the Abbott organization was led and finalized by its General Manager Edwin D. Feist, in April 2001.

This was another milestone in the company's — and the country's — history; as it did more than 60 years ago, Abbott once again affirmed its belief in the Philippines and the Filipinos by continuing to expand its business here.

The American Express Company was formed in1850 by Henry Wells and J.C. Fargo, the men of the legendary Wells, Fargo stagecoaches of the "wild, wild west." American Express initially handled shipments of valuable goods, then rapidly expanded with the introduction of Money Orders in 1882 and the invention of Travelers Cheques in 1891. An office was opened in Paris in 1895, and within five years a chain of offices could be found in all European capitols and port cities.

The Manila office of American Express was opened in 1916, first with freight, travel and banking services. Soon after, a network of offices spread throughout Asia.

The company has a proud history of helping Americans in times of conflict. The outbreak of World War I in Europe caught many Americans unprepared; American Express offices remained open and lent assistance with both currency and transportation, helping 150,000 American tourists trapped in Europe to get home. In the areas worst affected by war, locals traded in American Express checks rather than their own currency.

Again, in the three years prior to the US entry into World War II, American Express helped stranded Americans return home from Asia.

The company today is a global travel, financial and network services provider. Aside from charge and credit cards, it also offers financial planning, brokerage services, mutual funds, insurance and other investment products. It is the world's largest travel agency.

"Plastic money" has become increasingly popular as people recognize the convenience of carrying a card rather than cash. One gentleman used his American Express card to purchase a painting worth $2,477,500 at a Sotheby's auction.

Company policy states: "Not only is it appropriate for the company to give back to the communities in which it operates, it is also smart business. Healthy communities… provide an environment that helps companies such as American Express grow, innovate and attract outstanding talent."

Some of their grants have gone to protect the environment, others to supporting art and culture. In the Philippines, the company lent financial assistance for the preservation of the Kabayan Mummies, and Whale Shark and Philippine Eagle preservation. The parent American Express Foundation in New York, in support of cultural and historical preservation, gave a grant to the Angono Petroglyphs in Binangonan, Rizal — the oldest known Rock Art in the Philippines, dating back to about 1000 years B.C.

In 2001, Ian Fish, American Express country manager for the Philippines, on behalf of the company, presented new touch-screen computers to the National Museum. The technology allows museums around the Philippines to make multimedia presentations on the museum's features and content.

American Express office in Binondo, 1930s

American President Lines

The "California" (1850), the first American ship into San Francisco Bay.

Founded in 1848, the Pacific Mail Steamship Company was awarded a 10-year US government contract to carry mail between Panama and the Oregon Territory. In 1850, its first ship, the *California*, was the third steamer in history to sail through the Straits of Magellan at the tip of South America, and then north to become the first American steamer to enter San Francisco Bay.

A direct service from San Francisco to Manila was established in 1917. Pacific Mail was then the premier American steamship company operating the trans-Pacific route. By 1920 its fleet consisted of 46 steamers.

In 1925, the trans-Pacific steamers as well as the name, house flag and goodwill of Pacific Mail were acquired by Robert Dollar. Dollar Steamship Lines, APL's second predecessor company, pioneered round-the-world service with their fleet of seven *"President"* ships.

In 1938, the lingering effects of the Great Depression and the war in Europe were being felt worldwide; the

Dollar Steamship was failing. On November 1, 1938 the United States Maritime Commission took control of Dollar Steamship Lines, changing the company name to American President Lines, Ltd., and thereby reflecting the Dollar Lines' practice of naming some of its ships for American presidents.

In January 1942, operations stopped completely after all US and British residents in the Philippines were taken into custody and interned by the Japanese.

Like most Filipino employees of foreign firms during World War II, the APL staff cared for their imprisoned American bosses, providing food, medicines and money; whatever they could spare from the needs of their own families. This was an exceptional demonstration of loyalty.

Rebuilding after the war, in addition to passenger and international cargo loadings, the company also acted as an agent for inter-island and US Navy vessels. Eventually, inter-island transport operations were turned over to other carriers and APL concentrated on international traffic to the US and Europe.

By 1973, decreasing patronage, rising costs and the popularity of air travel became uncontestable. In April, the company's last remaining premier passenger ship, the *President Wilson*

completed her last voyage. APL was now a total containerized cargo carrier.

In July 1978, APL opened its first port branch in Cebu, followed later with Legaspi City and Mariveles branches. APL also served Subic Bay Naval Base, building the Sattler Pier in Subic to accommodate its huge commercial vessels.

The start of 1995 saw another transition in APL Manila's set up; Capt. Romeo L. Malig, became the company's first Filipino Managing Director. A direct call was introduced to Davao in 1996, which made APL the international carrier with the most branches in the Philippines.

On November 12, 1996, Neptune Orient Lines, Ltd. (NOL) merged with APL, becoming one of the world's top five shipping lines.

A century and a half later — from "round the world" to the "world wide web"— APL continues to increase its market share and reinforce its leadership role in the industry.

Today APL ships are a regular sight passing under the Golden Gate Bridge.

"Avon calling" has been a recognizable catchphrase for decades. The founder, David McConnell, called his company Avon after his favorite playwright, the Bard of Avon, Shakespeare.

Mrs. P.F.E. Albee of Winchester, New Hampshire pioneered the company's now famous direct selling method. Women have been selling Avon since 1886—34 years before they were allowed to vote in the US! In the Philippines, Avon first provided income opportunities to Filipinas in 1978 when it acquired Beautifont. Today there are 3 million Avon independent sales representatives worldwide—700,000 of them in the Philippines.

The world's leading direct seller of beauty and related products, Avon products are sold in 139 countries.

Avon Products, Inc. is now a global manufacturer and marketer of beauty and related products, including cosmetics, fragrances and toiletries; "Beauty Plus" consisting of jewelry, watches and accessories, and apparel; "Beyond Beauty" consisting of gift and decorative items, home entertainment, and health and nutrition products.

More beauty products carry the Avon brand name than any other in the world and it was also the first major cosmetics company to announce a permanent end to animal testing. This was done in 1989.

Avon has more women in management positions—86% — than any other Fortune 500 company.

Avon representatives are independent contractors or dealers; not agents or employees of Avon. Representatives purchase products directly from Avon and sell them to their customers. The Company's products are sold to customers through a combination of direct selling and marketing, utilizing independent representatives, licensed kiosks, Express Centers in urban areas, mail, phone, fax or online.

In the Philippines, Avon works with the Department of Education, Culture and Sports to recognize outstanding achievements of female public elementary and high school principals through the Gintong Ilawan Teodora Alonso Educator's Awards. In July 2000, the program was expanded to include private school principals.

Avon's Bigay Alam ay Bigay Buhay Women's Cancers Crusade, in partnership with the Department of Health and the Philippine Cancer Society, continues to disseminate life saving information on women's cancer prevention and detection.

A Worldwide Fund for Women's health was established in 1992 and has, to date, raised US$ 250 million with programs operating in 30 countries.

Avon Running: Global Women's Circuit launched the only global series of 10k races and 5k fitness walks for women, which promote cardiovascular health and make fitness accessible to women of every age and ability in 12 countries around the world, including the Philippines.

"Avon calling.." for health, education — and beauty.

Taan weir, one of the two weirs diverting water from the Casecnan and Taan rivers in Nueva Viscaya, Luzon; part of the Casecnan Project.

CalEnergy came to the Philippines in 1994. The business venture was its second in Asia, after Indonesia. It provides power to 3.4 million customers worldwide and to 750,000 homes in the Philippines.

CalEnergy International, headquartered in Des Moines, Iowa, is a subsidiary of MidAmerican Energy Holdings Company, global leader in the production, supply and distribution of energy from diversified sources including geothermal, natural gas, hydroelectric and coal.

In partnership with the Philippine National Oil Company–Energy Development Corporation (PNOC-EDC), CalEnergy owns and operates three geothermal power plants — Upper Mahiao, Mahanagdong, and Malitbog in Leyte. They provide 540 megawatts to Luzon, Cebu and Mindanao.

It also built the Casecnan Multipurpose Irrigation and Power Project in Nueva Ecija and Nueva Viscaya. Casecnan is a combined irrigation and hydroelectric power project meant providing 200,000 homes with electricity while irrigating 31,000 hectares of Central Luzon farmlands. It also stabilizes water supply to 137,000 hectares of existing irrigated farmlands. This should increase yields by approximately 465,000 tons of rice annually, a major boon towards food security.

CalEnergy is a collaboration of both US expertise and Filipino ingenuity. Its plants are run mostly by Filipinos; proof of its belief in the skills and talents of the Filipino.

CalEnergy International exists on a philosophy of service. Apart from serving its customers, it strives to help its communities and their people. When the firm came to the Philippines, it committed to provide not only light and power, but also empowerment of the people with whom they live and work. The company promotes education. It shares its expertise with villagers about caring for the environment, and trains villagers on new means of livelihood.

This is business philosophy. From 1996 to the 2000, CalEnergy International gave financial assistance amounting to an estimated P115 million for livelihood, education, construction, health, and environment preservation programs.

Caltex (Philippines), Inc. came to the Philippines in 1917 when Texas Company (as Texaco was then known) began marketing its products in the Philippines through local distributor Wise and Co. Four years later, Texaco (Philippines) was formally established and opened its office in Binondo, Manila. By 1936, Texaco joined forces with the Standard Oil Company (California) to form Caltex (Philippines) Inc. That same year, Caltex transferred to a new office and opened depots and service stations nationwide, making it the country's No. 1 oil company.

Three years of plunder and neglect during the Second World War wrecked havoc on the company's facilities. The Pandacan Terminal was destroyed and the Caltex network of depots and service stations were inoperative. Rebuilding was the mantra upon Liberation.

In 1951, the construction of a Caltex Refinery in San Pascual, Batangas began on a 125-hectare lot. Philippine President Ramon Magsaysay joined the 1954 inauguration of the US$60-million refinery, the first in the Philippines.

The roaring 1960s were marked with a series of milestones that helped Caltex reestablish itself as the country's premier oil company. By 1961, Caltex was operating five depots in Luzon, twelve in the Visayas region, and three in Mindanao. The following year, the Caltex Refinery supplied 50% of the country's national consumption for petroleum products. In 1969, two 108-kilometer pipelines were built bringing oil products from the Batangas refinery to Manila.

Caltex built and opened the country's first island wharf and storage complex at the Batangas complex in 1974 for very large crude carriers (VLCCs), which provided up to 10 days of the nation's crude oil needs at the time.

Caltex also spearheaded geothermal exploration in Kalinga, Apayao and studied alternative energy sources in 1977.

Aside from a new logo in 1996, Caltex entered convenience retailing in 1997, opening the first StarMart outlet in Sucat, Parañaque. In 1998, the Caltex Shared Services Center was established, one of the first regional headquarters to locate in the Philippines to concentrate on backroom operations.

Caltex supports several projects, including the Caltex Fund, a nationwide scholarship program for disadvantaged children that also provides assistance in skills/livelihood training and shelter; and Good Roots, an agro-forestry project that aims to preserve the environment through technology transfer to farming communities. Aside from monetary donations, Caltex employee volunteers helped build 42 houses to date for Habitat for Humanity Philippines. The company also supports Team Caltex Philippines, the national amateur boxing contingent that officially represents the country in international competitions and is a founding member of the Philippine Eagle Foundation.

The "Texas Company" offices, the beginnings of Caltex in the Philippines. (Photo: Carter Collection)

Cargill began as a small grain elevator in Conover, Iowa in 1865. From there, it has grown into a thriving company that merchandises, processes and distributes agricultural and other essential products and services throughout the world.

Cargill came to Manila in the 1950s. Starting as a representative office, its first business was buying copra for export to the US. In 1960 Granax Philippines was formed and the business expanded to trading wheat and other feed grains, as well as the export of sugar and molasses. This company was later renamed Granexport Corporation.

In 1971, Cargill sold Granex and formed a new company to conduct research and the test marketing of corn seeds, as well as to continue the molasses business. Later the company formed a subsidiary, Cargill Philippines, Inc. It began construction of a copra crushing plant in General Santos City, which started operations in 1991.

Cargill's Animal Nutrition unit produces various types of feed products for fowl, hogs, fish and specialty birds. Using state-of-the-art technology, it operates two modern plants in Baliwag, Bulacan and in General Santos, Mindanao.

Its Grains and Oilseeds unit, located in Subic, trades and distributes grain products such as corn, wheat, wheat meal, soybeans and protein meal. The Oilseeds unit is involved in originating copra, processing of oilseeds and trading coconut oil and copra meal in the international market. There is also a Sugar unit which trades and distributes sugar products, both in the domestic and the world markets.

Cargill also has a Financial Marketing group that trades in the money market, foreign exchange, fixed income equities, derivatives and trade structure finance.

The company has long focused on research. This has led to the creation of a "nutraceuticals business." A new product, chondroitin sulfate addresses the problem of osteoarthritis, a general wearing away of joint cartilage, which affects most people as they age. Nutraceuticals, as the name implies, combines nutrition with pharmaceutical properties. A simple example is orange juice fortified with calcium.

Cargill researchers have found a way to create polymer resins – the basic material of just about every kind of plastic – from renewable sources rather than petrochemicals. They created it from corn! In partnership with Dow, a US$300 million corn-to-plastic manufacturing facility is near Blair, Nebraska. This is typical of Cargill's policy of looking to the future and making it better.

Baliwag Feed Plant, Bulacan; inaugurated May 2000

Citibank's predecessor in the Philippines, The International Banking Corporation, opened July 14, 1902, within days of the first AmCham meeting at Clarke's.

Its first office was a stable at 86 Calle Rosario, Binondo leased from Don Carlos Palanca Tan Guinlay. The lease agreement stipulated that during times of flood, the bank would provide shelter in a dry area located behind the bank vault for two Palanca ponies. However unorthodox, the arrangement didn't seem to affect bank operations.

Initially, IBC concentrated on export markets, particularly for sugar, copra and hemp. In 1915, National City Bank acquired a majority stake in IBC, though the name change occurred only in 1927.

After the WWII, the bank focused on reconstruction, using its overseas network to stimulate trade. The Cebu branch re-opened May 1947, and in October, a military banking facility opened at Clark Field, Pampanga. A third branch opened in the Port Area, Manila, in October 1948.

In the 1960s, Citibank (it officially changed its name in 1976) provided significant support for Filipino entrepreneurs buying American-owned companies. It led a syndicate of banks to fund the Lopez family's purchase of the Manila Electric Company (Meralco), and the Villanueva group's purchase of

Atlantic Gulf and Pacific, then the largest construction and engineering firm.

A management-training program started in 1961 produced "The Golden Boys," who today hold top positions in Philippine banks and the private sector, including Rafael B. Buenaventura, the Bangko Sentral Governor.

The growing demand for consumer finance for education, medical, car and housing led to FNCB Finance opening in 1968.

Citibank led and was instrumental in persuading other New York banks to lend to the Philippines during the foreign exchange crisis in 1970. The maturing loans were repaid and the government paid off the new loans in five years.

After the oil crisis of 1973, it also led a consortium of banks to finance the development of the Nido oil complex in Palawan. It also offered financing to generate alternative energy from geothermal, nuclear, coal, bagasse and wood waste sources. Citibank backed the first geothermal plant, inaugurated in Laguna in May 1979.

Throughout the debt crisis years, Citibank actively mobilized support from the country's bank creditors to reschedule payments. Re-affirming its long-term commitment to the Philippines, it extended a US$125 million Concessional Financing

Facility for development projects in power, transportation, telecommunications and construction. With the liberalization of the telecommunications industry, Citibank provided bilateral and structured financing as well as advisories to the industry.

The bank financed build-operate-transfer power projects totalling 2,000 megawatts.

Citibank developed the local US Dollar clearing system in April 1994 and remains the only bank providing US dollar domestic settlement services.

The Citicorp and Travelers Group merger in April 1998 combined Citibank's consumer and corporate banking with Travelers' money-management, insurance, stock-broking and investment-banking operations. Citigroup emerged as the global leader in financial services with over 100 million customers in 100 countries.

It was advisor, funder, lead arranger and hedge provider in the largest investment in Philippine history — the US$4.5 billion Integrated Malampaya Deep Water Gas to Power project — in the development of the offshore field of natural gas discovered by Shell Philippines Exploration in Palawan,

In 2001, Citibank was cited Best Foreign Bank in the Philippines, Best in Cash Management and Philippine Peso by *Euromoney* — a long way from the stable in Binondo.

Coconut trees and rice fields are the typical rural scene in the Philippines, but the ubiquitous Coca-Cola logo is a part of it too. The story of Coca-Cola in the Philippines is interwoven with the country's modern history.

The first Coca-Cola produced locally rolled off the bottling line on March 19, 1927 at a production facility on General Solano Street in Manila, also used for a local soft drink brand owned by the San Miguel Brewery. The Coca-Cola Company granted an exclusive bottling and distribution franchise to San Miguel. Seven thousand cases of Coca-Cola were sold that year; a volume sold in a matter of minutes today.

WWII halted all bottling operations. But immediately after Liberation a temporary but complete facility was set up inside the "art deco"

Metropolitan Theater, one of the very few relatively intact structures left standing. Thousands of US troops then based in Manila benefited, as did the local population — "Rum and Coke" became a favorite at local watering holes.

By August 1, 1945, a new bottling plant went into operation opposite the ruins of the first plant. General Douglas MacArthur autographed a card attached to the first bottle off the production line. That bottle with its autographed card is on display at the Coca-Cola Pavilion at the Atlanta, Georgia, headquarters.

Growing demand in the 1950s led to significant investments in bottling facilities and sales offices outside Manila. Distribution systems (which at one time included refurbished military trucks) were rapidly expanded.

Coca-Cola broke new ground in the 1960s by featuring the country's biggest entertainers in its advertisements, utilizing the increased influence of media on the young during a time of major social change.

Fierce competition among soft drink makers characterized the 1970s, which left Coca-Cola the undisputed leader in the Philippine soft drinks industry by the early 1980s. The Philippines is one of the ten largest Coca-Cola markets in the world, with an expanded product line that includes bottled waters, juice and sports drinks.

With 22 bottling facilities, Coca-Cola is an important part of the economy. It provides thousands of jobs and business opportunities for allied and downstream industries. It is the single largest buyer of local premium sugar.

But beyond business, Coca-Cola invests heavily in community initiatives. The "Coca-Cola ed.venture" project funds the construction of state-of-the-art, Internet-ready computer labs in ten public high schools. And the Little Red Schoolhouse Project is building 50 schoolhouses in some of the country's most remote communities.

Coca-Cola will continue its remarkable story in the Philippines, continuing to invest as it has in a country – and people – that has welcomed it with open arms for 75 years.

ONLY

Through the use of a mild balmy and soothing soap like the popular

"PALMOLIVE" SOAP

can you remove all dirt, surplus cold cream and remains of rouge and powder.

"PALMOLIVE" Toilet Articles — Soap, Lotion, Vanishing Cream, Cold Cream, Shampoo, etc., for sale at all Drug-Stores and Perfumeries.

JUAN YSMAEL & CO., INC.

SOLE AGENTS

348 Echague   Tel. 2154

MANILA   ILOILO   CEBU

An early ad from the AmCham Journal.

Colgate-Palmolive watched the Philippines' evolve from colony to commonwealth to republic.

It started in 1926 under Arthur J. Brent as a small sales organization then known as the Palmolive Company. Among its first products were Octagon laundry powder, Crystal White laundry bar and Pompeia cosmetics, all imported from the US. Colgate Ribbon dental cream began selling in 1928.

During WWII the company's office and warehouse in Binondo were padlocked and subsequently looted; it's office manager, James H. Carpenter, was confined at the Sto. Tomas Interment Camp. (He instructed his employees, upon his capture, to surreptitiously enter the sealed office to rescue the company books. When they could not escape with the books, they copied all entries word for word. With these records intact, the company was able to collect all receivables from insurance after the war.)

Colgate-Palmolive resumed operations in 1946. With the economy back on its feet, it incorporated as Colgate-Palmolive Philippines, Inc. (CPPI) in 1949 — a wholly owned subsidiary of Colgate-Palmolive Company, New York.

The first locally produced Colgate Dental Cream rolled off CPPI's temporary plant in Intramuros in 1950. In 1951, the late President Elpidio Quirino presided over the inauguration of CPPI's modern manufacturing plant/office, billed as the "Industrial Project of the Year," at 1049 J.P. Rizal Avenue, Makati City. It produced previously imported products: Palmolive Soap (1951); Palmolive Shampoo (1965); Ajax Detergent Bar (1966); other products followed.

In 1955, with its concern for its employees, CPPI established a Retirement Pension Fund.

In 1976, CPPI organized the Colgate Sports Foundation, Inc. building or rehabilitating 32 sports facilities nationwide (basketball courts, swimming pools, sports complexes). CPPI is also involved in fund raising, relief operations, and in many community and educational development projects. Its "Bright Smiles, Bright Futures" oral health program has served millions of children in public schools and in 1998 was integrated into the elementary curriculum.

Today, CPPI markets a wide variety of personal and household care products. Many have become bywords to millions, making CPPI truly a part of every Filipino family. In fact Colgate has become synonymous with the term toothpaste in the Filipino vocabulary.

As the Philippines continues its journey towards political, economic and social development, CPPI intends not only to witness but to participate.

Connell Bros. Company Philippines, Inc.

It was two brothers from Minnesota who in 1898 envisioned the trade potential between the US Pacific Northwest and the "Far East." They took an opportunity offered by a Seattle bank to liquidate a distressed cargo of flour in Hong Kong.

A similar arrangement followed in Manila. J.J. Connell, arriving in Manila, asked Mr. A.G. Stephen (then manager of the Hong Kong and Shanghai Banking Corporation) to release the cargo to him, although the bills of lading had not yet arrived. "If you were to cross the Channel to those islands," said Stephen, pointing south, "the Bank could not bring you back." J.J. convinced him that he would not flee in any direction and Stephen released the flour.

The company expanded rapidly. Within 50 years it distributed Carnation Milk, Hershey Chocolate, Karo Corn Syrup, Sunkist Oranges, Welsh's Grape Juice, Kraft Cheese, Hormel Hams, Lipton Tea and many other brand names staple to Filipinos.

It also sold products under its own brand name "Morjon" (a combination of the brothers' Morris and John), is still on the market today.

Taking the risk out of marketing products overseas, Connell assumes responsibility for the financing, transportation, documentation, sales and marketing, warehousing and distribution. Their fiscal responsibility has resulted in a Dun & Bradstreet credit rating of 5Al, the highest available.

Fifty years ago the Connell Chairman said, "Our responsibilities in the economic field are many. First, we must continue our unprecedented levels of production so that we may continue to export to world markets the food, coal, steel and goods so urgently required. Second, we must carry out our role of world's banker in accordance with accepted banking practice, which is not to saddle debtor nations with still more debts but to encourage and assist them to become productive and financially sound.

Third, we must lead the way to revival of free trade by deed as well as promise.

"The encouragement today of free, unfettered and continuing exchange across sovereign boundaries of ideas, goods and cultural expression is the best guarantee for peace tomorrow."

His words ring eerily true five decades later.

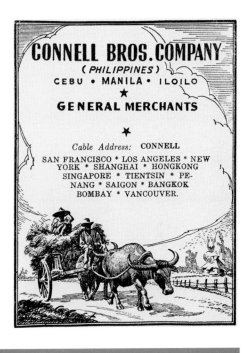

Connell's Matriarch Dita Wilber — the first "all-American" born in Manila....

Matilda "Dita" Wilbur, wife of Connell Bros. founder Brayton Wilbur Sr. was born in Manila on September 17, 1900. Her father, US Army Captain David Baker, was assigned as Director of the Bureau of Customs. Later he helped form the Philippine Constabulary and became its acting chief.

The Bakers returned to Texas in 1906. In 1918, after graduating from a convent in Illinois, Dita rejoined her parents at Fort Sam Houston where she met Brayton Wilbur, a first lieutenant in her father's regiment.

They met again when Wilbur worked in San Francisco and Dita's family had moved to Berkeley. They were engaged in 1921, but Dita's father decreed that his daughter could not marry until her groom had US$600. Brayton didn't have it, having borrowed US$1,000 to start a business with Floyd Ellis and Thomas Franck – the Wilbur-Ellis Company.

They finally married in 1923 – the same year that Wilbur-Ellis Company was incorporated. In 1931, Wilbur-Ellis purchased Connell Bros. Co. Ltd. and expanded trading to Asia.

While Brayton died in 1963, Dita has carried on – dynamic and involved as ever. As she continues past her centennial, her life has literally "spanned the decades."

DHL Worldwide Express (Phils.) Corp.

In July, 1969, Adrian Dalsey and Larry Hillblom both worked for a small delivery service company in San Francisco. Hillblom, a flying courier who had an "extra" US$ 3,000 made on the stock market, proposed they start their own company. Robert Lynn joined them and DHL was born. Their first route was between the US West Coast and Hawaii.

All self-financed, Dalsey once remarked, "...lucky I had so many credit cards!"

In the beginning, the three partners delivered shipping documents themselves — overnight, between San Francisco and Honolulu. It meant getting the documents to customs before the freight, getting goods through customs faster. In effect, DHL pioneered a process that revolutionized the way the world does business.

Along with shipping companies, banks were other early customers. Overnight delivery beat the postal system and ensured safe transport of sensitive documents.

In those early days DHL's billing was done by Marge Dalsey on a portable typewriter. She carried the typewriter and did the billing by hand in whatever hotel room the Dalseys happened to be at the end of each month.

When DHL began, the employment criteria were simple. You had to own a car, have a passport, and be prepared to jump on a flight at a moment's notice.

Since then the company has gone global, handling 162 million shipments a year with a fleet of 254 aircraft. It's the ninth largest airline in the world! On the ground DHL's 16,000 vehicles service 120,000 destinations.

DHL sponsored Rebecca Stephens, the first British woman to climb Mount Everest. She explained, "...DHL was my sponsor...in the spring of 1993, as a part of the DHL British Everest Expedition, I quit my job, jumped on a plane to the Himalayas. DHL's catchy signature tune, 'Ain't No Mountain High Enough,' may well have had something to do with it... and to this day I embarrass my friends by leaping up and down like a demented Labrador, waving at every DHL delivery van that passes by."

In 1971, DHL's founders saw the market for moving time-sensitive documents to the Far East. They chose two entrepreneurs, Guy Coombs and Rod Feliciano, to lead the expansion in the Philippines.

DHL Philippines was the fifth DHL station, the first outside the US and the first such service in the Philippines. From four employees servicing two clients, the Manila hub is DHL Worldwide express's largest and most sophisticated center in

Asia, with a nationwide network and staff of over 1,000.

In July 2002, DHL Worldwide Express (Phils) Corporation was incorporated as a joint venture company, 60% owned by DHL Philippines Corp., and 40% by DHL Worldwide Express B.V.I.

DHL Worldwide Express provides international inbound and outbound air express services to and from the Philippines; their local agent, DHL Philippines, is building Wide Wide World — responsible for handling all local courier services. The privately owned company's major shareholders are Deutsche Post World Net, Lufthansa and Japan Airlines.

Del Monte Fresh Produce (Philippines), Inc., an affiliate of Fresh Del Monte Produce, Inc., with its executive offices in Coral Gables, Florida, has roots which spring from the Philippine Packing Corporation (PHILPAK) established in the Philippines in 1920s.

Then, there was a recession in the US; agricultural firms were hard hit, and the California Packing Corporation (CALPAK) was threatened by its pineapple-canning operations, dependent on Hawaiian plantations, where an epidemic destroyed millions of dollars of produce.

CALPAK looked at other tropical regions suitable for growing pineapple. The choice was the Philippines.

PHILPAK was created January 11, 1926 as a subsidiary of CALPAK. But both were better known by the brand name Del Monte. In wasn't until June, 1967, that CALPAK changed its name to Del Monte Corporation, and in 1988 PHILPAK became Del Monte Philippines, Inc.

Throughout the years PHILPAK diversified beyond pineapple growing and processing, becoming a major supplier of fresh processed products in both domestic and international markets.

In 1968, Del Monte Corporation initiated a large-scale banana contract growing operation in Davao. They began with less than 2,000 hectares and two contract farms. By 1975, seven more contracted farms were producing on 5,100 hectares.

Del Monte Corporation was sold in December 1989 and the Davao Banana operations went to Polly Peck International (PPI). PPI Del Monte Tropical Fruit (Philippines) Inc. was the result. But in late 1992, PPI Del Monte Fresh Produce was sold to a Mexican group. The name of the Philippine operation was changed to Del Monte Fresh Produce (Philippines) Inc. ("DMFPPI"). And in 1996, Fresh Del Monte Produce, Inc. was acquired by its current owner, the IAT Group, Inc. It became a public company in November 1997.

Contracted hectares were approximately 9,300 in 2002 with an annual production of over 35 million boxes of primarily Cavendish bananas. In addition, one of DMFPPI's affiliates is in a joint venture producing Del Monte Gold pineapple. DMFPPI sources Champaka pineapple in Cagayan de Oro. The fresh produce is sold in Japan, Korea, China, Hong Kong, Singapore, New Zealand, the Middle East and Pacific Russia.

DMFPPI is certified ISO 2002 (International Standard for Quality Management System). It also provides education to approximately 60 students and supports the Adopt-A-Site project. DMFPPI employs 260 highly trained people with operations and offices in Davao City, Bugo, and Makati City.

INSPIRING JEALOUSY IN PINEAPPLES EVERYWHERE.

Del Monte Gold™
EXTRA SWEET PINEAPPLE

Dow Chemical Philippines, Inc.

The phrase, we live in a "plastic" society, proves far from being a bad thing. Modern society cannot function without chemicals and plastic. Dow Chemical Pacific Limited provides daily benefits in many, many ways — some quite surprising.

The Dow Chemical Company was originally incorporated in 1897, producing bleach on a commercial scale. In 1906 after a merger with Midland Chemical, Dow started its agricultural chemicals division.

In 1914, Herbert Dow shifted from the bleach business to chlorine as a raw material and in 1918, it adopted its diamond trademark. Ahead of its time, Dow hired its first woman researcher in 1929. In 1935, it entered plastics.

Just prior to World War II, the company expanded into Canada. And, during the war, it merged with Corning Glass, producing silicones for military use.

It was in 1953 that the now famous Saran® wrap for household use was introduced.

Always involved in research, the company introduced 23 new products in 1960 alone.

Asahi-Dow Ltd. became the first subsidiary outside North America. Although Dow had been doing business in the Philippines for some time, the company only formally established a Manila office in 1964.

Dow Chemicals are everywhere. Your bedding is likely made from polyurethane raw material supplied by Dow to the foam manufacturer. Your soap contains caustic soda; your shampoo uses emulsifiers, your air conditioner uses coolants. Your jogging shoes are made from polyurethane. Your breakfast cereal was packaged using polyethelene and the package ink comes from Dow chemicals. The refrigerator uses insulation of polyurethane (to increase efficiency and reduce energy consumption). Glass containers are made of polycarbonate.

Your telephone cables are likely wrapped in Dow-produced plastic.

The list goes on and on.

Dow is a "good" corporate neighbor. In 1972 it issued an 11-point Global Pollution Control Guideline. In 1993, Fortune magazine named Dow one of the "Top 10 Environmental Champions."

With its environmental protection focus, Dow has set up a seedling nursery at the Ninoy Aquino Park and Wildlife Nature Center in Quezon City and also provides recycling information to the Polystyrene Manufacturers Association.

Dow also works to improve the lives of the handicapped. In the Philippines, they consult with the Tahanang Walang Hagdanan (House with No Stairs); teaching paraplegics livelihood programs such as soap manufacturing.

During the term of President Ramos, Dow Chemical Pacific Ltd. was judged the "Mabini Presidential Awardee of the Year" for its "exemplary contribution to helping improve the lot of the handicapped."

The Herbert H. Dow Museum in Midland, Michigan. The building is a replica of the original Evans Mill complex where Dow started the Midland Chemical Company, the predecessor to The Dow Chemical Company.

The miracles of science®

When man first walked on the Moon he wore a suit made of 25 layers — 23 were from DuPont.

DuPont, a global science company that places an emphasis on discovery, was founded in 1802 by a French emigrant, Eleuthére Irénée du Pont on the banks of the Brandywine River in Wilmington, Delaware. It began with explosives growing to become a global chemicals, materials and energy company by the 20th century. Into its third century, it continues to deliver science-based solutions — making a difference to everyday lives.

From the small explosives company in Delaware, DuPont now operates in 70 countries worldwide with 135 manufacturing and processing facilities, employing about 85,000 people — approximately half outside the United States.

Through DuPont's research, clothes stretch with Lycra®, workers are protected with Kevlar® and Nomex® fibers, athletes break records with Coolmax®, and non-stick Teflon® is used in everything from fashion to cookware.

After several years of research in the 1930s, nylon, "synthetic silk," was introduced at the 1939 World's Fair in New York. It became a synonym for lady's stockings.

In the Philippines, DuPont opened in 1973 as DuPont Far East, Inc. Philippines. It provides automotive refinishing products, architectural laminating sheets, advance fiber systems, flexographic printing plates,

electronic materials, engineering plastics, industrial polymers, nylon textiles for apparel, polyester films, and specialty chemicals.

At its ISO 9000 certified Crop Protection Plant at Carmelray, Laguna, Dupont repackages fungicides (Manzate®, Curzate®), herbicides (Almix®, Karmex®) and insecticides (Londax® and Lannate®). Another plant in Polomolok, South Catabato, produces and markets Pioneer® premium quality hybrid corn seeds.

In Pasig City, the DuPont Performance Coating Refinish Systems began an automotive Refinish Training Center (RTC) in 1997. It supports training programs for local automotive shops and product distributors.

DuPont's Performance Coatings business works with Don Bosco Institute of Technology, Makati, extending the RTC program enrollment to its vocational program.

DuPont is also involved in various community projects in the Philippines; the reforestation of Mt. Makiling Forest Reserve Watershed; the Productivity Center for the Golden Acres' Home for the Aged, and a program providing free dental and medical clinics for farmers and their families; scholarships for less fortunate students of the Philippine Science High School and Family Farm Schools, and it has lent support to the Pasig River Heritage Marathon.

On July 19, 2002, DuPont began its third century, celebrating its 200th year of scientific achievement and innovation — providing products and services that improve the lives of people everywhere. DuPont delivers science-based solutions for markets that make a difference in people's lives in food and nutrition; health care; apparel; home and construction; electronics; and transportation.

DUPONT
200
YEARS

ExxonMobil

The "Kerosene Clipper", circa 1896

In 1892 it took a year to make the round trip to the Philippines from the east coast of the US. But fast "clipper" ships cut that time. Nicknamed the "Kerosene Clippers", they brought the company's "Cock" brand kerosene used for lighting and cooking.

The original company, Vacuum Oil Company, was formed in 1866 in Rochester, New York by Matthew Ewing and Hiram Everest. John D. Rockefeller of Standard Oil bought 75% interest in Vacuum Oil in 1879. Three years later, he formed the Standard Oil Company of New York (Socony).

Vacuum Oil Co. opened an office in the Philippines in 1896, introducing its lubricating oil for steamships. Previously, marine engineers used castor oil. To handle its growing business, Socony bought land in Pandacan near the Pasig River for future terminal operations. In 1905, the first car arrived in the Philippines. That same year, Socony opened an office in Cebu to handle operations in the Western Visayas and Mindanao.

In 1933 Socony-Vacuum and Standard Oil of New Jersey merged their Far Eastern interests into Standard Vacuum Oil (Stanvac). The company's Philippine business had grown to include 20 installations and sub-stations, 121 service stations, and 700 wholesale distribution agencies.

In 1946 Stanvac became the first oil company to resume operations after WWII. Army tank trucks made deliveries and rebuilding of the terminal finished in 1947. A new office was built on UN Avenue. With 42,000 feet of floor space and fully air-conditioned, it was a milestone for the time.

Stanvac signed a P 33.5 million agreement in 1957 to build a refinery in Limay, Bataan; at that time, the biggest single private investment in Philippine history. Construction started in 1958 and the refinery was inaugurated on April 8, 1961.

A split in 1960 led to another name change; Mobil Oil Corporation, the parent company of today's Mobil Philippines, Inc. which was, itself, incorporated a year later.

After 10 years of absence in the domestic lubricants market, Mobil Phils Inc. re-entered the lubricants business in 1993 offering the widely known "Mobil Lubricants" brand to the automotive, industrial, aviation and marine users.

Then in 2000, the worldwide merger of the two giant oil companies Exxon Corp. and Mobil Corp. brought Mobil Phils Inc and Esso Eastern Chemicals Inc. together. The integration was completed in December, 2001 giving birth to ExxonMobil Petroleum and Chemicals Holdings Inc. (EMPCHI) as the official corporate entity responsible for all aspects of ExxonMobil's business in the country.

In the words of CEO and Chairman Mr. Lee R. Raymond, "Social responsibility may be a comparatively new term now applied to corporations, but it is not a new concept to us. For many decades, ExxonMobil has vigorously adhered to policies and practices that guide the way we do business. The methods we employ to achieve results are as important as the results themselves."

General Electric Philippines, Inc.

General Electric was international in scope even before it was known as General Electric. Both parent companies, Edison Electric Light and Thomson-Houston, operated worldwide, through licensing and patent agreements by Edison, and technical and manufacturing agreements by Thomson-Houston.

In April of 1890 Thomson-Houston installed the first electric streetlights on Real Street in Manila. When the companies merged in 1892 to become General Electric their publication boasted: "Our incandescent and arc lamps extend in an unbroken line around the earth; they shine in the palace of the Mikado as well as in the Opera House in Paris." They could have added "the Metropolitan Opera House in Manila."

GE is a diversified technology, manufacturing and services company with a commitment to achieving worldwide leadership. It is in over 100 countries, with 250 manufacturing plants in 26 nations, employing 313,000 people.

The Manila Carnival of 1932 was huge and GE assisted Meralco in building a veritable "tower of light." The square tower rose 120 feet with a 42 sq. ft. base. Actually a shell of wood supported by a steel framework and covered with cloth, it looked like ordinary masonry. A tough grade of oiled paper diffused the light. The tower, a skyscraper of interesting architecture by day was a picture of beauty by night.

Wholly-owned GE Philippines was incorporated in 1935 to do a broad range of manufacturing, trading and service businesses. GE's gas and steam turbine technology is used by the National Power Corporation, the Manila Electric Company and independent power producers.

GE also supplies appliance manufacturers with thermostats, capacitors, push button switches and fan motors. It sells products ranging from industrial control components to integrated drive systems used in steel mills.

GE Medical Systems provides diagnostic imaging equipment and support services to hospitals and clinics throughout the country. It recently entered the area of networking products and services as well, providing advanced training for service engineers.

GE Philippines mission is to combine the global capabilities of GE with local expertise to bring the company's advanced technology, products and services to the Philippines, working closely with both government and private industry.

Scientific research is an increasingly important part of its activities extending to atomic research. Thus remaining faithful to the original founder, Thomas Edison, who is reputed to have more than a thousand patents on his various inventions. The electric light was only a beginning.

An ad from the AmCham Journal, 1954

Buick Motor Car Company, formed in 1902 by David Buick in Detroit, started it all. Moving to Flint, Michigan, control passed to William Durant, "King of Carriage Makers." Durant led Buick to being the largest automobile manufacturer in the US. His prophetic observation, "a million cars a year would someday be in demand." Quite an understatement today. General Motors was founded on September 16, 1908 and a year later posted sales of US$29,030,000, selling 25,000 cars and trucks; 19 percent of total US sales.

GM's leadership in automotive research and development started in 1912 with its introduction of the electric self-starter, phasing out dangerous hand-crank mechanisms. The firm became the General Motors Corporation on October 13, 1916 and by 1923 was the world's largest producer of cars and trucks.

The company's engineering and manufacturing skills were tested in World War I when it was commissioned to turn its civilian production facilities to that of war materials, within 18 months. Decentralized management and highly flexible local responsibility made possible the rapid conversion — a timetable never believed possible by the enemy. The result was an outpouring of weaponry credited with the winning of the war, changing the face of Europe and giving rise to the United States as a

The Chevrolet "Zafira"

world power. (The Corporation was again tasked to make a complete turnaround of its facilities for the production of war materials during World War II, the Korean Conflict and the Vietnam War.)

In the early 1970s, GM embarked on the "most comprehensive, ambitious, far-reaching, and costly program of its kind in the history of the automobile industry," the redesign of its entire lineup for better fuel economy. Engineers and designers kept the vehicle's comfortable interior, while reducing its weight and exterior size. The first "downsized" cars were GM's 1977 model, full size vehicles — but about a foot shorter and 700 pounds lighter than their predecessors. More vehicle innovations followed suit, including the 1980 model front-wheel drive compact and, in 1985, the first front-wheel drive luxury cars.

By the middle of the '90s, General Motors became the world's first automaker to market specifically

designed electric vehicles to the public — the new EV1 passenger car and the Chevrolet S-10 pick-up truck.

General Motors reestablished its presence in the Philippines in 1997 and today boasts of 5 GM AutoWorld outlets, each carrying the GM lineup of Chevrolet, Opel, Suzuki and Subaru products.

From its humble beginnings as a small motorcar firm in Michigan, General Motors currently sells its vehicles in 200 countries, employing more than 350,000 people worldwide.

An ad for GM's Buick from the AmCham Journal, circa 1924

The Goodyear Company began in a US$ 15,000 converted strawboard factory in Akron, Ohio in 1898. It is now the largest rubber company in the world, and it is also one of the most diversified corporations in the world. Its chief product is tires, and it makes about 2,200 different kinds of tires, including tires for the "moon wagon" that was used by the astronauts when they landed on the earth's satellite.

The first Goodyear offices were established in Manila in 1919, south of the Pasig River, on Muelle de Magallanes near the old insular Treasury building. In those days the city served as a warehousing point for tires and other Goodyear products sold by the country's representatives in China, Japan, the Dutch Indies and other Far East territories.

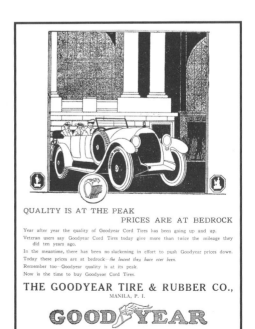

QUALITY IS AT THE PEAK
PRICES ARE AT BEDROCK

Year after year the quality of Goodyear Cord Tires has been going up and up. Veteran users say Goodyear Cord Tires today give more than twice the mileage they did ten years ago.

In the meantime, there has been no slackening in effort to push Goodyear prices down. Today these prices are at bedrock—*the lowest they have ever been.*

Remember too—Goodyear quality is at its peak.

Now is the time to buy Goodyear Cord Tires.

THE GOODYEAR TIRE & RUBBER CO.,
MANILA, P. I.

An early ad from the AmCham Journal

In 1928, when restrictions on the export of rubber seeds were eased, the company brought in "budded stumps" from their plantation in Sumatra to their nursery in Kabasalan, 80 miles from Zamboanga. There the trees thrived and the plantation added to the country's industry.

The original offices and warehouse were destroyed in WWII, but upon the return of American business after the war, the Goodyear offices were re-established in the Wilson Building on Juan Luna Street. In 1949, the headquarters was moved to the Port Area at the corner of 11th and Atlanta streets.

In 1956, with then vice-president Carlos P. Garcia, Goodyear opened a new P 12 million retread and repair plant in Las Piñas. The factory was erected on a 17-hectare plot with the main structure 1200 feet long. Over the years, Goodyear has continued to expand its manufacturing facility that has been certified to world quality management systems that includes the ISO9002, ISO14001 and the QS9000.

Globally, Goodyear is much more than a tire company. Its products range from chemicals, flowing to shoe products to a wide range of industrial products. It operates more than 85 production facilities and of these 45 are outside the United States; five are rubber plantations.

Goodyear-Philippines is proud of the fact that it serves the nation with the most complete line of quality

CHARLES GOODYEAR
Safety Pioneer
WHO DISCOVERED VULCANIZED RUBBER 100 YEARS AGO
1839 · 1939

consumer and commercial tires built with exclusive 'Trinuum Tyre Technology'.

The company maintains branches and warehouses in Cebu, Iloilo, Cagayan de Oro and Davao, and has Servitek and TyrePro dealership locations scattered all over the country distributing and marketing their products.

Johnson's Baby Powder is the rock upon which the success of Johnson & Johnson (Philippines), Inc. has been based for over four decades.

The company was incorporated in 1956; in a rented two-room office in the Cu-Unjieng Building on Dasmariñas Street, Manila with four employees.

It moved to the Port Area in 1957, where a filling line to manufacture Johnson Baby Powder was set up. Two years later products included Johnson's Baby Oil, Baby Shampoo, Baby Soap and Baby Cream. By 1960, Johnson's Baby Cologne was introduced.

A joint venture with Metro Drug Corporation, Philippine Medical Products, Inc., followed to manufacture and sell MODESS®, BAND-AID® Adhesive Bandages, medical tapes, and related products. This same year, the office was transferred to what is now the Filipinas Life Building, Makati.

In 1962, a new plant was constructed in Pasig, producing Johnson's Baby Products and Philippine Medical Products, and Johnson's Baby Lotion was introduced into the market. From 1965 to 1970 the launch of new baby toiletries products, first aid, dental and other products provided growth in the market by targeting adults as users of Johnson's Baby Products. In 1971,

Augusto C. Escueta, Jr., was appointed President, the first Filipino to hold this position in the company.

In the early 1970s the company expanded. An R & D department began in 1975, and a new manufacturing plant in Paranaque was inaugurated in 1977, with new high speed filling lines for powder and liquids to cope with growth. The first Philippine-made Johnson & Johnson disposable diaper was sold in 1978.

Like all Johnson & Johnson companies worldwide, Johnson & Johnson Philippines adheres strongly to "Our Credo," a statement of principles written in 1944 by Robert Wood Johnson, a son of one of the founders and long-time chairman of the corporation. It states: the company's first obligation is to its customers; the second is to it's employees; the community and the environment are its third; and its stockholders, its fourth.

In 1992, a formal contributions program was organized to strengthen its commitment to the Credo. This program had an impact on health care and education of under-privileged children and natural disaster relief. By 2001 the program had become a model for Johnson & Johnson companies in the Asia-Pacific region. The company was selected as one of 23 companies that best exemplified corporate social responsibility in the Philippines by the Financial Executives Institute of the Philippines (FINEX).

After months of negotiations in 1995 a merger between Scott Paper and Kimberly Clark was announced. The merger created a Fortune 100 global consumer products company, with new opportunities for growth in the international market.

KIMBERLY CLARK

Kimberly Clark was established in Neenah, Wisconsin in 1872 by four enterprising young businessmen — John Kimberly, Havilah Babcock, Charles B. Clark, and Frank C. Shattuck. By 1880 the company was incorporated.

The firm bought farmland and water power rights along the Fox River, three miles east of Appleton, Wisconsin, and built a large pulp and paper mill, a hotel and 60 houses, which were sold or rented.

The company began to manufacture creped cellulose wadding called Cellucotton as a substitute for cotton. It was used as bandages for wounded soldiers in World War I. After the war, Cellucotton led to the development of Kotex feminine pads and Kleenex facial tissue.

Growing use of cosmetics and cold cream led to disposable Kleenex facial tissues. First called "cold cream towels" and advertised as a "sanitary cold cream remover," a name change in 1930 to emphasize usage as a "disposable handkerchief" boosted sales.

In 1942 Kimberly Clark went to war. The company produced M-45 anti-aircraft mounts and fuses for heavy shells and other military goods.

The introduction of more "disposable" household products after the war spurred great growth. Big consumer hits included Huggies diapers and, in the early 1980s, the introduction of Depends diapers. Adult incontinence was a taboo topic but an ad campaign featuring actress June Allyson urging people to "get back into life" made the product acceptable. It gave people with this condition the ability to resume an active lifestyle.

SCOTT

Brothers Seymour and Irvin Scott ran a paper commission business for 12 years but the poor economy of the 1870s ran them out of business. Irvin and his younger brother, Clarence, then decided to form their own company. Irvin reportedly borrowed money from his father-in-law to form the Scott Paper Company.

By 1890 Scott Paper Company had become the leading producer of bathroom tissue in the US. They also introduced the first paper towels in American. Scott invented disposable paper towels for use in Philadelphia classrooms to help prevent the spread of the common cold from child to child.

In 1916, Scott Paper adopted the slogan "it's the counted sheet that counts" and took the lead against their competitors by selling bathroom tissue by the sheet. This changed the marketing strategy of the entire industry.

Working on a catchy title for a 1921 commercial motion picture portraying the entire process of ScotTissue towel manufacturing, people looked close at the towels themselves. They noticed the knit of the paper, it's cross-weave. Someone said, "it's the fibres, they're…" before the person could continue the sentence a chorus rang out, "They're thirsty!" This brought about "Thirsty Fibre" and the film was titled, "The Absorbing Story of Thirsty Fibre."

Scott Paper was the first to advertise bathroom tissue on national television.

Cover image from the company's publication "Shared Values" published in 1997

Mr. R.G. Miller (7th from right) and the first group of Production staff of Kraft Philippines

Our kitchens would be pretty empty if it weren't for Kraft. Kraft is the largest branded food and beverage company in North America and the second largest in the world.

Although Kraft Foods, along with Kraft Foods Philippines, Inc., was not formed as an integrated and fully merged company until 1989, its history goes back more than a century.

James Kraft started his cheese business in 1903 in Chicago, Illinois. C.W. Post introduced the first cereal meals in 1895 in Battle Creek, Michigan. Thomas McInnerney was a pioneer in the American dairy industry. And Oscar Mayer, a Bavarian immigrant, established a meat business in 1873 in Detroit, Michigan. They became the core of Kraft.

In 1892, a coffee blend developed by Joel Cheek for the Maxwell House Hotel in Nashville, Tennessee, became so popular, the hotel owner decreed no other coffee would be served to guests. Named MAXWELL HOUSE®, legend relates it was President Theodore Roosevelt who pronounced the blend "good to the last drop," as its slogan goes.

Jell-O™ is a brand recognized by 99% of Americans. It has also become familiar to Russian astronauts. In June 1996, Shannon Lucid, an astronaut on a 140-day mission to the Russian Mir space station, kept track of time by wearing pink socks and eating Jell-O on Sundays. After Lucid served her Russian crewmates their first Jell-O as a special Easter treat, they decided to share a bag every Sunday night. She wrote: "It is the greatest improvement in space flight since my first flight over 10 years ago." Since, back on earth, over 400 million boxes of Jell-O are sold every year; many people agree with Mrs. Lucid.

Kraft Foods Philippines, Inc. is an integration of two business organizations —Kraft Foods Philippines and General Foods Philippines — following the 1989 US merger of their mother companies. Kraft Foods Philippines, established in 1963, began its manufacturing of Kraft Cheddar Cheese in Paranaque, Rizal, on April 8, 1965. General Foods Philippines, incorporated in 1974, introduced TANG® Orange powder mix and Calumet® baking powder.

In 2000, Philip Morris acquired Nabisco Holdings Corp., a leading US food company and subsequently integrated it into the Kraft Foods business. In the Philippines, Nabisco's famous brands are now part of the Kraft Foods Philippines, Inc. array of products and brands locally available.

The Kraft Cares program of Kraft Foods International donated P 2 million to the "Project Big Brother" a program aimed at upgrading the quality of high school education in public schools, two of which are in Manila. The project also sponsors public schoolteachers in graduate schools, so they can update and enhance their teaching abilities.

Indeed, "Kraft Cares"....

Marsman-Drysdale Group

Established after the marriage of Jan Hendrik Marsman of Amsterdam, Holland and Mary Angus Blythe of Edinburgh, Scotland in September 1920, the Marsman business conglomerate started as a mining enterprise in Baguio — the Itogon Mining Company.

The Marsmans ventured into other industries and, on October 15, 1929, establilshed Marsman & Company, Inc. By 1939, Marsman conglomerates were in trading, and a slew of other industries in addition to gold mining.

In 1968 George W. Drysdale, Sr., husband of Anne Marsman, the Marsman couple's only child, took the helm. It was during Drysdale's tenure that Marsman — now called the Marsman-Drysdale Group (MDG) — diversified into pharmaceuticals, healthcare, trading, travel and tourism, food and agribusiness.

In 1969, the Marsman Estate Plantation, Inc. (MEPI) became one of the first banana plantations in Mindanao. This was followed by the Camarines Minerals, Inc. (CMI) in 1976, which is a holding company for the Group's more than 3,000 hectares of gold mining claims.

Marsman Tours and Travel Corporation (MTTC) started in 1979. It is an industry leader in outbound travel and the most multi-awarded tour operator in the country, with nine government-awarded Kalakbay Awards.

In 1986, Oro Verde Holding and Development Corp. (OVHDC) began

its 236-hectare orchard on Guimaras Island, with over 45,000 trees of highly esteemed Carabao mango.

Marsman-Drysdale Agribusiness Ventures, Inc. (MDAVI) began in 1994 in South Cotobato. It houses a cutting-edge processing facility that grades, packs and cools 12,000 kilos of exportable asparagus daily.

In 1997, George W. Drysdale, Sr. turned over MDG's chairmanship to his son, George Marsman Drysdale, Jr. Drysdale Jr. further developed the Group's agribusiness, expanding banana plantations from 1,300 hectares to 4,000; the number of agri-related MDG companies grew from five to fifteen. He also pioneered the development of organic bananas — the first of its kind in the international banana market, with global partners for marketing and sales.

In January 2000, the Group merged Pelican Agro Products, Inc. and Philippine Far East Agro Products, Inc. into Marsman-Drysdale Foods Corporation. The food processing company exports VHT-processed Carabao mangoes and produces Drysdale juices, as well as fruit and vegetable purees.

True to Jan and Mary Marsman's

commitment to make social responsibility a strong drive behind the Marsman group of companies, the Marsman-Drysdale Foundation, Inc. (MDFI) is the heart of the business conglomerate. The Foundation conducts Value Formation and Marriage Encounter seminars for managers, supervisors and other employees.

The Foundation also builds sanitary facilities, artesian wells, chapels and other multi-purpose structures. Free medical and dental clinics directly benefit 4,000 patients. Its cooperative development project provides training and seed funding for rural cooperatives, also running adult non-formal education programs.

A Marsman-Drysdale plantation in Mindanao.

Microsoft®

It was in 1975 when then college students Bill Gates and Paul Allen first came up with the idea of establishing a company focused on developing software. In Bill's dorm room, their eyes caught an ad in Popular Mechanics for a "personal computer" called MITS Altair 8800; a build-it-yourself kit for hobbyists.

Bill and Paul ordered the Altair. In the mail came bags of parts and photocopied instructions. After weeks of soldering, they had a computer roughly the size of a bread-box, with rows of switches and blinking lights.

The "brain" of the Altair—an inexpensive Intel 8080 microprocessor—made possible a truly human scale computer, as opposed to the bulky, heavy mainframes set in air-conditioned glass rooms and touched only by trained technicians.

The two realized the Altair needed software. Their business sense told them microprocessors would become more powerful and less expensive, allowing computers to reach more people, creating a huge demand for software.

They formed their own software company — calling it Micro-Soft.

Over the years, the PC has grown from a hobbyist's toy into an indispensable tool. It has revolutionized how we deal with information, how we communicate, how we work, learn and play.

From its roots in programming

Bill Gates and President Gloria Magapagal-Arroyo prior to the APEC meeting in Shanghai, October 2001.

languages and operating systems, Microsoft produces just about every kind of imaginable software...from industrial strength servers to games. "A computer on every desk and in every home"— the vision Microsoft helped turn into reality.

The US-based Microsoft Corporation entered the Philippines on August 30, 1995. Microsoft Philippines, Inc. provides innovative products, meeting the Filipino consumers' evolving needs. But more than that, Microsoft joins the country's pursuit of a better life for its people.

Each Microsoft product is dual purpose: one, to make it easier and more enjoyable to maximize the full power of personal computing; and two, to provide firms with efficient

solutions to maximize productivity.

Microsoft's corporate responsibility is clear. Through its Connected Learning Community (CLC) program, Microsoft Philippines reaches high school students from Batanes to Mindanao. The program provides underprivileged high schools with high-tech computer laboratories with networked PCs, software, peripherals (scanner, digital camera and printer), internet connection, and training for school administrators and teachers. The CLC program aims to uplift the quality of secondary education by giving Filipino students access to a technology they would otherwise not have the opportunity to tap. And they've made a good start.

Nestlé products have been on the scene for some time. In fact they were available in the Philippines in 1895, only 30 years after Henri Nestlé started selling his infant cereal product. From the trading houses in London and Paris came several condensed milk brands and, together with the infant cereal, all were available in Manila and Iloilo.

Before 1900 there were sales branches in Cebu and Zamboanga too, indicating the wide use of Nestlé brand products in the local market.

After WWII, the company started operations with a new name, Filipro, Inc., continuing to import Milo®, Nido®, Milkmaid® and Nescafé®.

When the government imposed import controls in the early 50s, Filipro was forced to become a distributor of peanut butter, fruit preserves and patis (fish sauce) to keep operations going. Success made Nestlé think seriously of building its own plant.

Today, Nestlé Philippines operates six factories supplying the local market, and it exports breakfast cereals. Built in 1962, the Alabang factory manufactures Nescafe® instant coffee and evaporated and sweetened condensed milk products.

In 1976, a second factory was built in Cabuyao, Laguna to make Milo®, milk brands and infant foods. Two more factories went up in Batangas and Bulacan. The company employs about 5,000 people and has become one of the top companies in the Nestlé world. It is also among the Top 10 corporations in the Philippines.

Together with General Mills it formed Cereal Partners Worldwide (CPW). Nestlé Philippines' factory in Lipa City exports the entire range of Nestlé breakfast cereal products under the ASEAN Industrial Joint Venture program. Recently, the company entered the pet care market with both Friskies® and Alpo® pet foods products.

Nestlé initiates community projects in areas where Nestlé operates. And they do not expect direct benefits. Graduates in skills development are not obliged to work for Nestlé; farmers from its

Henri Nestlé, Founder

agronomy programs may sell their crops to anyone. Nestlé also established the Cabuyao Integrated Community Development Foundation for four barangays in Cabuyao. This led to the formation of several NGOs working on livelihood programs such as pottery-making, balut-production and candle-making.

The Lipa factory runs the "Cut and Sew," program, providing jobs in producing factory uniforms and similar needs. The unemployed wives of the Lipa factory's barangay are engaged in the production of cut flowers.

All factories have tree planting programs; the Alabang Factory supports a local "clean up a creek" project and bamboo planting. The safety and preservation of the ecology and the environment are always on the agenda of Nestlé Philippines.

Transportando productos de la Nestlé & Anglo-Swiss Condensed Milk Co. en el Muelle del Rey (Filipinas).

The original Spanish reads:"Transportation of Nestlé products, and Anglo-Swiss Condensed Milk Co. on the Muelle del Rey." – Binondo, late 1890s

International Consultants, Inc.

OMNI Insurance Brokers, Inc.

William Ligenza, Founder

OMNI Insurance Brokers was founded in 1977 and incorporated in 1979. This Philippine based company is a licensed all-lines direct insurance brokerage firm, placing insurance on risks located primarily in the Philippines. The company began by specializing in medical, life and accident insurance plans. Within two years, Omni expanded in servicing all lines of general commercial, industrial and personal insurance.

Founded by William Ligenza with Jean Pierre Gautier, John Young, Teodita Gautier, Carissima Young, Ma. Trinidad Bonillo and Jesus Fortez, the company felt "no policy was too small." This charming attitude made it a favorite with the expatriate community that it primarily serves.

In 1971, the first Omni company was incorporated in Hong Kong. It was set up to provide various financial services, including insurance, to the expatriate community worldwide with a focus on those living and working in Asia.

Incorporated and managed by expats, OMNI Capital marketed its services to expats involved in the Vietnam War, the construction industry and also the ASEAN oilfields. It even worked with the motion picture industry and handled the insurance needs of co-productions filmed in the Philippines. Today the company handles the needs of thousands of families on almost every continent.

OMNI is known for its ability to service employee benefit plans. The company services all lines of insurance product to include policy design and wholesale development for underwriting firms.

Today the company continues to project its strength in Group Benefit Plans to new and existing clients. The company also has insurance specialization in certain industries: energy, mining and entertainment risks.

OMNI currently places a significant amount of business with Health Maintenance Organizations such as Lifecare, Blue Care, Philamcare, CAP Health and others. It also networks with other brokers in Malaysia, Hong Kong, Cambodia, Australia, Vietnam and are adding more locations.

Another program designed by OMNI for the Philippines is the OMNI Expat Benefits Associated

Phil., Inc. (OEBA). This is an organization established by a group of expats to provide other expats, regardless of nationality (including qualified Philippine nationals) with access to professional goods and services at group prices and/or with special benefits not normally offered to smaller groups or individuals.

Given the founder's love of the game of golf, it should come as no surprise that OMNI offers "Sportsman's Insurance." Coverage includes injury to the public, personal accident, the breakage of sport's equipment, fire and theft and, naturally, "Hole-in-one." The golfer is insured (even in a friendly game) proven that the hole-in-one is witnessed by at least two players in the same flight and is formally acknowledged by the Golf Club where the hole-in-one was scored.

PFIZER, Inc., celebrated its 150th anniversary in 1999. Pfizer, founded in 1849, still produces pharmaceuticals and still carries the same name as when it was established by Charles Pfizer and Charles Erhart, two young emigrant cousins from Germany.

In the beginning, Pfizer had one product and two employees. Stagecoaches provided the fastest transportation on land and steamboats on rivers. Medicine as we know it was in its infancy. Diphtheria, typhoid, tuberculosis and pneumonia took a terrible toll on people of all ages. Doctors had few remedies at their disposal.

Today, many diseases — such as smallpox, which once annihilated entire populations — have been almost eradicated. Others that were fatal can now be cured. Others, such as polio, have been greatly reduced.

Pfizer helped to achieve many of these breakthroughs. In what would be a significant contribution to humanity, they took Alexander Fleming's discovery, penicillin, and successfully mass-produced it. The discovery was made in 1928 but it was just before WWII that the company began to make it available in large quantities, saving the lives of millions and marking the beginning of modern medicine.

It was during the war years that Pfizer changed from a chemical manufacturing company into a pharmaceutical company, selling its products under its own label. Research was — and is — an important part of Pfizer's business, leading to newer and better antibiotics such as streptomycin.

Pfizer entered the Philippines in 1949, with it products imported and distributed by Metro Drug Corporation. In 1954 Pfizer was registered as a Philippine corporation with a total of 9 employees.

In 2000, Pfizer merged with Warner Lambert, making for one of the biggest mergers in global pharmaceutical history. This union also created the world's largest and possibly most talented biomedical research organization.

In line with its commitment to improving the quality of life, Pfizer works with various organizations, holding regular medical and dental missions, and sponsors programs such as the Polio Eradication Campaign, World Health Day and the Doctors-to-the-Barrios. Partnered with United Way International, the company provided disaster relief operations and livelihood support for victims of the Mayon Volcano eruption in 2001.

Pfizer also set up virtual libraries in the University of Santo Tomas and Philippine General Hospital, giving doctors access to critical information. In the Philippine Heart Center, the virtual library is also available for the use of patients.

William C. Steere, Jr., Chairman of the Board and CEO said, "…our most important achievement is this: In virtually every corner of the world, at every hour of the day and night, millions of people are benefiting from Pfizer medicines."

An Agricultural Division sales representative in the field

Philam Insurance Company, Inc.

The Philippine American Life and General Insurance Company, better known as 'Philamlife,' is a one-of-a-kind insurance company. Financed almost exclusively by US capital, it has 100 percent Filipino management.

From a single life insurance company established in 1947, the Group has grown to more than 30 affiliates and subsidiaries engaged in life and general insurance, health care, pre-need, banking, credit cards, mutual funds, property holdings and development, call center operations, information technology, and an exclusive membership club.

In its first year of operations, Earl Carroll, then president, anticipated outward dollar remittance would soon be difficult, with imports out-running exports. Exchange controls were imposed in 1949.

Carroll insisted that dependence on outside sources of finance ought to be lessened and, instead, "we should seek the latent savings of the masses of people."

How to do it? "Through insurance companies." He cited pre-war statistics showing the average annual payments of policyholders in the Philippines was only about P 200. His theory was to join thousands of policyholders to build a "mighty river of money… flowing into the great reservoir of capital that spurs the economy."

The "great reservoir of capital" spilled over into loans and investments. At first Philamlife channeled its excess funds into gilt-

In 1957, Philamlife constructed its headquarters along U.N. Avenue (formerly Isacc Peral), Ermita; it was a prizewinning design that remains a landmark today, though the company has recently built a modern skyscraper in Makati. (Photo: Lico Collection)

edged securities and first-mortgage loans. Later, it went into non-traditional areas, investing half its funds in construction or financing construction of residential units, office buildings and manufacturing plants.

In the 1950s, Philamlife developed a modern subdivision called "Philam Homes" in Quezon City. After the first four were completed, demand among policyholders wanting to buy forced Philamlife to a lottery to determine purchasers. This scenario was repeated when the company developed "Philam Village" in the Las Piñas area of Metro Manila in the 1960s.

In 1957, Philamlife constructed its headquarters along U.N. Avenue in Ermita, Manila; a prizewinning, landmark design housing its main offices. Philamlife likewise provided loans or equity to help the construction of hospitals such as the Makati Medical

Center, the Manila Doctors Hospital, and the Cebu Doctors Hospital.

The company also provided substantial financing for the construction of the SLEX Skyway, the Cavite Coastal Road and a number of power-generating plants.

On its 50th anniversary, the Philam Foundation was organized to contribute to improving the quality of life in livelihood generation, health, education and youth, arts and culture, and community development.

The ultimate accolade received by Philamlife is the Presidential Citation conferred in 1994 by President Fidel Ramos on its service to the country and the Filipino people.

In 1996, construction began on Makati's Philamlife Tower. Finished in time for the new millenium, it was then the tallest building in the country. Philamlife continues to grow.

Philip Morris, Esq. opened his retail tobacco shop on Bond Street in London in the middle of the 19th century. In 1900, the company was appointed tobacconist to King Edward VII and by 1902 the company was incorporated in the US. In the words of one of their more popular brands "they've come a long way."

In the 1950s Philip Morris started to diversify beyond tobacco products. In 1969 diversification was boosted with the acquisition of the 115 year-old Miller Brewing Company. In the mid-80s their purchase of General Foods and Kraft Foods, was the largest non-oil acquisition in US history.

Philip Morris entered the Philippines in 1955 under a licensing agreement with local manufacturer La Suerte Cigar and Cigarette Factory. It was its first such agreement outside the US. In 1993, Philip Morris Philippines, Inc. (PMPh) was formally established in the Philippines, the 15th largest tobacco market in the world.

PNPh's flagship brands Marlboro®, the world's Number One cigarette, and Philip Morris®, the premium menthol cigarette in the market, account for more than a quarter of the market. The two brands generate more than P 8 billion in annual excise taxes for the government.

As a responsible marketer of an adult product, Philip Morris leads the industry in keeping cigarettes out of the hands of children. Their Youth Smoking Prevention program, which consists of three components: the "I am S.T.R.O.N.G...I am Responsible" values education program, the Youth Retail Access Prevention program and a multi-media YSP advertising campaign has been endorsed by the Secretary of Education to become part of the curriculum of every public secondary school.

But Philip Morris is also the world's largest consumer packaged goods company. It is the number one tobacco company; Kraft Foods is the second largest food firm in the world, and Miller Brewing Company is the second largest beer company in the US.

Philip Morris supports a host of socio-civic projects, including reforestation and construction of school buildings for the communities of its key shareholders. For the tobacco-growing provinces, PMPh funds several projects to improve the lives of tobacco farmers and their families as well as to modernize farming techniques to improve agricultural yield.

PMPh is also recognized as a corporate leader in the promotion of arts and culture in the Philippines.

Its Jazz Concerts have been enjoyed by a great many. The company is the proponent and exclusive sponsor of the Philippine Art Awards. They have attracted thousands of participating artists since 1994.

The company profile states: "We truly believe that we can make a difference in the world, and we will continue our unwavering efforts to do just that...wherever there are people in need."

The Lincoln Center Jazz Orchestra (LCJO) headed by multi-awarded trumpeter Wynton Marsalis with veteran Pinoyjazz statesman, Lito Molina, and former first lady, Ming Ramos, a jazz afficionado herself, at a perfromance held at the Cultural Center of the Philippines in 1998 as part of the "Philip Morris Rhythms" concert series. (Photo: Ritchie Quirino collection)

Philippine Long Distance Telephone Co.

Governor General Henry Stimson signed into law Act No. 3436 on November 28, 1928. The bill passed by the Philippine Legislature gave Philippine Long Distance Telephone Company (PLDT) the franchise to establish and operate telephone services.

The franchise stipulated that the company would establish lines to the following points: Baguio within one year, Manila-Legaspi within three years, Manila-Cebu-Negros within another four years and connections within Ilocos province and Aparri within another four years. PLDT was ahead of time on all.

By 1936, a nationwide telephone system linked the Philippines at strategic points in Luzon, in the Visayas and in Mindanao. Overseas radio telephone services were established in 1933. By the end of their first decade there were 28,579 telephones in service, the company employed 927 people and the flat monthly rate of service was P 7.50.

Now, of course, approximately 10 out of every 100 Filipinos have a fixed-line telephone; there are nearly two million cellular phone subscribers and roughly 300,000 Internet subscribers. The monthly rate is also slightly higher.

PLDT also went into space. In 1996 it launched the Philippines first (and one of Asia's most powerful) international communications and broadcast satellites—Aguila II.

PLDT's franchise, which extends to 2028, authorizes it to provide virtually every type of telecommunications service throughout the country. It has a network of 177 central office exchanges serving the Metro Manila area and 191 other cities and municipalities. At the end of 1998, the number of access lines in service was 1.6 million, which represented about 60% of all access lines in the country.

PLDT operates the only nationwide digital microwave backbone, which connects its own exchanges with 1,010 other local exchanges, including those operated by the government. The company also put into service the country's first nationwide all-fiber-optic network designed to handle heavy volumes of voice, data and video transmissions. To provide international long distance services, PLDT uses three international gateway switching exchanges, submarine cables and satellite systems that give it worldwide connection capability.

Ramon Cojuangco, the first Filipino PLDT president, headed the corporation from 1967 until his death in 1984. It was under his watch that the company grew to the multi-billion giant it is today. Cojuangco initiated a series of expansion and modernization programs.

In 1998, the company's controlling ownership was transferred from the Cojuangco Family to the Hong Kong-based First Pacific Group.

Commonwealth President Manuel Quezon, with J.E. Hamilton Stevenot (Vice President of PLDT) inaugurating Hong Kong-Manila radiophone – 1933.

Procter and Gamble has been a part of Filipino life for over sixty-seven years. The company traces its roots to 1908, when two American ex-troopers, Edwin Burke and Ernest Young, formed a partnership—the Manila Refining Company. The business was initially engaged in the manufacture of candles and fertilizer. Their factory was originally located at the foot of the Maypajo Bridge in Caloocan City.

By 1913, and business flourishing, the company was incorporated and given a new name—Philippine Manufacturing Corporation (PMC) and in the same year operations were moved to Velasquez, Tondo—a growing commercial area.

Crisscrossing canals in the area allowed delivery of raw materials to the factory and the Tutuban rail station aided in the distribution of finished goods to the provinces. In addition, the area bordered the Escolta—Manila's early "downtown." The Tondo plant played a significant role in the company's history. (It became the first Procter and Gamble plant in Asia after P&G bought PMC in 1935.)

In 1914, PMC built its own coconut oil mill. It also launched two brands that survived up to the last quarter of the century: Purico®, the first vegetable shortening manufactured in the country (1919-1985), and Star® margarine (1931-1994).

At the outbreak of World War II, PMC's US officials were held at the Sto. Tomas Interment Camp, and the operation of the plant was taken over by the Japanese. Operations stopped in 1944 when fuel oil ran out. And the plant was totally destroyed during Liberation.

When the war ended, reconstruction of the plant started. PMC resumed operations in 1947. New facilities were installed, including a canning plant. New brands were introduced in quick succession: Perla® (1949); Sunshine bulk margarine (1949) and Camay® soap (1950), the first quality beauty soap manufactured in the country.

The 1950s saw the emergence of two of the company's more famous products—Tide® (1957) and Dari Crème® (1959), the country's first refrigerated butter-like margarine. The 1960s produced Safeguard® soap (1966), touted as the stellar brand launch of the decade.

In 1987, the Company merged with Richardson Vicks Corporation and adopted a new corporate name, Procter and Gamble Philippines (P&GP). In May, 1996, P&PG moved to its state-of-the-art facilities in Cabuyao, Laguna.

It is no accident that Procter and Gamble is one of the most dynamic business firms today, marketing an array of leading household consumer products. Sixty-seven years of listening, adapting, and experimenting have produced an organization truly responsive to the needs of Filipino consumers.

After 60 historic years, the Tondo plant formally closed down in mid-1997 and all operations moved to Cabuyao, Laguna. (Photo: AmCham Journal, March 1950)

The Prudential Insurance Company of America was founded by John F. Dryden in 1875. It was then called the Prudential Friendly Society and held office in a Gothic building on Broad Street in Newark, New Jersey.

Prudential was the first life insurance company in the US to introduce a basic insurance plan that cost as little as three cents a week.

Since then it has become one of the largest financial services companies in the world. Prumerica Life Insurance Company, Inc. was established in the Philippines in 1998 and is a wholly owned subsidiary of Prudential. Prumerica is the name used for their satellites outside the US. The entire group is easily recognizable by its famous logo – the Rock of Gibraltar.

More and more people in the Philippines are recognizing the fact that they will have to take responsibility for securing their own financial well-being. As the standard of living of the Filipino people improves, most look for ways to protect their lifestyle and provide for their family's financial security and for their children's education. They also plan for their future retirement.

The primary purpose of life insurance is to provide protection against the unforeseen events in life. Prumerica trains its "Life Planners" as specialists in analyzing customer's protection insurance needs. They are also experienced in designing

Courtesy of Prudential Financial, Inc.

Prumerica Financial
The Prumerica Life Insurance Company, Inc.
A Prudential Financial company

programs specifically tailored to meet a client's needs.

Obviously, everyone is unique. Each person's situation, age, family, annual income and assets are different. Therefore, no one insurance plan could possibly meet everyone's need. For this reason, Life Planners attempt to understand a person's requirements before proposing an appropriate insurance program. These programs can be easily altered and revised should the requirements change.

The company's Life Planners are selected carefully and then trained to ensure they fulfill Drydens' dream of

providing the best possible service to each customer.

Global Volunteer Day started as Prudential's National Volunteer Day. The first Volunteer Day was held on October 28, 1995. More than 5,000 Prudential employees and their families volunteered in over 100 community service projects.

Prudential's Global Volunteer Day has grown to become one of the largest corporate-sponsored volunteer programs in the world. During the Global Volunteer Day held on October 6, 2001, 37,000 Prudential Financial employees and friends joined together and donated an unprecedented 300,000 hours to 849 organized community projects in 17 countries around the world, including the Philippines.

The founder's fundamental concept "to practice the eternal principle of love toward others and one's family, which is the foundation of society" continues more than a century later.

SINGER®

Singer Sewing Machine Company

Isaac Singer invented his sewing machine in 1851, and news of the invention spread as he traveled with his demonstration machine around US country fairs. In 1855, it was awarded first prize at the World's Fair in Paris. Singer joined forces with Edward Clark to form I.M. Singer & Co.

Clark developed a hire-purchase plan, the prototype for installment or time payment. It moved a lot of machines profitably.

Since then, the red "S" has become familiar around the world. One of Singer's early ads relates two friends debating the possibility of the moon being inhabited. "There is a simple way of settling the matter," he said, "Across the street is a Singer shop. Go into it and ask the manager. For assuredly, if there is anyone on the moon, the Singer Sewing Machine Company will have a shop there."

They may not be on the moon, but the company has certainly been in the Philippines since 1875. However, it was only on October 24, 1910 the company formally received its license to operate.

Its growth was assured by setting up company-managed retail shops in the provinces. Through its hundreds of sales and service representatives, Singer successfully promoted the machine concept of sewing.

Consumer acceptance was then, and still is, largely due to three factors: the proven quality of the machines themselves, the availability of reliable service throughout the country and the liberal payment terms offered. Singer became the generic term for sewing machine.

Singer machines are standard equipment in factories, shops and homes throughout the country. As an export product, clothes manufactured in the Philippines— sewn on Singer machines—add greatly to the national income and to the welfare of the manufacturers employees.

The Singer Company has evolved over the last century and a half to become a major distributor of consumer products. It offers a wide range of home audio and video equipment, kitchen appliances, home aids and furniture. And it still offers alternative purchase plans and affordable financing terms.

Perhaps not yet on the moon, but Singer showrooms are located in strategic locations in key cities. There are 210 dealers nationwide and a complement of 1,000 sales agents.

Portion of a vintage Singer Company ad on a postcard. (From the Jonathan Best Collection)

St. Luke's
Medical Center

World Class Technology and Expertise
in Caring Hands

St. Luke's Medical Center was established in 1903 as a dispensary by Episcopalian Missions. Originally located in Calle Magdalena, Manila, "San Lucas" was a consistent Model Hospital Awardee and ultimately a Hall of Famer in the pre-war years.

World War II found its Filipino and American staff intact, its building spared. After Liberation patients increased and a larger space was needed.

In August 1959, St. Luke's moved to its current site in Cathedral Heights, Quezon City. The succeeding years saw the hospital continue advancing in medical expertise and technology.

But by 1971, St. Luke's was having financial difficulties. In 1974, liquidity problems brought the hospital to a standstill. Bishop C. Cabanban, the first Filipino Episcopal Bishop and the head of the Philippine Episcopal Church, stepped in. He overhauled the hospital's management system; disbanded the Board of Governors and created an all-volunteer Board of Trustees. Incorporating it as a non-stock, non-profit, charitable institution, he sought help from prominent US lawyer William Quasha.

Quasha's appointment proved the turning point for the 72-year old institution. He and his team immediately worked to restore the hospital to its former standing; new organizational and operational concepts were adopted. Funds were sourced to acquire up-to-date, revenue-generating equipment.

Thus St. Luke's, largely due to

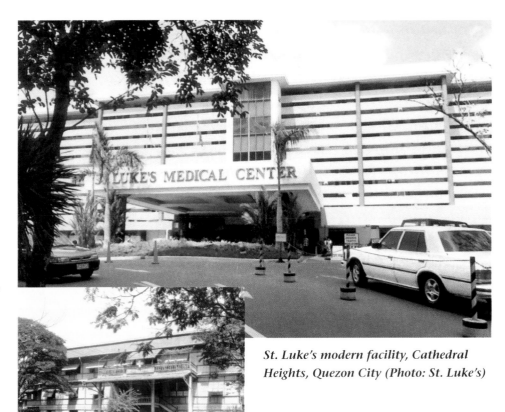

St. Luke's modern facility, Cathedral Heights, Quezon City (Photo: St. Luke's)

St. Luke's Hospital, Calle Magdalena, Manila – 1928 (Photo: AHC)

Quasha's persuasive powers, saved money through donations from suppliers and gained in technology through subsidized training by distributors of the new state-of-the-art equipment. Additional rooms were built, advanced equipment acquired, and medical excellence established.

In 1984, St. Luke's was renamed St. Luke's Medical Center. In 1991, it was recognized as the "Best Philippine Company in Financial Management" by the World Executive Digest and the Asian Institute of Management.

The once ailing and nearly bankrupt hospital is now one of Asia's most progressive. The management system ensures that every peso earned reverts back to the hospital and is invested in the best facilities and recruiting of the best-trained and most-experienced professionals.

St. Luke's also aspires to achieve a holistic approach to healing, one that looks after a patient's total well being. This dictates attending to a person's mental, emotional and psychological needs aside from just the physical. By undertaking new projects to imbibe more holistic methods of healing, St. Luke's continues to break new ground in medicine and total patient care.

United Parcel Service

In 1907 an enterprising 19-year-old from Seattle, Washington, James E. Casey, and some teenage friends borrowed US$ 100 and started a messenger service—the United Parcel Service. From a basement office they delivered anything from hand-written notes and telegrams to bail money, later switching to home delivery service for local retail outlets. Casey patterned UPS to military precision and emphasized reliability, round-the-clock service and low rates.

Since its inception, UPS understood its reputation depends almost exclusively on the front-line people making the daily pickups and deliveries. Ted Gradolf, UPS's VP of worldwide sales said: "It certainly started with Jim Casey... The only thing we have to offer is service, and to the extent that we offer and provide good service we will continue to be successful."

UPS's tracking system monitors packages throughout the delivery process; customers can check shipment status any time. The computerized clearance system, transmitting customs documents to authorities while the shipments are en route, means UPS shipments are frequently cleared before they arrive.

UPS began operations in the Philippines in April 1997, a joint venture with Delbros, Inc., with their intra-Asia air hub at Subic Bay Freeport. By 2002, UPS invested over US$ 300 million, setting up its new

President Gloria Macapagal-Arroyo at the launching and inaugural flight of UPS Intra-Asia Hub at Clark, Pampanga, April 4, 2002.

hub in the Clark Special Economic Zone.

The company's focus has always been on people. One company manager explained, "The ultimate measure of leadership is really how well the people around you develop and respond."

This policy proved invaluable when disaster struck the World Trade Center, New York on September 11, 2001. When Joe Liana, UPS district manager for Manhattan—30 years with the company—was informed of the attack, he raced into the city. Flagging down the first UPS truck he saw he went to their complex on 43rd Street. Sending messages to every driver's computerized clipboard, telling them to call in, within three hours he knew his only casualties were four trucks, crushed in the buildings' collapse.

With his dedication to service Mr. Liana called 4,000 employees to the UPS complex. Sorting through tens of thousands of packages, looking for

medical supplies, they made 200 deliveries to hospitals, doctors and pharmacies, helping to save lives. The company bounced back within a few days.

UPS was saved by a combination of corporate culture and technology. Its decentralized system empowers district managers such as Liana to make key decisions.

From running errands in Seattle, the company now delivers more than 13 million packages per day. It boasts access to four billion of the earth's six billion people. From a few guys and a bike — what a success story!

Wyeth

Wyeth Philippines was the first Philippine-American joint venture in the pharmaceutical industry. In 1959 A.T. Suaco & Co. and American Home Products Corporation joined to set up a Philippine company.

The company was founded in Pennsylvania in the 1860s by the Wyeth brothers. They began as a small drugstore and, from the very first, their history was one of innovation. They transformed the way drugstores operate and were more a research laboratory than a drugstore—at least for that time. They "advance manufactured" frequently prescribed medicines in bulk.

Wyeth developed the "compressed pill" or tablet and the first rotary tablet press. It also made the first soluble gelatin capsules. Possibly the most important for humanity was their development of a heat-stable, freeze-dried vaccine and the bifurcated needle, which helped lead to the worldwide eradication of smallpox. Wyeth waived the patent royalties on its bifurcated needle, thus aiding in the delivery of 200 million smallpox vaccinations per year.

On his death in 1929, Stuart Wyeth, the son of one of the original founders, left controlling interest in the firm to Harvard University. Two years later, American Home Products bought Wyeth from Harvard. That same year, AHP purchased Petrolager Laboratories. Over the next two decades, AHP merged with or purchased a number of companies including laboratories and food manufacturers.

Nearly a century after Wyeth's founding, the Suaco family organized A.T. Suaco and company in 1946 in Manila. This enterprise pioneered the local manufacture of various pharmaceutical preparations. In 1958, A.T. Suaco negotiated with American Home Products Corporation to establish the first Philippine-American joint venture in the pharmaceutical industry. In 1964, the joint venture assumed a new name, Wyeth Suaco Labortories Incorporation.

1964 was also the inauguration of the first manufacturing plant for infant products. Two revolutionary formulas were introduced— S-26 was the first whey-dominant infant mild powder in the country, especially formulated to closely resemble human milk. Then came Bonna, a breakthrough in the company's effort to provide the Filipino masses with a premium yet affordable quality infant formula.

Increased demand required larger facilities. A nutritional manufacturing plant in Canlubang, Laguna opened in 1992. The new plant doubled production capacity and employed latest drying technology, high speed packaging lines and a centralized warehousing facility.

In 1987, AHP bought Bristol-Myers Company's animal health division and assimilated the new business into Fort Dodge Animal Health. It also acquired Parke-Davis Animal Health Products, making them the third-largest animal health products manufacturer in the US.

Into the 21st century, Wyeth is a global research-driven pharmaceutical company committed to solving the world's health problems through leading-edge biotechnology.

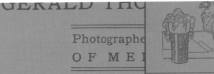

AmCham Presidents 1920-1971

Herbert L. Heath
1920 – 1921
1924 – 1928

Charles Mason Cotterman
1922- 1924

Robert E. Murphy
1928

Paul A. Meyer
1929 - 1932
1935- 1938

Howard M. Cavender
1933 – 1934

Samuel F. Gaches
1939 – 1941
1945

William H. Rennolds
1946

Frederic H. Stevens
1947- 1949

Paul H. Wood
1950
1956 – 1958
1959 – 1960

Joseph A. Parrish
1951

John L. Manning
1952
1958

J. H. Carpenter
1953

W.C. Palmer III
1953- 1954

Paul R. Parrette
1954 –1956

R. W. Pockmire
1960 – 1961

Harold D. Carl
1961 – 1962

Calvin C. Crawford
1963

Newland Baldwin
1964 – 1965

William W. Donnelly
1965 –1966

Albert W. Dunn
1966 – 1967

Andres Soriano, Jr.
1967 – 1968

William R. Daly
1968 – 1969

William A. Powers
1969 –1970

James A. Wolahan
1970 – 1971

AmCham Presidents 1971-2002

Robert D. Wales
1971 – 1972

William E. Mitchell
1972 – 1973

Sam R. Eastabrooks
1973 – 1974

Jose M. Soriano
1974- 1975

George Suter
1975 – 1976
1978 – 1979
1980 – 1981

James H. Brennan
1976- 1977

William C. Dunning
1977

Harold R. Butler
1979 – 1980

Rodrick J. O'Connor
1981 – 1982

A. Lewis Burridge
1982 – 1985

Fred C. Whiting
1985 – 1986

George W. Drysdale
1986 – 1987

Gordon Westly
1987 – 1988

Robert M. Sears
1988 – 1989

Mark C. Blacker
1989 – 1990

Thomas J. Leber
1990 – 1994

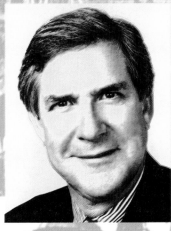

William S. Tiffany
1994 – 1996

Carlos A. Contreras
1996 – 1998

George M. Drysdale
1998 – 2001

Terry J. Emrick
2001 – 2002

Donald R. Felbaum
September 2002

George P. Henefeld
2002

Contributors

Guy Sacerdoti has lived in Southeast Asia for nearly three decades as a writer and consultant. He was correspondent for the *Far Eastern Economic Review* in Malaysia, and bureau chief in Indonesia and the Philippines, where he also served as president of the Foreign Correspondents Association of the Philippines from 1984-85. He currently does client specific consulting producing political and macro-economic risk analysis. He also plays keyboards, guitar and sings with the classic rock band "SNAFU!"

Leslie Ann Murray first came to Manila as an infant, in time to be "a guest of the Emperor" when the Japanese Imperial forces entered Manila. A year after liberation she moved to her native California, returning to Hong Kong to finish her education several years later. She ran a Hong Kong cultural magazine afterwards. Serendipitously she returned to Manila in 1961 as a bride, raised two children, worked in the travel industry as country manager for SAS and contributed articles and photographs for travel publications worldwide. Most recently she was Executive Director of Asia Society.

Barbara (Bobby) Greenwood was the original "Coordinator" for this book project until her death in May 2002. She arrived in the Philippines in the early 1960s with degrees in Journalism and Drama and worked extensively in the motion picture industry—both local and foreign—particularly in Vietnam in 1968 and with the filming of the modern classic "Apocalyse Now" in the mid-1970s. She came back to journalism working with "What's On/Expat" and freelancing, contributing to a variety of publications, including the AmCham Journal.

Beth Day Romulo is the widow of Philippine statesman Carlos P. Romulo, first Asian President of the United Nations General Assembly, army general, Philippine ambassador to the US, and Foreign Secretary. Beth Day's books —some of which were printed in 16 foreign editions—and her steady flow of articles have been published in the US and abroad for over half a century. She is currently a columnist for the *Manila Bulletin*.

Andrew Gonzalez, FSC. is a former Secretary of the Department of Education, Culture and Sports. A former president of De La Salle University, he is now Vice-President for Academics and Research and President of the Manila Bulletin Publishing Corporation. Published extensively in the field of higher education, socio-linguistics, language teaching, and religious education, he received his doctorate degree in Linguistics from the UC, Berkeley.

Dr. Mary Racelis is a sociologist and Director of the Institute of Philippine Culture, Ateneo de Manila University. She has produced several books and numerous articles on Philippine society and culture in the course of her distinguished research and writing career. Racelis served in Eastern and Southern Africa as UNICEF Regional Director from 1983-92, returned to the Philippines as the Country Representative of the Ford Foundation until 1997.

Dr. Alexander Calata is the Executive Director of the Philippine-American Educational Foundation (PAEF), which administers the Fulbright scholarship program for the Philippines. He studied at the Divine Word College, Ateneo de Manila University, and University of Santo Tomas. He was a Fulbright grantee to UCLA, and British Council fellow at the University of Bradford in England, and a FAPE-Ford Foundation at Educational Testing Service (ETS) in Princeton. He taught at the De La Salle University.

Luis Guerrero Nakpil was a columnist for the now defunct newspaper, *The Philippine Post*. For more than a year, he expounded on trends and developments in the design and construction activities in and around Manila with his column "Concrete Terms". Nakpil is a contributor to the design magazine *BluPrint* and the art magazine *Araw*. He is also the Principal Architect for LGNakpil+PMMoran+Associates. Nakpil is the son of the late architect, Angel E. Nakpil and journalist Carmen Guerrero-Nakpil.

Gerard Rey A. Lico is an Assistant Professor at the College of Architecture and College of Arts and Letters at University of the Philippines. He graduated from the University with a B.S. in Architecture and a Masters Degree in Arts History. Aside from publishing articles popularizing architecture in the *Philippine Daily Inquirer* and in the *BluPrint* magazine, he has also published on the Internet. He has received several awards for his research.

Alice Guerrero Guillermo teaches at the Department of Art Studies at the University of the Philippines. She studied at the Holy Ghost College, at the Universite-d'Aix-Marseille in France as a scholar of the French government, and at the University of the Philippines where she finished her Ph.D. in Philippine Studies. She has won several awards, and in 1999 was named Centennial Honoree for the Arts (Art Criticism) by the Cultural Center of the Philippines.

Raul L. Locsin runs BusinessWorld Publishing Corporation, and is Publisher and Editor of BusinessWorld newspaper and its ancillary publications. "A newspaper is a public trust" has always been his motto. His first nationwide paper was BusinessDay, the only national daily that remained unscathed during 1972-81 martial law period. Eschewing politics, it became known for its objectivity, and kept that reputation when it added political reporting in the early 1980s. The combination of a labor issue and the advent of computerized publishing led him to dissolve BusinessDay and start up BusinessWorld in 1987.

Phylita Joy Gamboa Virata is Vice President for Audience Development at Repertory Philippines Foundation, Inc. She has been a professional actress, director, producer since 1976, and was founder and Artistic Director of the Repertory Children's Theater. Virata wrote the book, lyrics, was production coordinator and assistant director for MIONG—an original historical musical about Gen. Emilio Aguinaldo and the declaration of independence in 1898. She holds a Masters in Industrial Management from the University of the Philippines.

Patis Tesoro is a fashion designer deeply involved with the revival and improvement of Philippine arts and crafts. After high school she studied Art Education and Textile Design at Marygrove College in Detroit. After returning to Manila she married Jose Claro Tesoro and began designing for Tesoro Handicrafts. Tesoro started her own label in 1982, frequently exhibiting overseas. She has received several major awards for her work.

Ted Lerner is the author of the book, *Hey, Joe - a Slice of the City, an American in Manila*. He has spent much of the last decade writing on cultural and social issues in his man-on-the-street style. His "Hey Joe" column ran for several years in the respected newspaper *BusinessWorld*. Lerner's penchant for gab is often as good as his pen. Coupled with a love of boxing, he can often be found in center ring as emcee for top-ranked fights.

Isabel Caro Wilson is Chairman of the Board of Business Machines Corporation, Datagraphics, Inc., Rhine Marketing Corp., and Metals Engineering Resources Corp. She was Philippine Ambassador to Spain from 1993-1998. She remains Senior Advisor for Spain and Portugal for the Philippine Chamber of Commerce and Industry. She is active in civic work, and is currently President of the Dasmariñas Village Association and the Asian Cultural Council Philippines.

Carlyn Truax Manning is one of the long-time US residents of Manila, she is originally from Chicago by way of New York where she was a top model and dancer. After marriage to John (Jack Manning) in 1948 she made Manila her home and has been active in a multitude of volunteer organizations as well working in the travel industry. She is also the only female member of the Elk's B.P.O.E. Lodge 761. She is currently writing her memoirs of her life and experiences in the Philippines.

Acknowledgments

A book project of this scope involves the cooperation and participation of many, many people. From access to research materials to offering ideas, to writing from personal expertise and experience to providing logistical support, the following people helped in making this piece of history.

From AmCham Philippines – The Board of Directors, Executive Director Robert M. Sears, George Drysdale, Jr., Terry Emrick, Laurie Lofgren, Shiela Nichols, Donald Felbaum, Ben Hughes, Demetrio ("Jun") Salipsip, J. Marsh Thomson, Daisy Palor, Ernesto Rivera, Aurora Galvez, Divina Coombes, Belinda Soliman, Ivy Marzean, Lynn Acejas, Lynnie Buyco, Florenda Dumagan, Elmer Yanuaria, Dominador Borres, Summer Serrano, Czarina Ebarvia, Roberto Cardinal, Lilia Balomaga, Benito Millo, Leo Juego and Roy Fulgado. Ellison Quijano (from New York's Fil-Am Chamber), COCUSA (Washington, D.C.), APCAC (Hong Kong) and all the AmCham member companies and personnel who contributed time and effort in support of this project.

From the American Historical Collection – Jose M. Cruz, S.J., Waldette M. Cueto. Gabriel L. Garbo.

We also wish to thank Marc and Reni Singer, Guillermo ("Ige") Ramos, Lynn Cadorniga, James Saunders, George Vastardis, Barbara Gonzalez, Fr. James Reuter, Ken Metcalf, Richie Quirino, Elizabeth L. Enriquez, Murray Hertz, Fr. Tyler Strand, Joseph Mock, Hilda Clofe, Edna Paterno, Bert Olbes, Peter Parsons, Thomas Walsh, James Halsema, Ralph Graves, Serge Grynkewich II, Dr. Michael Anderson, Antonio Perez, Josefina Sopia, Molly Stephenson, Ben Baguyo, Ambeth R. Ocampo, Cora Alvina, Angus Campbell, Joan Orendain, Sara Collins Medina, Jonathan Best, John Silva, Datu Michael Mastura, Carmen Guerreo Nakpil, Ethel G. Roberts, Josemarie Zabaleta, Rosario ("Charing") Westly, Elsie and Paul Perrine, Jeff Phillips, Aurora Phillips, Leo and Leila Larkin, Merv Simpson, Dr. Florinda Capistrano-Baker, Ramon E.S. Lerma, William E. Bright II, Nigel M. S. Rich, CBE, Lope V. Juban, Jr., Tomas O. Del Castillio, Jr., Alfonso Ancheta, Santiago Robles, Lillibeth V. Fajardo, Silverio ("Rio") Ambrosio, Roberto Eugenio, Mardy Cristobal, Millie Dizon, John Young, Marie Bonillo, Ceto Dideles, Jose F. Reandelar, Chit Itchon, Junie Lutian, Anne Marie Chua, Maggie A. Angeles, Ana Esperanza Ong, Cherry Pinga, Ramon Abadilla, Deborah Roxas, Roger Salazar, Alice Orleans, Ruth Canillas, Remigo Ramos, Rene Silva, Dina Mendez, Dave Gomez, Joji Domantay, Billy Marisigan, Mae Rivera, Evelyn Morales del Rosario, Stephanie Belmonte, Karen Villanueva, Amee Tomboc, Lali Suzara, Nenita Rull, Portia Sto. Domingo, Arlita Narag, Anna Joy Dalma, Digna Santos…with sincere apologies for any errors or omissions.

Also, special thanks to the Sacerdoti and Murray families and friends who have borne with this project – and those long hours – in making this project a reality.

Index

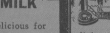
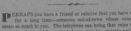